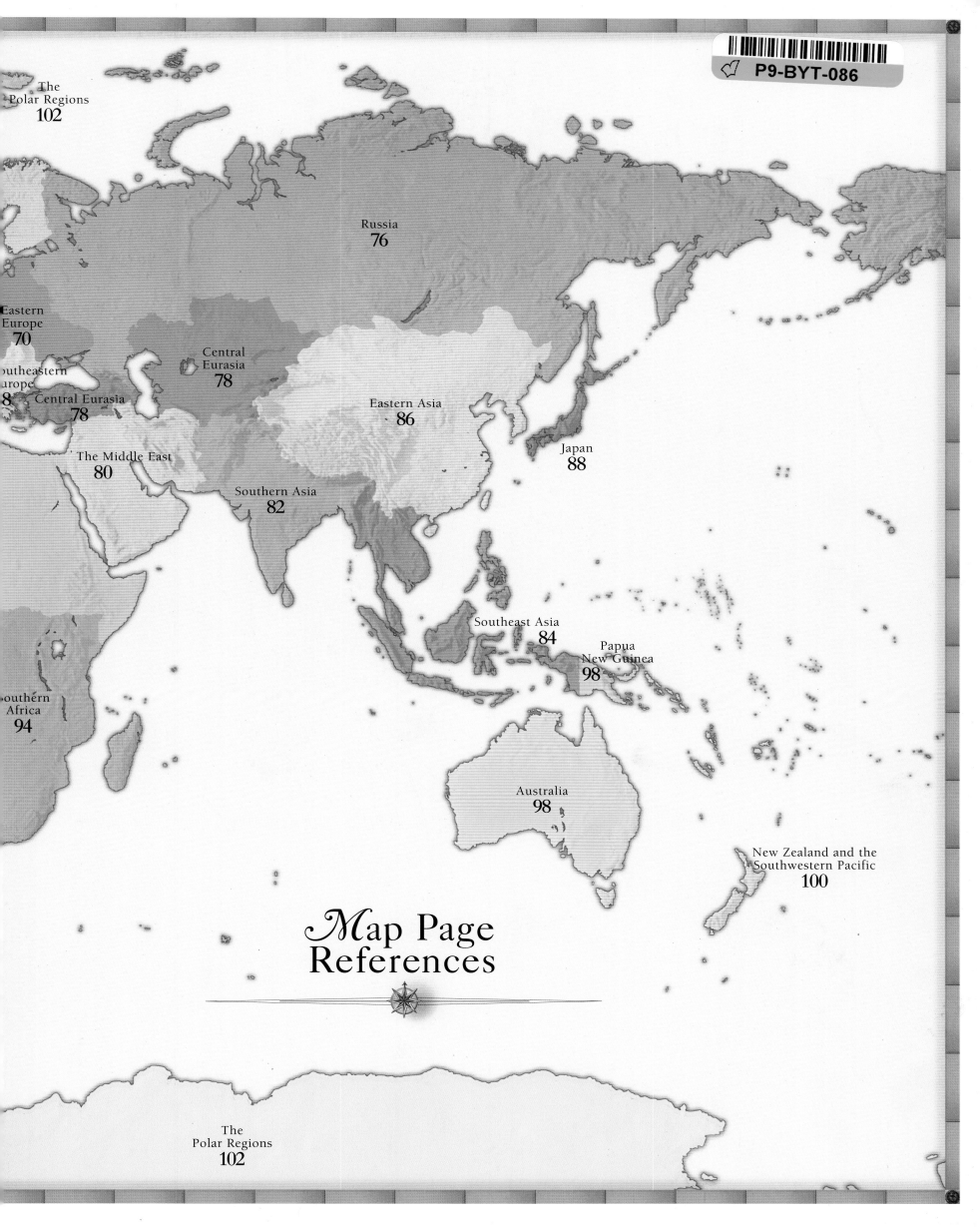

The
Polar Regions
102

Russia
76

Eastern
Europe
70

Central
Eurasia
78

Southeastern
Europe
8

Central Eurasia
78

Eastern Asia
86

Japan
88

The Middle East
80

Southern Asia
82

Southeast Asia
84

Papua
New Guinea
98

Southern
Africa
94

Australia
98

New Zealand and the
Southwestern Pacific
100

$\mathcal{M}$ap Page References

The
Polar Regions
102

P9-BYT-086

THE READER'S DIGEST
Children's Atlas
of the World

$\mathcal{T}$HE READER'S DIGEST
Children's Atlas of the World

A Reader's Digest Children's Book
Published by Reader's Digest Children's Publishing, Inc.
Reader's Digest Road, Pleasantville, NY 10570–7000

Conceived and produced by Weldon Owen Pty Limited
59 Victoria Street, McMahons Point, NSW, 2060, Australia
A member of the Weldon Owen Group of Companies
Sydney • San Francisco • Auckland • London

Copyright © 1998 Weldon Owen Pty Limited
Revised edition copyright © 2000 Weldon Owen Pty Limited
Third edition copyright © 2003 Weldon Owen Pty Limited

READER'S DIGEST CHILDREN'S PUBLISHING, INC.
President: Vivian Antonangeli
Creative Consultant: Michael J. Morris
Group Publisher: Rosanna Hansen
U.S. Editor: Sherry Gerstein
Creative Director: Ira Teichberg
U.S. Production Coordinator: Debbie Gagnon
Director of Sales and Marketing: Rosanne McManus
Director of U.S. Sales: Lola Valenciano
Marketing Director: Karen Herman
U.S. Consultant: Stephen F. Steiner

WELDON OWEN PTY LTD
Chief Executive Officer: John Owen
President: Terry Newell
Publisher: Sheena Coupe

Design Concept: John Bull
Managing Editor: Ariana Klepac
Art Director: Sue Burk

Project Editor: Scott Forbes
Consulting Editor: Colin Sale
Editorial Assistant: Anne Ferrier
Text: Scott Forbes
Editorial Coordinator, Third Edition: Jessica Cox

Senior Designer: Hilda Mendham
Designer, Thematic Spreads: Lena Lowe
Pre-press Co-ordinator: Jocelyne Best
Computer Production: Laura Sassin, Amanda Woodward
Computer Graphics: Stuart McVicar
Jacket Design: John Bull
Senior Picture Researcher: Anne Ferrier
Picture Researcher: Peter Barker
Archives: Rita Joseph

Illustrators: Susanna Addario, Andrew Beckett/illustration, André Boos, Anne Bowman, Greg Bridges, Danny Burke, Martin Camm, Fiammetta Dogi, Simone End, Giuliano Fornari, Chris Forsey, John Francis/Bernard Thornton Artists, U.K., Jon Gittoes, Ray Grinaway, Terry Hadler/Bernard Thornton Artists, U.K., Tim Hayward/Bernard Thornton Artists, U.K., David Kirshner, Frank Knight, Mike Lamble, James McKinnon, Peter Mennim, Nicola Oram, Tony Pyrzakowski, Oliver Rennert, Barbara Rodanska, Claudia Saraceni, Michael Saunders, Peter Schouten, Stephen Seymour/Bernard Thornton Artists, U.K., Marco Sparaciari, Sharif Tarabay/illustration, Steve Trevaskis, Thomas Trojer, Genevieve Wallace, Trevor Weekes, Rod Westblade, Ann Winterbotham

Maps: Digital Wisdom Publishing Ltd
Flags: Flag Society of Australia

Production Managers: Helen Creeke, Caroline Webber
Production Assistant: Kylie Lawson
Vice President International Sales: Stuart Laurence

Library of Congress Cataloging–in–Publication Data

The Reader's Digest children's atlas of the world / consulting editor, Colin Sale; [maps, Digital Wisdom Publishing Ltd.].—Third ed.
p.   cm.
"Copyright 2003 Weldon Owen Pty Ltd"—Prelim.p.[2].
Includes bibliographical references and index.
SUMMARY: Includes more than fifty maps; a fact file on each country and territory; illustrations of places, people, landscapes, and wildlife; an introduction to map making and map reading; projects; activities; and quizzes.
ISBN 0–7944–0207–0 (trade hard cover : alk. paper).
1. Children's atlases. [1. Atlases. 2. Geography.] I. Sale, Colin. II. Weldon Owen Pty Limited. III. Digital Wisdom Publishing Ltd.
IV. Title: Children's atlas of the World.

G1021   .R563   2003   99-26619
                                                                           CIP
912—dc21   MAPS

Color Reproduction by Colourscan Co Pte Ltd
Printed in Singapore by Imago Production

A WELDON OWEN PRODUCTION

THE READER'S DIGEST
Children's Atlas
of the World

Consulting Editor: Colin Sale

Reader's Digest
Children's Books™

Pleasantville, New York/Montréal, Québec

CONTENTS

NORTH AMERICA 32

SOUTH AMERICA 48

EUROPE 54

ASIA 74

AFRICA 90

AUSTRALIA AND OCEANIA 96

How to Use This Atlas

THE READER'S DIGEST CHILDREN'S ATLAS OF THE WORLD takes you on a fascinating tour of our extraordinary world. Before you set off, read the sections called Maps and Mapmaking and How to Read a Map. There you will find out about different kinds of maps and how they are made, and learn how to read and use maps. The remaining introductory pages are a guide to our planet, Earth. They show you where it is located in space, what it is made of, how its landscapes have been shaped, and how weather, wildlife and peoples vary around the world. The atlas maps are divided into seven parts—one for each of the continents of North America, South America, Europe, Asia, Africa, and Australia and Oceania, and one for the polar regions. Each part begins with a continent map that includes country lists and shows the most important features of the landscape. The continent map is followed by a series of illustrated maps which are packed with facts, pictures and activities. The sample maps and notes on these two pages explain the features on both types of map. At the back of the atlas you will find the World Fact File. This provides useful information on all of the world's countries and major territories. Finally, there is a glossary of terms used in this book, as well as a gazetteer—a geographical index that helps you to find places on the maps.

ILLUSTRATED MAP

Country list This is a list of the countries or states on the map, their populations and capital cities.

France

FRANCE, THE LARGEST COUNTRY in western Europe, has a varied climate and landscape. In the north, the weather is mild and wet, and much of the land is flat. As you travel south, the climate becomes warmer and the land more mountainous. Three-quarters of the population live in towns and cities, but most of the country is farmland, and France is Europe's leading farming country. The northern plains are covered in fields of wheat and sugar beets, and in central and southern France vineyards dot the hillsides—more wine is produced in France than in any other country except Italy. The area around Paris, the capital, is the most densely populated region. It is home to one-fifth of the country's population and most of its industries. Several great rivers, including the Seine and the Loire, cross France's northern and western plains. These waterways were once the country's main transportation routes, and their banks are lined with historic villages and magnificent castles known as châteaus. In the south, the mountains of the Pyrenees and the Alps separate France from Spain and Italy. Among their snow-capped peaks lie popular ski resorts and national parks that are home to eagles, marmots and goatlike antelopes called chamois. Along the Mediterranean coast there are many busy beach resorts. Near the Italian border lies Monaco, the second-smallest country in the world. Monaco is famous for its casinos and its annual Grand Prix motor race.

FRANCE
POPULATION: 59,765,983 • CAPITAL: Paris
MONACO
POPULATION: 31,987 • CAPITAL: Monaco

Amazing Fact This box contains fascinating facts about the area on the map.

• AMAZING FACT •

France is now connected to Great Britain by an undersea rail link known as the Channel Tunnel. The tunnel took seven years to build and includes two rail tracks. Trains take 35 minutes to pass through the tunnel. Travelers can journey from London to Paris in about three hours.

Continent Facts This includes the size of the continent, its population and the names of its countries.

CONTINENT MAP

Records This is a list of the tallest, longest and largest features of the continent.

Size comparison These pictures show how the continent's most important mountains and rivers would look if you could see them side by side.

Political map This map shows all the countries in the continent.

Physical map This map shows the main features of the landscape.

Colored border
Each part of the atlas has a different colored border.

Map reader's grid The letters and numbers on the border help you find places on the map. See page 10 to find out how to use the grid.

Projects By trying out these activities and experiments, you can learn more about a topic or a part of the world.

See page 10 to find out how to use the grid.

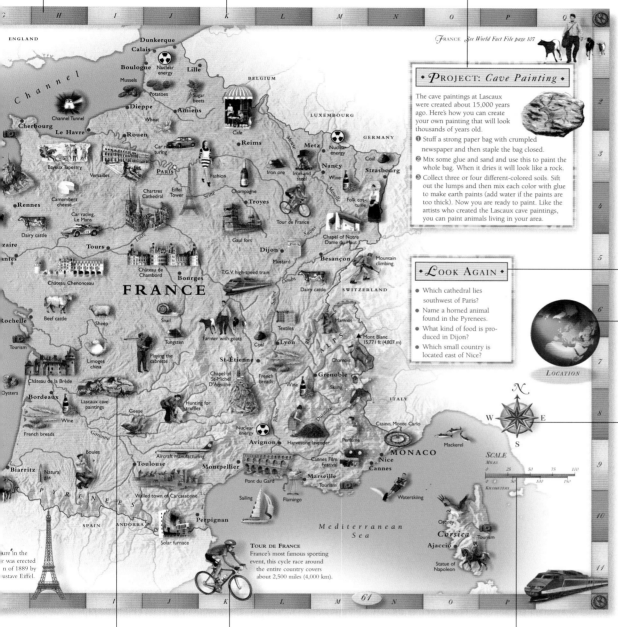

*F*RANCE *See World Fact File page 107*

· P*ROJECT*: *Cave Painting* ·

The cave paintings at Lascaux were created about 15,000 years ago. Here's how you can create your own painting that will look thousands of years old.
❶ Stuff a strong paper bag with crumpled newspaper and then staple the bag closed.
❷ Mix some glue and sand and use this to paint the whole bag. When it dries it will look like a rock.
❸ Collect three or four different-colored soils. Sift out the lumps and then mix each color with glue to make earth paints (add water if the paints are too thick). Now you are ready to paint. Like the artists who created the Lascaux cave paintings, you can paint animals living in your area.

· L*OOK AGAIN* ·

• Which cathedral lies southwest of Paris?
• Name a horned animal found in the Pyrenees.
• What kind of food is produced in Dijon?
• Which small country is located east of Nice?

LOCATION

Look Again
To answer these questions, you'll need to take a close look at the information on the map.

Locator globe
This globe shows where the area on the map is located.

T*OUR DE* F*RANCE*
France's most famous sporting event, this cycle race around the entire country covers about 2,500 miles (4,000 km).

Illustrations These show the people, places, wildlife and activities in the area on the map.

Feature illustrations
These pullout features provide extra information on some of the map illustrations.

Scale The scale bar helps you to calculate distances on the map. To find out how to do this, see page 10.

Compass The compass helps you find north. To find out how to use the compass, see page 10.

see page 10.

*K*EY TO MAP COLORS

Desert and semidesert

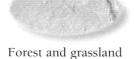
Forest and grassland

Tundra

Ice cap

*K*EY TO MAP SYMBOLS

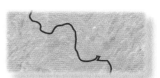
country border

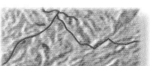
regional (state) border

disputed border

CHANNEL ISLANDS (U.K.)

territory and country to which it belongs

●**Baltimore**
⊙**ANNAPOLIS**
✪**WASHINGTON, D.C.**

✪ national capital
⊙ regional capital
● city or town

river

lake

▲ **Ben Nevis**
4,406 ft (1,343 m)

▲ major mountain

Ⓔ African elephants

Ⓔ endangered animal

Maps and Mapmaking

A MAP IS A PICTURE that shows you what an area of land looks like from above. Any area, no matter how large or small, can be drawn as a map. Some maps show small areas such as a town; others show the whole world. Because maps usually show areas that are much larger than the page they are printed on, objects have to be drawn much smaller than they really are. This is called drawing to scale. The bigger the area of a map, the smaller the real objects have to be drawn. Maps that show a small area and a large amount of detail are called large-scale maps. Maps that show a large area and a small amount of detail are called small-scale maps. On most maps, real objects are represented by lines, colors and symbols. For example, on a map of a town, black outlines may indicate streets, and colored shapes may show buildings. On a map of a country, towns may appear as simple black dots, and rivers as blue lines. A book of maps—like the one you are reading now—is called an atlas. An atlas usually contains maps of the whole world as well as maps of countries and continents.

MAPPING THE WORLD
Each of these maps shows the location of Riverford School, but each is drawn at a different scale.

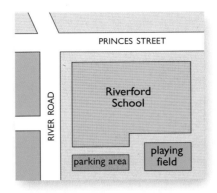

In this map of Riverford School, lines, colored shapes and labels are used to show the school, nearby streets and other features. Maps of small areas like this are often called plans.

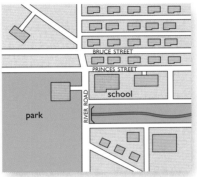

This is a map of Riverford town. Because the area of the map is larger, less detail can be shown. You can now see that the school is near houses, a park and a river, but you can no longer see the school parking area or playing field.

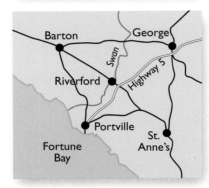

This map shows the region around Riverford. The town is now represented by a simple black dot, so you can no longer see the school or the streets. But you can see that Riverford is near water, and that it is linked to other towns by major and minor roads.

◆ AMAZING FACT ◆

In Greek mythology, Atlas was a man who led a rebellion against the gods. As a punishment for this act, he was made to support the world on his shoulders. When the first books of maps were published in the 16th century, many had an illustration of Atlas carrying a globe on their covers. As a result, a book of maps soon became known as an atlas.

◆ PROJECT: *Mapping Your Neighborhood* ◆

You can draw a map of your neighborhood. To do this you will have to think about where places are, how far apart they are, and what shape they are. You may need to go for a walk and make a list of the things you want to show on your map.

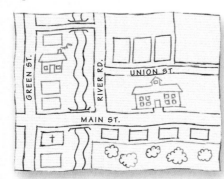

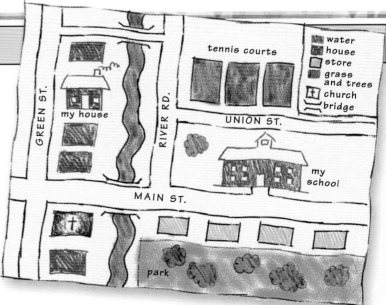

❶ Once you have decided what you are going to include, draw in the streets.

❷ Then add shapes to represent features such as buildings, parks and rivers. Label the streets.

❸ Now color your map. Use one color for houses, one for streets, and so on. Draw a key to show what the colors represent. Finally, add labels for important places such as your home and school.

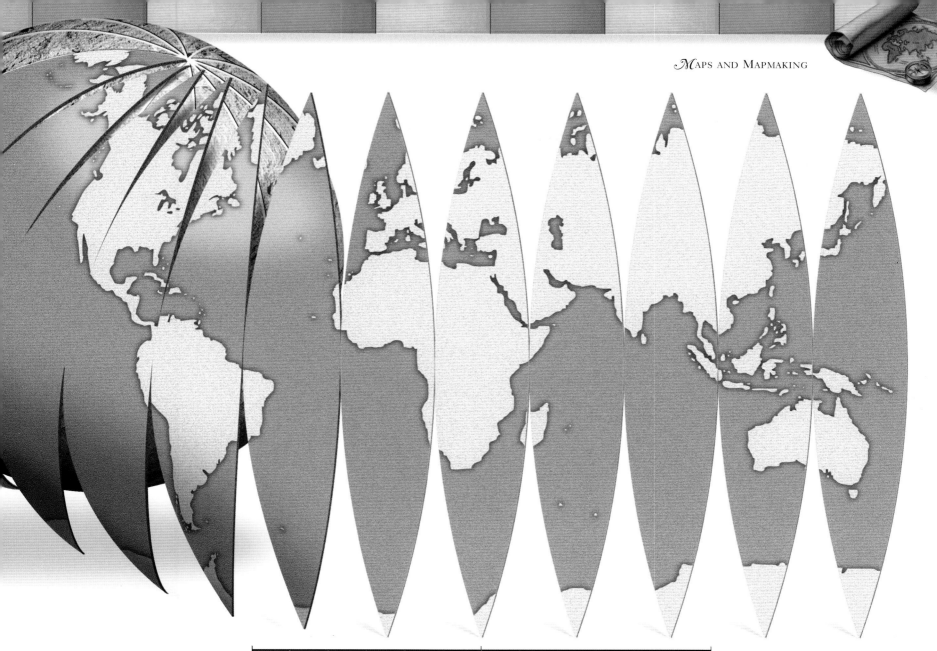

MAKING MAPS

People who make maps
are known as mapmakers
or cartographers. Before
airplanes and spacecraft
were invented, mapmakers
used information supplied
by travelers and explorers to
make maps. Nowadays, most
maps are based on surveys
and on photographs taken
by satellites positioned in
space, high above Earth.
Mapmakers face one major
problem: Earth is round, but
most maps have to be flat.
A globe is the most accurate

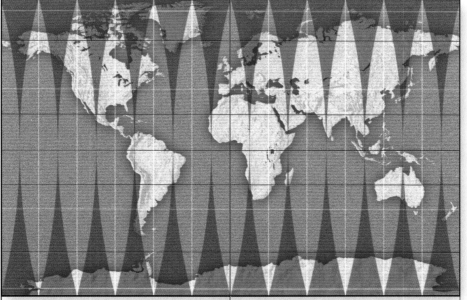

Arctic
Circle
(66.5°N)

Tropic of
Cancer
(23.5°N)

Equator
(0°)

Tropic of
Capricorn
(23.5°S)

Antarctic
Circle
(66.5°S)

180°   Greenwich meridian (0°)   180°

A FLAT EARTH
As shown above, the
surface of the globe
can be divided into
segments. To create
a flat, rectangular
map like the one on
the left, mapmakers
must fill in the gaps
between the segments.
To help them do this
and plot locations,
mapmakers use lines
of latitude (horizontal
lines) and longitude
(vertical lines).

kind of map because it is the same shape as Earth. But if you
tried to create a flat map by simply peeling the surface of a
globe, you would end up with a world map made up of pieces,
or segments. You can test this for yourself by carefully peeling
an orange and trying to flatten out the skin. You will find that
it is impossible to make the peel lie flat without breaking it.
In order to create a flat map, mapmakers have to stretch and
squash the segments of the globe. The different ways in which
they do this are known as projections. There are many types of
projections, and each creates a slightly different map.

LINES AROUND THE WORLD
Mapmakers use a grid system to plot locations on the globe.
Lines of longitude are drawn between the North Pole and
the South Pole and are measured in degrees east or west
of the Greenwich meridian (0°). Lines of latitude are
drawn in a west-east direction and measured in degrees
north or south of the equator (0°). The equator
divides the world into the Northern and Southern
hemispheres. The Greenwich meridian and the 180°
line separate the Eastern and Western hemispheres.

How to Read a Map

Maps are packed with information. They tell you where places are, what size and shape they are, and how far and in what direction they lie from each other. Maps can also tell you about a region's climate, landscape, vegetation, towns and cities, and transportation routes. Once you have learned how to read maps, you can use an atlas to find out many things about countries all around the world.

FINDING PLACES

Most maps and atlases use a gazetteer and grid system to help you find places. You look for the place name in the gazetteer—an index of place names which usually appears at the back of the atlas—and then use the grid reference to find the location on the relevant map. Normally, a map grid consists of a series of letters along the top and bottom of the page and a series of numbers down the sides. Take a look at the map of Australia on the right. The grid reference for the city of Melbourne is H8. To find Melbourne, look at the letters on the top or bottom border and find H. Then find 8 on the left- or right-hand border. Imagine a line running down the page between the two Hs and another running across the page between the two 8s. (You can use a ruler to help you line up the numbers.) You will find Melbourne near the intersection of these lines.

USING THE MAP GRID

In the gazetteer of this book, each place name is followed by a grid reference. The grid reference for the city of Nashville, Tennessee, in the United States is 41 L4. To locate Nashville, turn to page 41 and find L and 4 on the grid. Trace a line down from L and another across from 4. Nashville is near the intersection of the two lines.

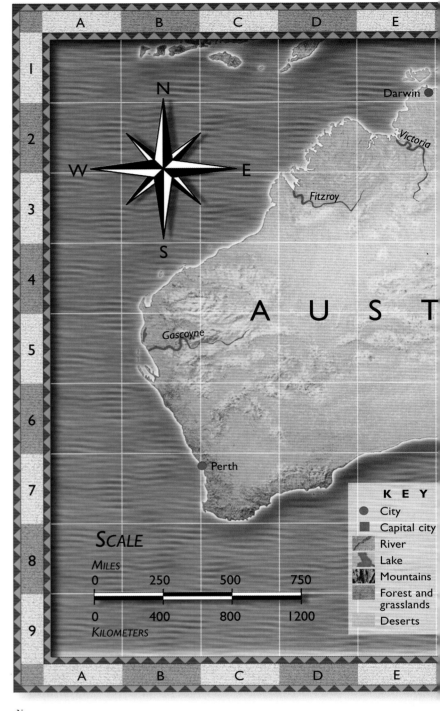

KEY
- City
- Capital city
- River
- Lake
- Mountains
- Forest and grasslands
- Deserts

SCALE

MILES
0   250   500   750

0   400   800   1200
KILOMETERS

DESCRIBING DIRECTION

A map usually has a compass symbol, which indicates the direction of north (N) on the map. Sometimes, as on the map above, it also shows the directions of south (S), east (E) and west (W). You can use the points of a compass to describe where places are. For example, on the map above we can say that Sydney is east (E) of Adelaide and that Brisbane is north (N) of Sydney. Brisbane is both north and east of Adelaide, so we can use a combination of compass points and say that Brisbane is northeast (NE) of Adelaide. But Brisbane is farther to the east of Adelaide than it is to the north of it. So, if we want to be even more accurate, we can describe Brisbane as being east-northeast (ENE) of Adelaide. The compass above left shows all the combinations of compass points that you can use to describe direction.

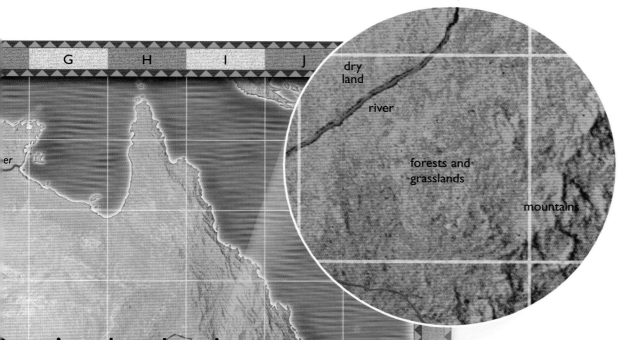

dry
land

river

forests and
grasslands

mountains

COLOR KEYS
On this map of Australia, dark shading indicates mountains. Green represents forests and grasslands, and orange shows desert and other dry land. Areas of water such as oceans, lakes and rivers are all colored blue.

THE LAY OF THE LAND
The colors of a map may tell you something about a region's landscape, vegetation and climate. Often, shading is used to show mountain ranges, and colors are used to represent different kinds of vegetation. Green normally represents forests or grasslands, while yellow or orange indicates an area of dry land such as desert. On many maps, a special symbol, such as a square or star, is used to indicate a capital city. Most maps and atlases have a key that explains these features. In this atlas, you will find the key on page 7.

◆ PROJECT: *Using a Scale* **◆**

To measure the distance between Perth and Sydney on the map at left, follow these steps:

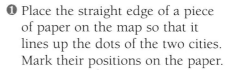

❶ Place the straight edge of a piece of paper on the map so that it lines up the dots of the two cities. Mark their positions on the paper.

❷ Place the paper next to the scale so that one of the dots lines up with zero. The scale is shorter than the distance, so mark the paper where the scale ends and note the distance it represents.

Place the mark back at zero and repeat these steps as often as necessary. Add the figures to calculate the distance between the cities.

You can also use the scale to measure distances along curved lines.

❶ Place a piece of string on the map along the Darling River, bending it to match the course of the river.

❷ Grasp the string at each end of the river, then straighten it out and measure it against the scale. You can then calculate the length of the river.

MEASURING DISTANCE
Most maps have a scale. This shows how distance on the map compares with real distance. Many scales appear as a bar that is divided into sections, as do the ones used in this book. In the scale shown on the map above, each section on the top part of the bar is equal to 250 miles, and each section on the bottom of the bar represents 400 kilometers. The project on this page shows you how to use this type of scale to measure distances on a map. Scales can also be written like this:

1:1,000,000

This shows that the map has been reduced 1,000,000 times. Distances on the ground are therefore 1,000,000 times greater than they are on the map. Thus 1 inch on the map is equal to 1,000,000 inches, or 15¾ miles, and 1 cm on the map is equal to 1,000,000 cm, or 10 km. Other scales are written like this:

1 inch = 10 miles

This shows that 1 inch on the map corresponds to 10 miles in real distance.

Planet Earth

WE LIVE ON A SMALL PLANET in a tiny part of a vast universe. Our part of the universe is called the solar system. There are nine planets in the solar system, and they move around, or orbit, a star that we call the Sun. Enormous groups of stars are known as galaxies. Our galaxy is called the Milky Way and it is made up of at least 100 billion stars! There are many millions of galaxies in the universe and each one is surrounded by a vast, empty space. The solar system formed about five billion years ago from a large, swirling cloud of dust and gases. The hot, central part of the cloud became the Sun, while farther out, rocks and gases combined to form the planets. Other rock fragments became asteroids, or minor planets.

◆ AMAZING FACTS ◆

- Our galaxy looks like this. The faint, glowing arms of this galaxy are clouds of stars. Each of these stars is like our Sun and may have its own system of planets.
- Jupiter is bigger than all the other planets, moons, comets and asteroids put together. Yet, it is still only about a hundredth as large as the smallest star.

ROUND AND ROUND

As each planet orbits the Sun, it also spins, or rotates, on its axis—an imaginary line through its center. Earth rotates once every 24 hours, and takes one year to orbit the Sun. Planets near the Sun orbit more quickly than those farther away. Asteroids also orbit the Sun. Most are located between Mars and Jupiter, in an area known as the asteroid belt. The planets and asteroids are all held in their orbits by gravity, a powerful force that pulls them toward the Sun. Without this force, they would fly off into space.

THE PLANETS IN PERSPECTIVE

The illustration below shows the relative distances between the planets, as well as how long the planet takes to orbit the Sun (a year on that planet) and how long it takes to spin on its axis (a day on that planet).

Sun | Mercury Year: 88 Earth days. Day: 59 Earth days.
    Venus Year: 225 Earth days. Day: 243 Earth days.
    Uranus Year: 84 Earth years. Day: 17.9 hours.
    Earth Year: 365.25 days. Day: 24 hours.
    Jupiter Year: 11.9 Earth years. Day: 9.8 hours.
    Mars Year: 1.9 Earth years. Day: 24.6 hours.
    Saturn Year: 29.5 Earth years. Day: 10.2 hours.
    Asteroid Belt

◆ PROJECT: *Space Mobile* ◆

You can make your own mobile of the solar system to hang up in your bedroom or in your classroom at school.

❶ First, collect some paper, colored pens, string or cotton thread, scissors and a coat hanger.

❷ Draw the Sun and each of the planets and color them. Make sure you copy the colors and relative sizes of the planets as shown in the illustrations on these pages.

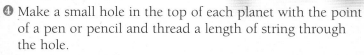

❸ Carefully cut out each planet using a pair of scissors.

❹ Make a small hole in the top of each planet with the point of a pen or pencil and thread a length of string through the hole.

❺ Tie the Sun and the planets to the bottom of the coat hanger. Place the Sun in the middle and arrange the planets on either side of it in the order shown in the illustration on these pages. Don't forget that some planets are closer together than others.

❻ When all the planets are in place, the mobile is ready to hang.

WORLD IN MOTION

As Earth turns on its axis, we move in and out of the Sun's light. Day begins as we move into the light. As we turn away from the Sun, night falls. Because Earth is tilted at an angle, the amount of sunlight reaching different parts of the world varies throughout the year. When part of Earth is tilted toward the Sun, it is summer there. When it is tilted away from the Sun, it is winter.

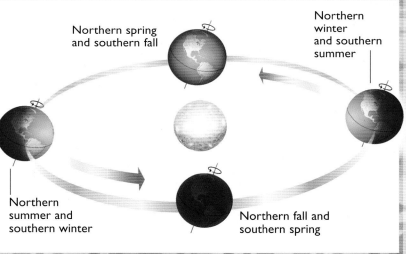

Northern spring and southern fall

Northern winter and southern summer

Northern summer and southern winter

Northern fall and southern spring

FIT FOR LIFE

Some planets are surrounded by a layer of gases called an atmosphere. As far as we know, Earth is the only planet in the solar system with an atmosphere that contains sufficient water and oxygen for life to flourish. Our atmosphere is so thin that if the planet were the size of an apple, the atmosphere would be only as thick as the peel.

Neptune Year: 165 Earth years. Day: 19.2 hours.

Pluto Year: 248 Earth years. Day: 6.4 Earth days.

13

An Ever-Changing Planet

EARTH IS SHAPED LIKE a large ball. Inside are several layers made of different materials. As Earth formed, heavy minerals such as iron and nickel sank to the center, while lighter materials rose to the middle and upper levels. At first, the upper levels consisted entirely of hot, liquid rock, but as Earth cooled, the outside solidified to form a thin, hard crust. This crust broke into several pieces, known as lithospheric plates. These plates float on the liquid, molten rock—or magma—underneath and are constantly moving, although you cannot feel the movement. Energy from Earth's core creates powerful convection currents that force the plates together and apart. This happens extremely slowly, but over millions of years these movements shape and shift the surface of Earth, causing earthquakes and volcanic eruptions and forming mountains and islands.

Inner core
Outer core
Lower mantle
Asthenosphere
Lithosphere
Upper mantle
Ocean crust
Continental crust
Convection currents

INSIDE EARTH

Our planet's solid iron inner core is surrounded by an outer core of liquid iron and nickel. Above this is a layer of solid rock called the lower mantle and a wide band of liquid rock known as the asthenosphere. Earth's outer layer is called the lithosphere. It consists of the solid rock of the upper mantle, and the crust. Crust under the land (continental crust) is usually thicker than crust under the sea (ocean crust). In Earth's core, temperatures reach an amazing 5,400°F (3,000°C). This heat creates strong convection currents that push the crust in different directions.

◆ PROJECTS: *Folding the Crust* ◆

❶ Cut a paper plate in half. These halves represent two of Earth's lithospheric plates.

❷ Using adhesive tape, attach a sheet of paper to the plate halves. The paper represents Earth's crust.

❸ If you slide one half of the plate under the other, the paper buckles. Similarly, when two of Earth's plates collide, their crusts fold, forming mountains.

❶ Take a sheet of paper, fold it in half and continue to fold it.

❷ After six folds, it becomes difficult to fold the paper any further. In the same way, the thicker Earth's crust, the greater the force required to fold it.

Spreading plates

Hot-spot volcanoes

Coastal collisions

Coastal Collisions
When thin ocean crust meets thick continental crust, the thin crust slides under the thicker crust. Magma rises to the surface and forms a line of volcanoes. This process formed Mount St. Helens in the United States.

Hot-Spot Volcanoes
Weaknesses in the middle of plates, known as hot spots, allow magma from the asthenosphere to burst through the crust and form volcanoes. The Hawaiian Islands were created by hot-spot volcanoes.

Spreading Plates
Circulating magma may force plates apart. Where the plates separate, magma rises through the gap and cools and hardens to form a ridge. Normally this happens under the sea, but in Iceland it can be seen on land.

WORLD IN MOTION
Convection currents cause Earth's plates to collide, separate and slide past each other. The effects of these movements are shown in the illustration above and in the photographs on the right.

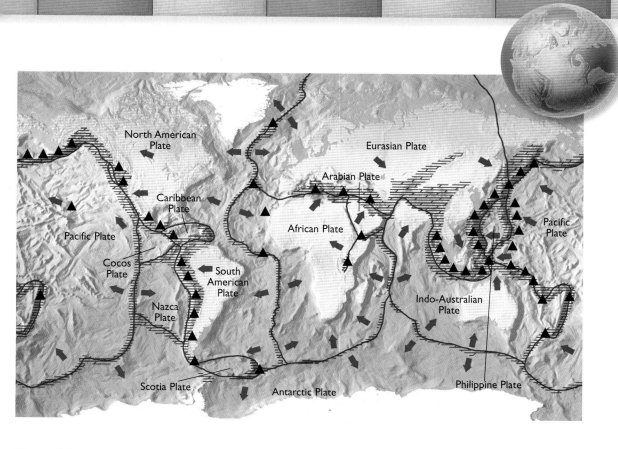

North American Plate

Eurasian Plate

Arabian Plate

African Plate

Caribbean Plate

Pacific Plate

Pacific Plate

Cocos Plate

South American Plate

Nazca Plate

Indo-Australian Plate

Scotia Plate

Antarctic Plate

Philippine Plate

200 million years ago

90 million years ago

Present

60 million years from now

ON THE MOVE

Over millions of years, plate movements have joined and divided Earth's landmasses. Two hundred million years ago, there was a single "supercontinent." It split into two landmasses, which then broke up to form the continents we know today. Further changes to these landmasses will occur as Earth's plates continue to drift.

PLATE MOVEMENTS

Earth's plates fit together like the pieces of a jigsaw puzzle, but the plates are constantly moving. This map shows the direction in which each plate moves. Most volcanoes and earthquakes occur where plates meet. This means that countries in the center of plates, such as Australia, have few earthquakes and volcanoes, whereas countries at the edges of plates, such as Japan, have many.

← Direction of movement

▲ Volcanoes

Earthquake zones

◆ AMAZING FACTS ◆

- When the volcano on the island of Krakatoa in Indonesia erupted on August 27, 1883, the explosion was heard 3,000 miles (4,800 km) away!

- More than 500,000 earthquakes occur every year. Fortunately, most of these are too weak to cause any damage.

Sliding plates

Folding crust

Undersea collisions

Sliding Plates

A fault line forms where two plates slide past each other. The friction between the plates creates earthquakes. These occur regularly along the San Andreas fault in California as part of the coastline slides northward.

Folding Crust

When two plates with crusts of similar thickness collide, the edge of one plate slides under the other, and the crusts buckle and fold to form mountains. This process created the massive Himalayas mountain range in Asia.

Undersea Collisions

When two plates with ocean crust collide, one may sink beneath the other, forming a deep trench. In places, magma bursts through the crust to form volcanic islands. The islands of Japan formed in this way.

◆ LOOK AGAIN ◆

- What is Earth's inner core made of?

- What kind of volcanoes formed the Hawaiian Islands?

- Where are earthquakes most likely to occur?

Weather and Climate

OUR WEATHER MAY CHANGE from day to day, but we usually experience the same kind of weather from year to year. The pattern of weather that occurs in a region over a long period is known as the climate. The climate of an area depends on three main factors: how far north or south of the equator it is (its latitude), how high it is (its altitude), and how close it is to the sea. As a result of Earth's orbit and its round shape, sunlight warms areas near the equator more than areas near the poles. Tropical regions are therefore hot year-round, and the poles are always cold. Areas between the tropics and the poles are temperate. This means that they have warm summers and cool winters. Mountains are colder than lowland areas because as you climb higher the atmosphere becomes thinner and retains less heat. In coastal regions, sea breezes and ocean currents prevent the weather from becoming too hot or too cold, so these areas have a milder climate than inland areas. Where winds blow inland from the sea, they are usually moist and bring high rainfall.

WIND PATTERNS

Because hot air rises and cold air sinks, the Sun's uneven heating of Earth's surface causes air to circulate as shown in the large diagram below. These patterns of air circulation are deflected by the planet's rotation, and form the major wind systems shown on the globe below right. These winds carry warm or cold, moist or dry air, and are an important influence on Earth's climates.

Air Circulation

Warm and cold air meet, creating a belt of stormy, wet weather.

Cold easterly winds blow from the poles.

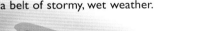
Air flows poleward from the southwest

60°N

30°N

Air flows toward the equator from the northeast

Equator

WORLD CLIMATES

The world can be divided into eight major climate zones, which are shown on this map and described on these pages. Ocean currents influence many of these climates. For example, northwestern Europe has a mild climate as a result of the warm waters of the Gulf Stream.

warm currents   cool currents

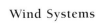

Cold Temperate
These regions have long, bitterly cold and snowy winters. Their summers are usually mild and damp.

Mountain
Mountains are normally colder, wetter and windier than neighboring regions that lie nearer sea level.

Polar
The polar regions are extremely cold for most of the year. Although snow falls regularly, the poles are relatively dry.

Upper air cools and sinks, creating dry conditions.

Warm, moist air rises at the equator, clouds form and rain falls.

Wind Systems

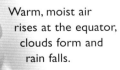

Polar easterlies ——

Westerlies ——

Trade winds ——

Westerlies ——

Polar easterlies ——

Wet Temperate
Wet temperate regions have four distinct seasons, with cool, wet winters and warm, wet summers.

Dry Temperate
Rainfall is relatively low in these regions. Most areas have mild, wet winters and hot, dry summers.

Desert and Semidesert
These are dry, barren areas with very low rainfall. They are usually hot by day, but may be cold, or even frosty, at night.

Subtropical
In summer, these regions are hot and wet like tropical areas. In winter, they are dry and mild like deserts.

Tropical
The tropics are hot and wet. In some areas, it rains all year round. In others, most of the rain falls in summer.

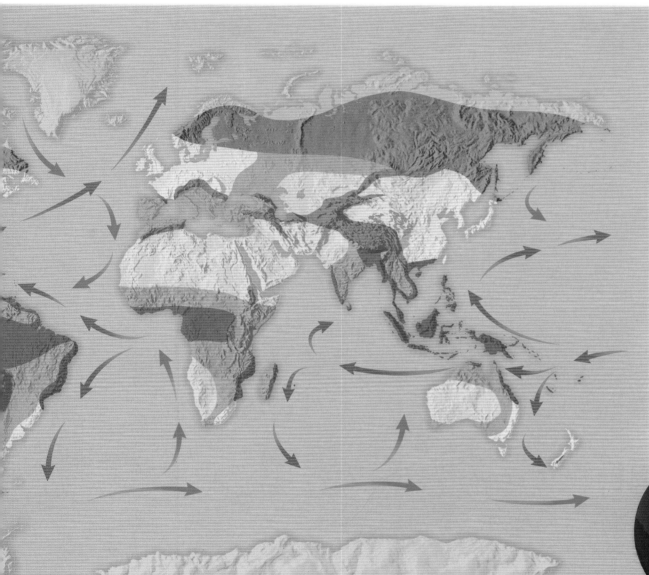

◆ AMAZING FACT ◆

Thunderstorms are most common in tropical areas, but occur all over the world. At least 20,000 storms occur each day, and at any one time about 2,000 may be taking place. Lightning from these storms strikes the ground as frequently as 100 times every second.

ENERGY FROM THE SUN
Because Earth is shaped like a ball, the Sun strikes it more directly near the equator than at the poles. This is why tropical areas are hot and the polar regions are cold.

◆ PROJECT: *Why the Poles Are Colder Than the Equator* ◆

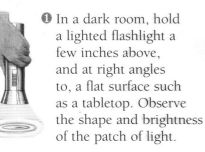

❶ In a dark room, hold a lighted flashlight a few inches above, and at right angles to, a flat surface such as a tabletop. Observe the shape and brightness of the patch of light.

❷ Tilt the flashlight and note how the light changes. When the light strikes the surface from directly overhead, the patch of light is small and intense. When the light strikes the table at an angle, the patch is larger and weaker.

In a similar way, sunlight is most intense at the equator, where it strikes the ground from directly overhead. At the poles, the light strikes Earth at an angle and is spread across a wider area, making it much weaker.

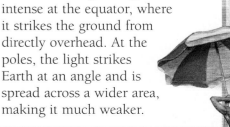

The Living World

ALMOST EVERY PART OF OUR PLANET is inhabited by an amazing variety of living things. So far, scientists have named about two million kinds, or species, of plants and animals, but there may be between 10 and 100 million species on Earth! All living things inhabit the biosphere, which is made up of the land, oceans and atmosphere. Within the biosphere, there are many kinds of environments. Over millions of years, plants and animals have gradually altered their bodies and behavior to suit their particular environments. This process is known as adaptation. Together, an environment and its inhabitants form an ecosystem. The members of each ecosystem depend on each other for food and other resources. For example, vegetation provides food for plant-eating animals (herbivores) which may in turn be eaten by meat-eating animals (carnivores). These close relationships mean that damage to one part of an ecosystem is likely to affect every other part of it.

GLOBAL ECOSYSTEMS
Each of Earth's environments has its own community of plants and animals. This illustration shows how ecosystems change between the tropical rain forests (far left) and the polar ice caps (far right).

Oceans
The oceans contain a huge variety of species that have adapted to life under water. Marine plants include many kinds of seaweed. Animals include sea mammals such as seals and whales, coral, and thousands of fish species.

Tropical Rain Forests
The hot, humid weather of the tropics creates dense forests that are home to more species than any other environment. Monkeys and birds live high in the trees, while jaguars and other mammals prowl the forest floor.

Subtropical Savannas
With rain falling only in summer, subtropical areas have few trees. The African savanna grasslands support herds of herbivores such as zebras, which are hunted by lions and other carnivores. Vultures and other scavengers eat the leftovers.

Deserts and Semideserts
Desert species have adapted to drought. Some plants, such as cacti, store water in their stems. Others have long roots that reach water far underground. In hot deserts, many animals come out only at night, when it is cooler.

WORLD ENVIRONMENTS

Because the weather determines the types of plants that grow, Earth's environments are closely related to its climate zones.

- Tropical rain forests
- Subtropical savannas
- Deserts and semideserts
- Temperate grasslands and shrub woodlands
- Temperate forests
- Coniferous forests
- Mountains
- Polar ice caps and tundra

• AMAZING FACT •

The world's largest flower, the rafflesia, is found in the rain forests of southeast Asia and can measure up to three feet (1 m) in diameter. It gives off a smell like rotting flesh which attracts insects.

Mountains

The higher the land, the less vegetation there is and the colder and windier it gets. Thick fur coats keep many mountain animals warm. Some species, such as mountain goats, have special hooves that help them climb rocky slopes.

Polar Ice Caps and Tundra

The ice caps are bitterly cold and offer little shelter. Some animals have fur and a thick layer of fat to keep them warm. Tundra is treeless land that surrounds the Arctic ice cap. Its low shrubs feed hares, lemmings and other herbivores.

Temperate Grasslands and Shrub Woodlands

Moderate rainfall creates grasslands and shrub woodlands. Grasslands attract herbivores such as bison and are ideal hunting grounds for birds of prey. There is little shelter, so some animals live in burrows.

Temperate Forests

Trees grow well in wet temperate regions. In areas with cold winters, most of the trees are deciduous, which means that they shed their leaves in fall. Some animals migrate in winter; others survive on food stored during summer.

Coniferous Forests

Cold temperate regions are covered by forests of evergreen trees called conifers. Shaped so that snow slides off them, these trees are well adapted to the cold winters. Many animals have thick fur, and some hibernate for the winter.

• LOOK AGAIN •

- Name a plant-eating animal that lives on the African savanna.
- Which plants store water in their stems?
- How have animals adapted to mountain environments?

Our Natural Resources

EARTH PROVIDES US with everything that we need to live. Its atmosphere, rivers and lakes supply fresh water which, with sunshine and soil, enables plants to grow. In turn, plants produce vital supplies of oxygen and provide us and other animals with food. Animals supply humans with meat, wool and dairy products. Plants also provide timber, fuel, and textiles such as cotton. All these resources—water, plants, crops, animals—are renewable. This means that if we manage them carefully they will never run out. Other resources are nonrenewable. They do not regrow or replenish themselves and will eventually be used up. They include minerals, precious stones and fossil fuels (coal, oil and gas). Minerals—such as clay, chalk and many metals—and precious stones—such as diamonds and emeralds—have a wide range of uses, particularly in industry. Coal, oil and gas supply most of the energy we need for lighting and heating our homes and for fueling our cars. They are known as fossil fuels because they are the remains of animals and plants buried deep underground. Some of these nonrenewable resources may run out within the next 50 years. Because of this, and because burning fossil fuels creates pollution, scientists are trying to find ways of using renewable resources to supply more of the energy we need.

ENERGY SUPPLIES
The illustration below shows our principal sources of energy. As the chart on the right indicates, coal, oil and gas still supply most of our fuel. But alternative energy supplies such as wind and solar power are being developed in many parts of the world. As reserves of fossil fuels run out, these sources will become increasingly important.

Energy Use

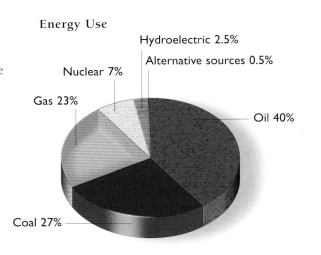

- Hydroelectric 2.5%
- Alternative sources 0.5%
- Nuclear 7%
- Gas 23%
- Oil 40%
- Coal 27%

EARTH'S RESOURCES
The map above shows how land is used in different parts of the world, and where major fuel reserves are located.

- Major gas field
- Major coal field
- Major oil field

- Urban areas: towns, cities and industries
- Areas with large farms where people grow crops and raise animals for sale

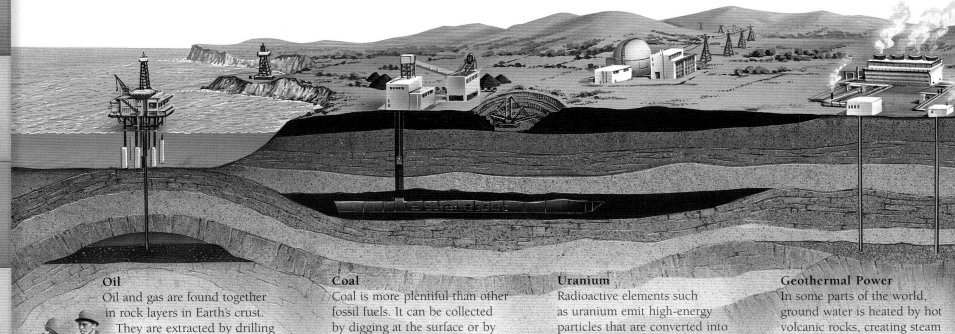

Oil
Oil and gas are found together in rock layers in Earth's crust. They are extracted by drilling from sea- or land-based rigs.

Coal
Coal is more plentiful than other fossil fuels. It can be collected by digging at the surface or by mining deep underground.

Uranium
Radioactive elements such as uranium emit high-energy particles that are converted into electricity at nuclear power plants.

Geothermal Power
In some parts of the world, ground water is heated by hot volcanic rocks, creating steam that is used to generate power.

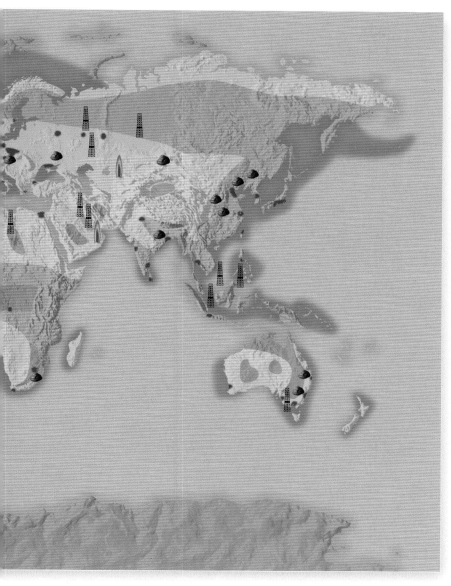

THE WATER CYCLE

A process known as the water cycle provides us with a regular supply of fresh water. Water in oceans, lakes and rivers is constantly evaporating into the air, where it exists as water vapor. The warmer the air, the more water vapor it can hold. When air cools, its ability to hold water decreases, and some of the water vapor turns, or condenses, into tiny water droplets or ice crystals. These droplets or crystals form clouds. If the droplets or crystals combine and become heavy enough, they fall as rain or snow. Water that falls on land drains into rivers, lakes and underground channels. It then flows into the sea, replenishing the oceans and completing the water cycle.

Areas with small farms where people grow crops and raise animals mainly for their own use

Grassland areas used for grazing large numbers of animals

Deserts, dry grasslands and tundra used for grazing small numbers of animals

Forested areas with some farming, hunting and mining

Areas that are too cold or dry for farming, but include some mining and hunting

Major fishing grounds

◆ PROJECT: *Create a Water Cycle* ◆

This simple experiment will show you how the water cycle works.

❶ Cool a long, metal spoon or ladle by placing it in a freezer for a few minutes. Choose a spoon with a wooden handle.

❷ Ask an adult to help you boil some water in a kettle or saucepan.

❸ As the water boils, the warm air above the water rises. As it starts to cool, it condenses and forms clouds of steam.

❹ Hold the cold spoon over the steam, being careful not to burn yourself. The cooling effect of the cold metal causes the water vapor to condense more quickly and form droplets of water on the underside of the spoon.

❺ The droplets grow in size until they become heavy enough to fall, just like rain. Some of the droplets may fall back into the kettle or saucepan, replenishing the water supply.

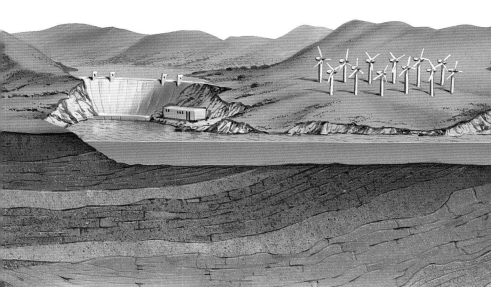

Hydroelectric Power
Hydroelectric power is created when water is passed through electricity-generating turbines at the bottom of a dam.

Wind Power
Windmills convert the power of the wind into electricity. The wind turns the windmills, which drive electrical generators.

Solar Power
Clusters of mirrorlike solar panels reflect the Sun's rays onto a solar furnace, where the intense heat is converted into electricity.

Sea Power
At a tidal dam or barrage, waves pass through narrow tunnels, driving huge turbines that produce power.

The Human Family

OUR PLANET IS HOME to about 6 billion people. This population is not spread evenly over Earth's landmasses. Instead, people are concentrated where resources are plentiful, or can be easily obtained by trade. Therefore, few people live in deserts or polar regions, but many live in fertile areas, close to energy sources, and near rivers and coasts. The world's population is now growing more quickly than ever before. In the time it takes you to read this sentence, more than 20 babies will have been born. Since 1950 the number of people on Earth has more than doubled. This growth is the result of a longer life expectancy due to improved medical services, and a high birth rate in some parts of the world. The most rapid population growth occurs in developing countries—poorer countries with little industry or technology. It is difficult for these countries to feed and take care of their growing populations, so many of them are urging their people to have fewer children.

NATIONAL POPULATIONS
This diagram shows the 10 countries with the world's largest populations. China has by far the biggest population—in fact, one in every five people in the world lives in China!

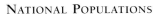

China	India	U.S.A.	Indonesia	Brazil	Pakistan	Russia	Bangladesh	Nigeria	Japan
1.28 billion	1.05 billion	281 million	231 million	176 million	148 million	145 million	133 million	130 million	127 million

WHERE PEOPLE LIVE
The dots on this map show the world's most densely populated areas.

- Developed countries
- Developing countries

CROWDED COUNTRIES
Some countries are densely populated—a large population lives in a small area. Others are sparsely populated—a small population occupies a large area.

The Netherlands:
1,000 people per square mile
(400 per sq. km)

Australia:
6 people per square mile
(2 per sq. km)

GROWING CITIES
As countries develop, people move to cities to look for work in factories and businesses. As shown by this comparison of the populations of Paris, France, and Jakarta, Indonesia, cities in developing countries are now growing more rapidly than those in developed countries.

Paris   Jakarta

1970		1990		2010	
8.5 million	3.9 million	9.3 million	9.3 million	9.6 million	19.2 million

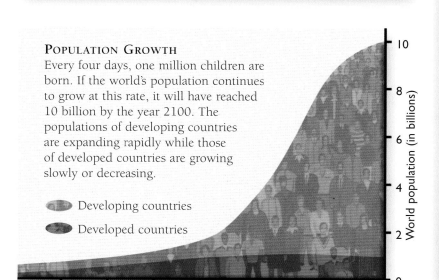

◆ *A*MAZING FACTS ◆

- Every second, three babies are born.
- If the world's population were spread out evenly over its landmasses, each person would occupy an area larger than four football fields.
- Standing side by side, everyone in the world could fit onto the island of Jamaica.

POPULATION GROWTH

Every four days, one million children are born. If the world's population continues to grow at this rate, it will have reached 10 billion by the year 2100. The populations of developing countries are expanding rapidly while those of developed countries are growing slowly or decreasing.

- Developing countries
- Developed countries

Year 1750 1800 1850 1900 1950 2000 2050 2100

World population (in billions)

RICH AND POOR

Countries with large industries and high levels of technology are called developed countries. People in these parts of the world are generally wealthy and have many possessions. In countries with little industry and technology, people are poorer and have few possessions. These countries are known as developing countries. Although they are home to far fewer people, developed countries are much richer and use a much larger proportion of the world's resources than developing countries.

Developed countries:
make up 20% of the world's population
own 80% of the world's wealth
use 70% of the world's energy

Developing countries:
make up 80% of the world's population
own 20% of the world's wealth
use 30% of the world's energy

◆ *P*ROJECT: *Languages* ◆

More than 3,000 languages are spoken around the world, but more than one-third of the world's population speaks one of the following six languages. So you can learn to say "hello" to more than two billion people!

hello
English
(350 million speakers)

你好
*ni **hao***
Chinese
(1 billion speakers)

مرحبا
*mar-ha-**ban***
Arabic
(150 million speakers)

¡holà!
o-la
Spanish
(250 million speakers)

नमस्ते
*na-ma-**stay***
Hindi
(200 million speakers)

привет!
pree-vyet
Russian
(150 million speakers)

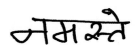

Planet in Peril

THE FUTURE OF OUR PLANET is at risk, now more than ever before. In the last 200 years, rapid population growth and the development of industry and technology have magnified the effect of our activities on the environment. Supplies of fossil fuels and other nonrenewable resources are running out. We are overusing the soil, forests and fishing grounds, and no longer giving these renewable resources a chance to recover. Waste from our homes and industries is poisoning water supplies, and gases from our cars and factories are polluting the air we breathe. Increasing air pollution may even be changing the climate. Scientists all over the world are trying to find ways to preserve resources and limit the damage we are doing to Earth. Through simple activities such as recycling, using our cars less and buying environmentally friendly products, we can all play a part in protecting Earth and preserving its resources for future generations.

◆ AMAZING FACTS ◆

- An acre (0.4 ha) of Brazilian rain forest is destroyed every nine seconds.
- Every day, more than 50 species become extinct. This is mainly the result of human activities such as forestry and hunting.

A GLOBAL CRISIS

This map shows that environmental problems affect almost every part of Earth. The most serious problems are described and illustrated on these pages.

 Existing deserts

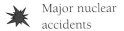 Areas at risk of becoming deserts

Existing rain forest

Cleared rain forest

● Cities with severe air pollution

Areas affected by acid rain

Polluted waterways

Heavy oil slicks created by shipping

Light oil slicks created by shipping

✳ Major nuclear accidents

Major oil tanker disasters

Major oil rig explosions

Holding Back the Desert

In dry parts of the world, overgrazing and clearing the land of its natural vegetation can turn fertile areas into desert. To keep deserts from spreading farther, we need to better manage the land we farm and replant trees and shrubs.

Saving the Forests

Vast areas of natural forest are being cleared to supply timber, fuel and paper, and to make way for towns and farms. You can help protect the world's forests and reduce the need for more wood by recycling paper. Replanting trees also helps.

Reducing Air Pollution

Cars and factories fill the air with grime and poisonous gases. Industries and car manufacturers are trying to reduce such pollution. You can also help by walking, cycling or using public transportation instead of traveling by car.

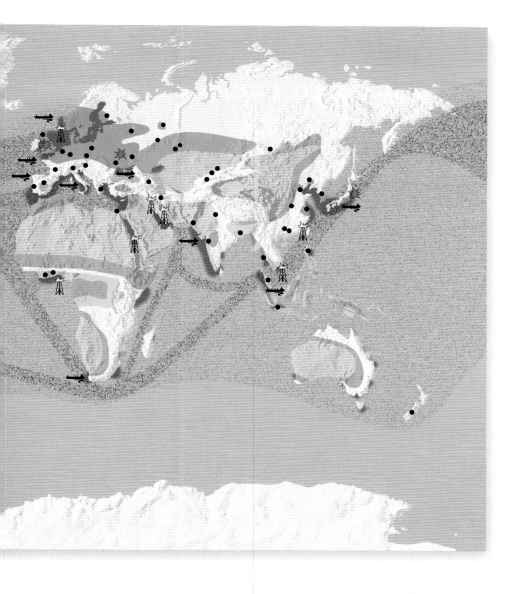

Oil Spills

Oil and other pollutants spilled by ships are a threat to wildlife. In 1989, oil spilled by the tanker *Exxon Valdez* off the coast of Alaska, in the United States, killed thousands of animals, including 350,000 seabirds.

Nuclear Accidents

Nuclear accidents occur rarely but can be devastating. In 1986, an accident at the Chernobyl nuclear power plant in the Ukraine released a cloud of radioactive gas across Europe, poisoning land, crops and people.

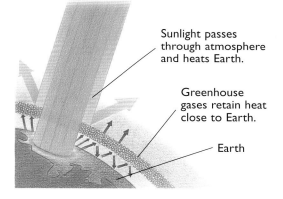

Oil Well Explosions

Accidents on oil and gas rigs can cause major environmental problems. During the Gulf War in Kuwait in 1992, hundreds of oil wells were set on fire, causing serious water and air pollution throughout the region.

Eliminating Acid Rain

Air pollution can turn rain into a strong acid. Acid rain kills trees, pollutes rivers and even damages buildings. The only way to stop acid rain is to reduce air pollution.

Saving the Ozone Layer

A layer of ozone in the upper atmosphere filters out harmful radiation from the Sun. This layer is being damaged by chlorofluorocarbons (CFCs)—chemicals found in some aerosols and refrigerators. Always buy CFC-free products.

Keeping Our Water Clean

The world's rivers and oceans are being poisoned by waste from factories and shipping, and sewage from homes and offices. To help protect water supplies, support local cleanup programs, and never dispose of garbage in or near waterways.

Sunlight passes through atmosphere and heats Earth.

Greenhouse gases retain heat close to Earth.

Earth

GLOBAL WARMING

Gases in the atmosphere, known as greenhouse gases, keep Earth warm by trapping some of the energy that comes from the Sun. But the burning of fossil fuels is raising the levels of these gases, causing the planet to warm too much. If this continues, some fertile land may turn into desert, and ice caps may melt, causing flooding in lowland areas. Most countries are trying to reduce greenhouse gas emissions.

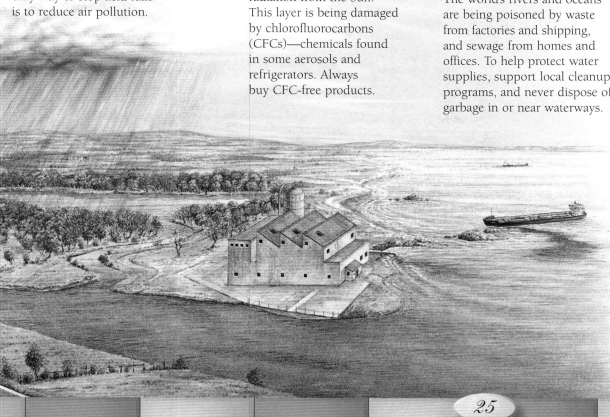

• $\mathcal{L}$OOK AGAIN •

- How can we prevent acid rain?
- What gases keep Earth warm?
- How can you help protect the ozone layer?

The Physical World

WE CALL OUR PLANET EARTH, but more than two-thirds of its surface is covered by salt water. Large areas of salt water are called oceans, and smaller areas are known as seas. There are four oceans—the Pacific, Atlantic, Indian and Arctic—and many seas. The Pacific Ocean alone is larger than all of Earth's landmasses combined. Land covers only 29 percent of our planet's surface. Its shape and the kind of soil and vegetation that cover it vary enormously from place to place. Throughout the world there are hills, mountains and areas of flat land called plains. Trees and other plants cover many parts of Earth, but some places have almost no vegetation. Deserts—very dry areas with sparse vegetation—cover about one-fifth of the world's land. The polar regions and many mountaintops are covered in ice and snow. The seas, too, have their mountains and valleys. Deep trenches are found in most oceans, and mountains on many islands are actually the tops of undersea mountains. For instance, Mauna Kea, on the island of Hawaii in the Pacific Ocean, is 33,480 feet (10,205 m) high, measured from the sea floor to its highest point. That's far taller than Mount Everest, the highest mountain on land.

PHYSICAL FACTS

Circumference of Earth around the equator:
24,902 miles (40,067 km)
Area of sea: 139,433,000 square miles
(361,132,000 sq. km)
Area of land above sea level: 57,156,000 square
miles (148,940,000 sq. km)
Largest ocean: Pacific Ocean, 60,061,000 square
miles (155,557,000 sq. km)
Largest landmass: Eurasia (Europe and Asia),
20,733,000 square miles (53,698,000 sq. km)
Deepest ocean trench: Mariana Trench, Pacific
Ocean, 35,840 feet (10,924 m)
Largest island: Greenland, 840,000 square miles
(2,175,000 sq. km)

◆ AMAZING FACT ◆

Almost all of the water on Earth—97.3 percent— is salt water. Less than 3 percent is fresh water, and two-thirds of this is locked up in icecaps and glaciers. That leaves less than 1 percent in rivers, lakes and underground channels.

ARCTIC OCEAN

SEVERNAYA ZEMLYA

FRANZ JOSEF LAND

Spitsbergen
SVALBARD

Greenland Sea

Laptev Sea

NEW SIBERIAN ISLANDS

East Siberian Sea

Barents Sea

NOVAYA ZEMLYA

Kara Sea

Chukchi Sea

Jan Mayen Island

Iceland

Norwegian Sea

SCANDINAVIA

Dvina

CENTRAL SIBERIAN PLATEAU

Lena

Bering Strait

FAEROE ISLANDS

Ireland

North Sea

BRITISH ISLES

EUROPEAN PLAIN

Volga

URAL MOUNTAINS

Ob'

WESTERN SIBERIAN PLAIN

Ob'

Yenisey

Angara

SIBERIA

Lena

Amur

Bering Sea

Sea of Okhotsk

ALEUTIAN ISLANDS

ALEUTIAN TRENCH

IC RIDGE

EUROPE

Dnieper

CARPATHIAN MTS.

ALPS

Danube

ASIA

THE STEPPE

Aral Sea

Lake Balkhash

Lake Baikal

AZORES

CHANNEL ISLANDS

Black Sea

Caspian Sea

TIAN MTS.

GOBI DESERT

KURIL ISLANDS

KURIL TRENCH

IC

MADEIRA

ATLAS MTS.

Mediterranean Sea

Euphrates

Tigris

ZAGROS MTS.

HINDU KUSH

KUNLUN MTS.

PLATEAU OF TIBET

Huang (Yellow)

Sea of Japan (East Sea)

Hokkaidō

Honshū

NORTHWEST PACIFIC BASIN

PACIFIC

CANARY ISLANDS

Red Sea

Nile

NUBIAN DESERT

ARABIAN PENINSULA

HIMALAYAS

Indus

Ganges

Chang (Yangtze)

East China Sea

MIDWAY ISLANDS

OCEAN

VERDE ISLANDS

N

SAHARA DESERT

Arabian Sea

DECCAN

Bay of Bengal

Mekong

Taiwan

Luzon

South China Sea

PHILIPPINE BASIN

MARIANA TRENCH

Wake Island

MID-PACIFIC MOUNTAINS

Niger

SAHEL

AFRICA

LACCADIVE ISLANDS

ANDAMAN ISLANDS

NICOBAR ISLANDS

Sri Lanka

PHILIPPINE ISLANDS

Philippine Sea

MARIANA ISLANDS

Guam

MICRONESIA

MARSHALL ISLANDS

CENTRAL PACIFIC BASIN

Johnston Atoll

Uele

Ubangi

Congo

Kasai

CONGO BASIN

Lake Victoria

GREAT RIFT VALLEY

MID-INDIAN RIDGE

MALDIVES

SUNDA ISLANDS

NINETYEAST RIDGE

Sumatra

Borneo

Palau

CAROLINE ISLANDS

MELANESIA

Nauru

OCEANIA

GILBERT ISLANDS

Ascension

St. Helena

MID-ATLANTIC RIDGE

SEYCHELLES

COMOROS ISLANDS

Mayotte

MID-INDIAN BASIN

Java

JAVA TRENCH

Christmas Island

New Guinea

SOLOMON ISLANDS

Tuvalu

Tokelau

MARTIN VAZ ISLANDS

Zambezi

Madagascar

Mauritius

Réunion

INDIAN OCEAN

COCOS (KEELING) ISLANDS

WHARTON BASIN

Coral Sea

Vanuatu

FIJI ISLANDS

SAMOA ISLANDS

Niue

NAMIB DESERT

KALAHARI DESERT

Orange

GREAT SANDY DESERT

SIMPSON DESERT

GREAT DIVIDING RANGE

New Caledonia

Tonga

TONGA TRENCH

Tristan da Cunha

Gough Island

CAPE OF GOOD HOPE

AUSTRALIA

GREAT VICTORIAN DESERT

Lake Eyre

Darling

Norfolk Island

KERMADEC ISLANDS

KERMADEC TRENCH

SOUTHWEST INDIAN RIDGE

Amsterdam Island

St. Paul Island

CROZET ISLANDS

KERGUÉLEN ISLANDS

SOUTHEAST INDIAN RIDGE

Great Australian Bight

Murray

Tasmania

Tasman Sea

NEW ZEALAND

North Island

CHATHAM ISLANDS

SOUTH SANDWICH ISLANDS

Bouvet Island

PRINCE EDWARD ISLANDS

HEARD AND McDONALD ISLANDS

ATLANTIC-INDIAN BASIN

Macquarie Island

AUCKLAND ISLANDS

South Island

WALVIS RIDGE

SOUTH INDIAN BASIN

ANTARCTICA

Ross Sea

2
3
4
5
6
7
8
9
10

Countries of the World

APART FROM ANTARCTICA, which has no permanent population, all the land on Earth is divided into countries. There are almost 200 countries in the world, and each country has its own government and its own laws. The world's smallest country, the Vatican City, measures only one-fifth of a square mile (0.44 sq. km). That's about the size of 100 football fields. The largest country in the world, Russia, is 39 million times bigger! The lines that separate countries are called borders. On this world map, the countries are shown in different colors so that you can see the borders clearly. Borders may be straight or curved. Some are formed by rivers or mountain ranges; others cross lakes or seas. The sizes of countries and the shapes of their borders often change. Sometimes a large country divides into smaller countries because groups of people want to form separate countries. Neighboring countries often disagree about where a border ought to be. Such disputes have led to wars in many parts of the world. In this atlas, disputed borders are shown by a dotted line. Many countries govern areas of land in other parts of the world. These are called territories. On a map, the name of the governing country usually appears in parentheses after the name of the territory.

POLITICAL FACTS

Number of countries: 193
Number of territories: 65
Largest countries:
Russia, 6,592,812 square miles (17,075,383 sq. km)
Canada, 3,851,809 square miles (9,976,185 sq. km)
China, 3,705,386 square miles (9,596,960 sq. km)
Smallest country: Vatican City, 0.17 square miles (0.44 sq. km)
Longest border: U.S.-Canada, 3,987 miles (6,416 km)

· LOOK AGAIN ·

The following shapes represent countries shown on the world map on the right. Can you find and name them?

KEY TO NUMBERED COUNTRIES

1 THE NETHERLANDS
2 BELGIUM
■3 LUXEMBOURG
4 CZECH REPUBLIC
5 SLOVAKIA
6 SWITZERLAND
■7 LIECHTENSTEIN
8 SLOVENIA
9 CROATIA
■10 ANDORRA
■11 MONACO
■12 SAN MARINO
■13 VATICAN CITY
14 BOSNIA-HERZEGOVINA
15 MOLDOVA
16 YUGOSLAVIA
17 ALBANIA
18 MACEDONIA
■19 GIBRALTAR (U.K.)
20 ARMENIA
21 AZERBAIJAN
22 UNITED ARAB EMIRATES

ARCTIC OCEAN

SVALBARD (NORWAY)

JAN MAYEN ISLAND (NORWAY)

ICELAND

FAEROE ISLANDS (DENMARK)

SWEDEN FINLAND

NORWAY

ESTONIA
LATVIA
LITHUANIA

RUSSIA

DENMARK

UNITED KINGDOM

IRELAND

GERMANY
POLAND
BELARUS

FRANCE
AUSTRIA HUNGARY
ITALY
ROMANIA
BULGARIA

UKRAINE

KAZAKSTAN

MONGOLIA

PORTUGAL SPAIN

GREECE
MALTA
TUNISIA

TURKEY
CYPRUS
LEBANON
SYRIA

GEORGIA
UZBEKISTAN KYRGYZSTAN
TURKMENISTAN
TAJIKISTAN

NORTH KOREA
SOUTH KOREA
JAPAN

PACIFIC OCEAN

MADEIRA (PORTUGAL)

MOROCCO

ISRAEL
JORDAN
IRAQ
IRAN
AFGHANISTAN

CHINA

TAIWAN

MIDWAY ISLANDS (U.S.A.)

CANARY ISLANDS (SPAIN)

WESTERN SAHARA (MOROCCO)

ALGERIA
LIBYA
EGYPT

KUWAIT
BAHRAIN
QATAR
SAUDI ARABIA
OMAN

PAKISTAN
NEPAL
BHUTAN

INDIA

BANGLADESH
MYANMAR (BURMA)
LAOS

WAKE ISLAND (U.S.A.)

NORTHERN MARIANA ISLANDS (U.S.A.)

GUAM (U.S.A.)

JOHNSTON ATOLL (U.S.A.)

MAURITANIA
MALI
NIGER
CHAD
SUDAN
ERITREA
YEMEN

LACCADIVE ISLANDS (INDIA)

ANDAMAN ISLANDS (INDIA)

THAILAND
VIETNAM
CAMBODIA

PHILIPPINES

MARSHALL ISLANDS

SENEGAL
GAMBIA
GUINEA-BISSAU
GUINEA
SIERRA LEONE
LIBERIA
CÔTE D'IVOIRE (IVORY COAST)

BURKINA FASO
NIGERIA
CENTRAL AFRICAN REPUBLIC

DJIBOUTI
ETHIOPIA

NICOBAR ISLANDS (INDIA)

SRI LANKA

MALDIVES

BRUNEI
MALAYSIA

PALAU

FEDERATED STATES OF MICRONESIA

NAURU

KIRIBATI

CAMEROON
EQUATORIAL GUINEA
GABON
CONGO
SÃO TOMÉ AND PRÍNCIPE

DEMOCRATIC REPUBLIC OF THE CONGO (ZAIRE)

KENYA
UGANDA
RWANDA
BURUNDI
SOMALIA

TANZANIA

SINGAPORE

BRITISH INDIAN OCEAN TERRITORY (U.K.)

CHRISTMAS ISLAND (AUSTRALIA)

COCOS (KEELING) ISLANDS (AUSTRALIA)

INDONESIA

EAST TIMOR

PAPUA NEW GUINEA

SOLOMON ISLANDS

TUVALU

TOKELAU (N.Z.)

ASCENSION (U.K.)

ANGOLA
ZAMBIA
MALAWI

SEYCHELLES

COMOROS
MAYOTTE (FRANCE)

VANUATU

WALLIS AND FUTUNA (FRANCE)

SAMOA
AMERICAN SAMOA (U.S.A)

NIUE (N.Z.)

ST. HELENA AND DEPENDENCIES (U.K.)

IN VAZ ISLANDS (BRAZIL)

NAMIBIA
BOTSWANA
ZIMBABWE
MOZAMBIQUE

MADAGASCAR
MAURITIUS
RÉUNION (FRANCE)

NEW CALEDONIA (FRANCE)

FIJI
TONGA

SWAZILAND

LESOTHO
SOUTH AFRICA

INDIAN OCEAN

AUSTRALIA

NORFOLK ISLAND (AUSTRALIA)

KERMADEC ISLAND (N.Z.)

ATLANTIC OCEAN

TRISTAN DA CUNHA (U.K.)

GOUGH ISLAND (U.K.)

AMSTERDAM ISLAND (FRANCE)

ST. PAUL ISLAND (FRANCE)

NEW ZEALAND

CHATHAM ISLANDS (N.Z.)

PRINCE EDWARD ISLANDS (SOUTH AFRICA)

CROZET ISLANDS (FRANCE)

KERGUÉLEN ISLANDS (FRANCE)

AUCKLAND ISLANDS (N.Z.)

SOUTH SANDWICH ISLANDS (U.K.)

BOUVET ISLAND (NORWAY)

HEARD AND McDONALD ISLANDS (AUSTRALIA)

MACQUARIE ISLAND (AUSTRALIA)

CAMPBELL ISLAND (N.Z.)

PACIFIC OCEAN

ANTARCTICA

The Power of Politics

EXACTLY HOW DID countries form? Early on, people lived in small family groups and their ways of life, or cultures, were shaped by the physical demands of the regions they lived in. Eventually, as the family groups grew larger, relations between the groups helped form the regions into countries—a fact that has created many of the conflicts we've recently seen. Africa, for example, was divided into countries by outside colonial powers, splitting up many ethnic groups and mixing others together. Today, more than 60 borders or territories are causing conflict within and between countries, and disputes that start as local affairs can soon escalate into something bigger. For instance, when the Serbian leader Slobodan Milosevic tried to purge Kosovo of ethnic Albanians, the United States, United Kingdom, and other NATO countries stepped in and launched air strikes to stop him. In the midst of so much conflict, many people keep working for peaceful solutions. The United Nations was established in 1945 to preserve peace through international cooperation, and almost every country in the world is now a member. It encourages fighting sides to negotiate and can send in peacekeeping forces to maintain order.

KASHMIR

In 1947, when British India was divided into India—a state populated mostly by Hindus—and Muslim Pakistan, both countries claimed Kashmir. The United Nations drew the "Line of Control" and most of Kashmir went to India. Many Muslim Kashmiris have since rebelled against Indian rule. And now that India and Pakistan both have weapons of mass destruction, nuclear war is a possibility.

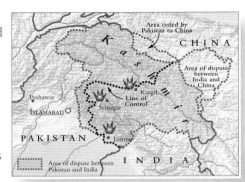

• AMAZING FACT •

On achieving independence, countries often change their names: Belize used to be called British Honduras, Sri Lanka was Ceylon, and Botswana was Bechuanaland.

☆ Hot spot

🕊 Peacekeepers

GLOBAL HOT SPOTS

Wars can be internal disputes, such as civil wars and independence struggles, or conflicts involving two or more countries, often caused by disagreements over borders or territory. Since September 11, we've seen a new kind of war appear—a global war on terrorism, rather than against a country.

SEPTEMBER 11, 2001

When terrorists hijacked passenger planes and flew them into the World Trade Center and the Pentagon, the United States declared war on terrorism. The hijackers were linked to Osama bin Laden's al Qaeda organization, an international terrorist network run largely from Afghanistan. The United States led a military attack that helped to bring down Afghanistan's Taliban regime, and continues to pursue networks of terrorists throughout the world.

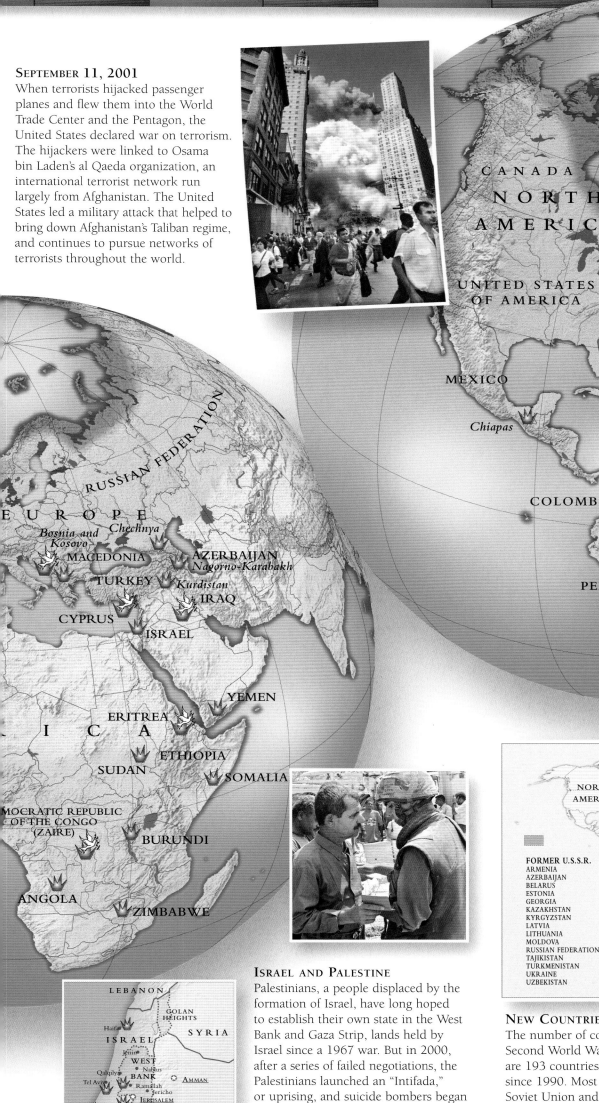

CANADA
NORTH AMERICA

UNITED STATES OF AMERICA

World Trade Center, New York
The Pentagon, Arlington, Virginia

60°N

30°N

MEXICO

HAITI

Chiapas

VENEZUELA

COLOMBIA

Equator

SOUTH AMERICA

PERU

BRAZIL

30°S

RUSSIAN FEDERATION

EUROPE

Bosnia and Kosovo
Chechnya
MACEDONIA

AZERBAIJAN
Nagorno-Karabakh

TURKEY

Kurdistan
IRAQ

CYPRUS

ISRAEL

YEMEN

ERITREA

...ICA

ETHIOPIA

SUDAN

SOMALIA

DEMOCRATIC REPUBLIC OF THE CONGO (ZAIRE)

BURUNDI

ANGOLA

ZIMBABWE

ISRAEL AND PALESTINE

Palestinians, a people displaced by the formation of Israel, have long hoped to establish their own state in the West Bank and Gaza Strip, lands held by Israel since a 1967 war. But in 2000, after a series of failed negotiations, the Palestinians launched an "Intifada," or uprising, and suicide bombers began targeting Israeli civilians. Israel has responded with military force to try to root out terrorists.

LEBANON
GOLAN HEIGHTS
Haifa
ISRAEL
SYRIA
Jenin
WEST
Nablus
Qalqilya
BANK
Tel Aviv
Ramallah
AMMAN
Jericho
GAZA
JERUSALEM
STRIP
Bethlehem
JORDAN
Gaza
Hebron

Areas occupied by Israel since 1967

NEW COUNTRIES

The number of countries in the world has nearly tripled since the end of the Second World War. In 1946, there were just 74 countries, while today there are 193 countries. The world map above shows the new countries created since 1990. Most of these appeared when Communism collapsed in the Soviet Union and people in Eastern Europe and the Balkans formed their own governments. Some countries, such as East Timor and Palau, achieved independence from other nations. Others, such as Yemen and Germany, formed when two countries reunited.

NORTH AMERICA
EUROPE
ASIA
MARSHALL ISLANDS
PALAU
SOUTH AMERICA
AFRICA
MICRONESIA
EAST TIMOR
AUSTRALIA

FORMER U.S.S.R.
ARMENIA
AZERBAIJAN
BELARUS
ESTONIA
GEORGIA
KAZAKHSTAN
KYRGYZSTAN
LATVIA
LITHUANIA
MOLDOVA
RUSSIAN FEDERATION
TAJIKISTAN
TURKMENISTAN
UKRAINE
UZBEKISTAN

FORMER YUGOSLAVIA
BOSNIA AND HERZEGOVINA
CROATIA
MACEDONIA
SLOVENIA

OTHERS
CZECH REPUBLIC
EAST TIMOR
ERITREA
FEDERAL REPUBLIC OF GERMANY
FEDERATED STATES OF MICRONESIA
MARSHALL ISLANDS
NAMIBIA
PALAU
REPUBLIC OF YEMEN
SLOVAKIA

North America

THE CONTINENT OF NORTH AMERICA extends from just south of the North Pole to just north of the equator. It includes almost every kind of environment, from ice caps to forests, mountains, deserts and jungles. In the west, an almost unbroken chain of mountains stretches from Alaska to Costa Rica and includes the Rocky Mountains, one of the world's most famous mountain ranges. The United States (often called the U.S.A. or America) and Canada are the largest of the continent's 23 countries. The United States is made up of 50 states. Canada is divided into ten provinces and three territories. North America includes some of the world's biggest cities, but also vast areas of wilderness. Most North Americans are the descendants of European immigrants, but there are also many people of African origin as well as groups of native peoples.

CONTINENT FACTS

Regional land area: 8,522,127 sq. miles (22,078,049 sq. km)
Regional population: 486,069,988
Independent countries: Antigua and Barbuda, The Bahamas, Barbados, Belize, Canada, Costa Rica, Cuba, Dominica, Dominican Republic, El Salvador, Grenada, Guatemala, Haiti, Honduras, Jamaica, Mexico, Nicaragua, Panama, St. Kitts–Nevis, St. Lucia, St. Vincent and the Grenadines, Trinidad and Tobago, United States of America

WORLD RECORDS

WORLD'S LARGEST GORGE
GRAND CANYON, U.S.A., 277 MILES (446 KM) LONG, 10 MILES (16 KM) WIDE, 1 MILE (1.6 KM) DEEP

WORLD'S LARGEST FRESHWATER LAKE
LAKE SUPERIOR, U.S.A.-CANADA, 31,800 SQ. MILES (82,350 SQ. KM)

WORLD'S LONGEST CAVE SYSTEM
MAMMOTH CAVES, U.S.A., 351 MILES (565 KM)

WORLD'S LARGEST ACTIVE VOLCANO
MAUNA LOA, HAWAII, U.S.A., 13,680 FT (4,170 M) HIGH, 75 MILES (120 KM) LONG, 31 MILES (50 KM) WIDE

WORLD'S LONGEST BORDER
U.S.-CANADIAN BORDER, 3,987 MILES (6,416 KM)

WORLD'S TALLEST ACTIVE GEYSER
STEAMBOAT GEYSER, YELLOWSTONE NATIONAL PARK, U.S.A., 380 FT (115 M)

WORLD'S LARGEST THEME PARK
WALT DISNEY WORLD, U.S.A., 47 SQ. MILES (122 SQ. KM)

CONTINENT RECORDS

HIGHEST MOUNTAIN
MOUNT MCKINLEY (DENALI), U.S.A., 20,320 FT (6,194 M)

LOWEST POINT
DEATH VALLEY, U.S.A., 282 FT (86 M) BELOW SEA LEVEL

LONGEST RIVER
MISSISSIPPI-MISSOURI, U.S.A., 3,740 MILES (6,020 KM)

LARGEST COUNTRY BY AREA
CANADA, 3,851,809 SQ. MILES (9,976,185 SQ. KM)

LARGEST COUNTRY BY POPULATION
UNITED STATES OF AMERICA, POPULATION 280,562,489

LARGEST CITY BY POPULATION
MEXICO CITY, MEXICO, POPULATION 18,330,000

MAJOR MOUNTAINS AND RIVERS

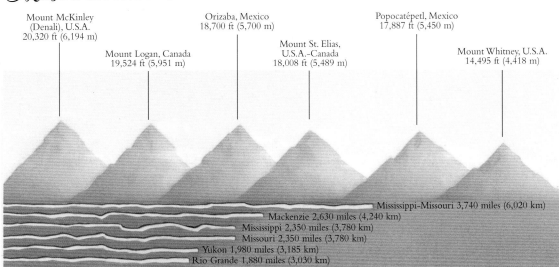

Mount McKinley (Denali), U.S.A. 20,320 ft (6,194 m)

Mount Logan, Canada 19,524 ft (5,951 m)

Orizaba, Mexico 18,700 ft (5,700 m)

Mount St. Elias, U.S.A.-Canada 18,008 ft (5,489 m)

Popocatépetl, Mexico 17,887 ft (5,450 m)

Mount Whitney, U.S.A. 14,495 ft (4,418 m)

Mississippi-Missouri 3,740 miles (6,020 km)
Mackenzie 2,630 miles (4,240 km)
Mississippi 2,350 miles (3,780 km)
Missouri 2,350 miles (3,780 km)
Yukon 1,980 miles (3,185 km)
Rio Grande 1,880 miles (3,030 km)

POLITICAL MAP

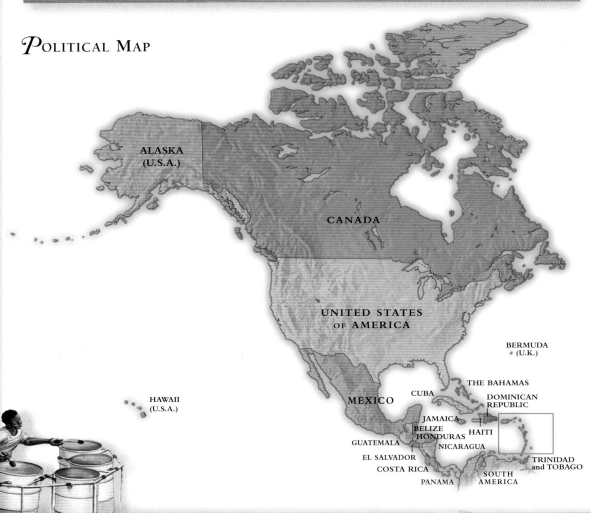

ALASKA (U.S.A.)

CANADA

UNITED STATES OF AMERICA

HAWAII (U.S.A.)

MEXICO

BERMUDA (U.K.)

THE BAHAMAS

CUBA

DOMINICAN REPUBLIC

JAMAICA

BELIZE
GUATEMALA
HONDURAS
NICARAGUA
EL SALVADOR
COSTA RICA
PANAMA

HAITI

TRINIDAD and TOBAGO

SOUTH AMERICA

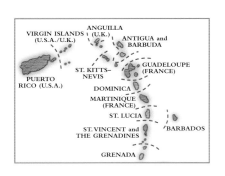

ANGUILLA (U.K.)
VIRGIN ISLANDS (U.S.A./U.K.)
ANTIGUA and BARBUDA
ST. KITTS–NEVIS
GUADELOUPE (FRANCE)
PUERTO RICO (U.S.A.)
DOMINICA
MARTINIQUE (FRANCE)
ST. LUCIA
ST. VINCENT and THE GRENADINES
BARBADOS
GRENADA

PHYSICAL MAP

ASIA

ARCTIC OCEAN

× NORTH POLE

Chukchi Sea

Beaufort Sea

Banks Island

QUEEN ELIZABETH ISLANDS

Ellesmere Island

Greenland

Baffin Bay

EUROPE

Bering Sea

BROOKS RANGE

Yukon

Victoria Island

Baffin Island

ALEUTIAN ISLANDS

Mt. McKinley (Denali)

Mt. Logan

Mt. St. Elias

Mackenzie

Great Bear Lake

Arctic Circle

Labrador Sea

Gulf of Alaska

Great Slave Lake

C A N A D I A N

Hudson Bay

LABRADOR

Newfoundland

QUEEN CHARLOTTE ISLANDS

ROCKY MOUNTAINS

COAST MTS.

G R E A T   P L A I N S

S H I E L D

ATLANTIC OCEAN

Vancouver Island

Lake Winnipeg

Missouri

Lake Nipigon

Lake Superior

Lake Huron

Lake Ontario

St. Lawrence

PACIFIC OCEAN

COAST RANGES

GREAT BASIN

Great Salt Lake

Mt. Whitney

Colorado

Mississippi

Lake Michigan

Lake Erie

APPALACHIAN MOUNTAINS

WAIIAN LANDS

Missouri

Ohio

Bermuda

SIERRA MADRE OCCIDENTAL

SIERRA MADRE ORIENTAL

Rio Grande

Mississippi

Mississippi

THE BAHAMAS

Tropic of Cancer

Gulf of California

Gulf of Mexico

GREATER ANTILLES

LESSER ANTILLES

Popocatépetl

Orizaba

Bay of Campeche

Caribbean Sea

Lake Nicaragua

SOUTH AMERICA

Equator

GALÁPAGOS ISLANDS

Western Canada and Alaska

CANADA, THE WORLD'S SECOND-LARGEST country, covers more than half of North America. Northern Canada is a vast wilderness where bears fish icy rivers for salmon, and wolves hunt caribou across snow-covered plains. The new Arctic territory of Nunavut, occupying the eastern mainland of the Northwest Territories and most of the Arctic islands, came into existence in 1999. Nunavut means "our land" in the language of its Inuit inhabitants. Few people live in this cold environment. Eighty percent of Canada's residents live within 185 miles (300 km) of the southern border, where the climate is milder and the land is more fertile. The prairie grassland that covers parts of Alberta, Manitoba and Saskatchewan is one of the world's most productive farming regions. These provinces also supply most of Canada's oil and gas. West of the towering Rocky Mountains is the Pacific coastline, a maze of islands and narrow waterways. In the Gulf of Alaska, glaciers creep down the mountains toward the shore, while seals and whales swim in the bays. Alaska is the biggest of the United States, but it is separated from the rest of the country by Canada. More than half of Alaska's lands are wildlife refuges, and the state contains some of North America's largest oil fields.

ALASKA (U.S.A.)
POPULATION: 634,900 ∗ CAPITAL: JUNEAU

ALBERTA
POPULATION: 3,064,200 ∗ CAPITAL: EDMONTON

BRITISH COLUMBIA
POPULATION: 4,095,900 ∗ CAPITAL: VICTORIA

MANITOBA
POPULATION: 1,150,000 ∗ CAPITAL: WINNIPEG

NORTHWEST TERRITORIES
POPULATION: 40,900 ∗ CAPITAL: YELLOWKNIFE

NUNAVUT
POPULATION: 28,200 ∗ CAPITAL: IQALUIT

SASKATCHEWAN
POPULATION: 1,015,800 ∗ CAPITAL: REGINA

YUKON TERRITORY
POPULATION: 29,900 ∗ CAPITAL: WHITEHORSE

∗ AMAZING FACT ∗

The United States bought Alaska from Russia in 1867 for $7.2 million. At the time, many people thought that this was a waste of money. But once the state's large reserves of gold and oil were discovered, the deal seemed like a bargain.

ALASKAN BROWN BEAR
At 9 ft (2.7 m) long, these huge bears are the largest meat-eaters living on land. They often fish for salmon in rivers and streams.

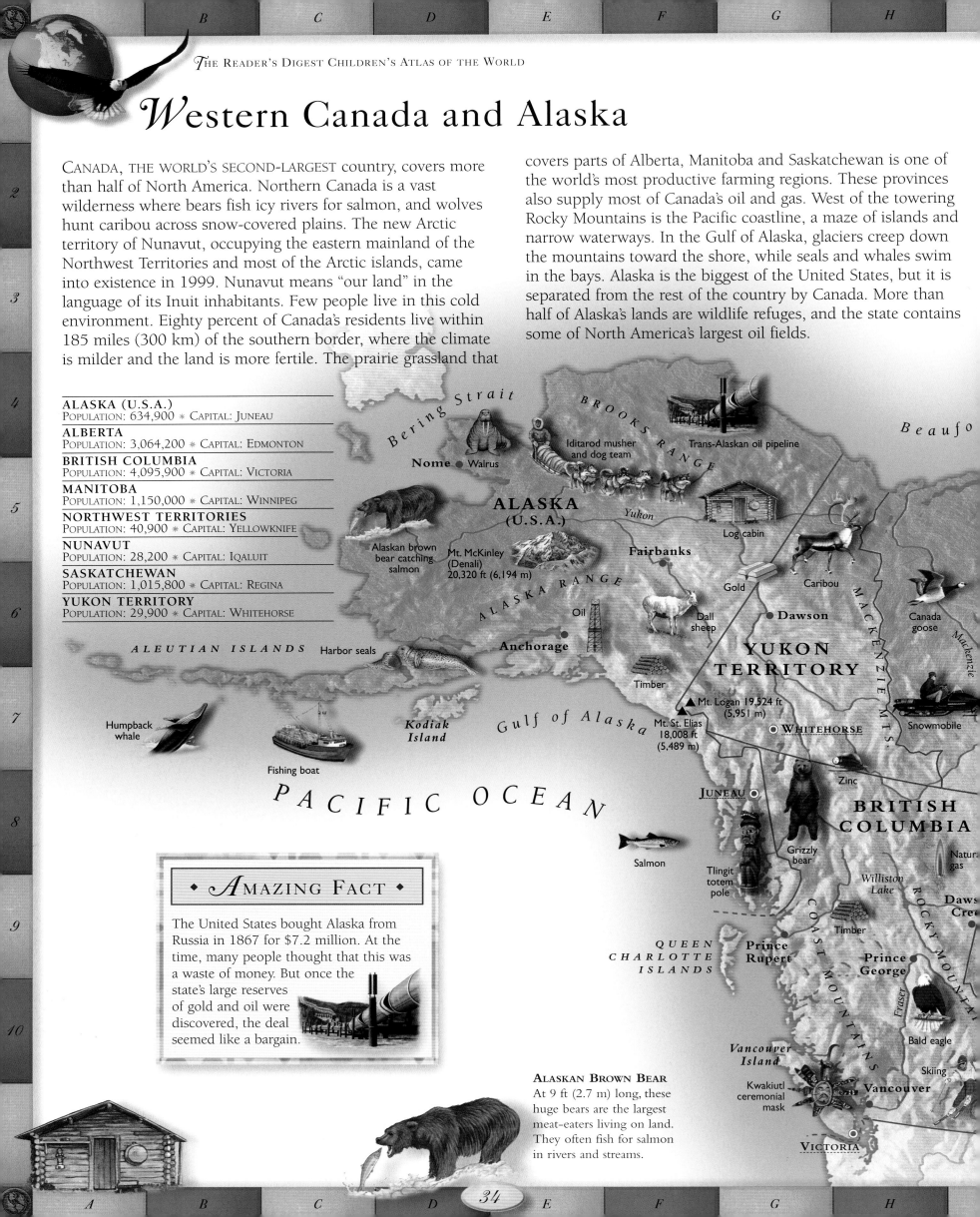

Bering Strait

Beaufo[rt]

BROOKS RANGE

Iditarod musher and dog team

Trans-Alaskan oil pipeline

Nome ● Walrus

Log cabin

ALASKA (U.S.A.)

Yukon

Alaskan brown bear catching salmon

Mt. McKinley (Denali) 20,320 ft (6,194 m)

Fairbanks

Gold

Caribou

ALASKA RANGE

Oil

Dall sheep

● Dawson

Canada goose

Anchorage

YUKON TERRITORY

Timber

MACKENZIE MTS.

Mackenzie

ALEUTIAN ISLANDS

Harbor seals

Mt. Logan 19,524 ft (5,951 m)

Mt. St. Elias 18,008 ft (5,489 m)

◎ WHITEHORSE

Snowmobile

Humpback whale

Kodiak Island

Gulf of Alaska

JUNEAU ◎

Zinc

BRITISH COLUMBIA

Fishing boat

PACIFIC OCEAN

Salmon

Grizzly bear

Natura[l] gas

Tlingit totem pole

Williston Lake

ROCKY MOUNTAIN[S]

Daws[on] Cree[k]

QUEEN CHARLOTTE ISLANDS

Prince Rupert

Timber

Prince George

Vancouver Island

Fraser

Bald eagle

Skiing

Kwakiutl ceremonial mask

Vancouver

COAST MOUNTAINS

VICTORIA ◎

WESTERN CANADA AND ALASKA *See World Fact File page 104*

Narwhal

ARCTIC OCEAN

Ellesmere Island

Musk ox

QUEEN ELIZABETH ISLANDS

Polar bears

PARRY ISLANDS

Arctic fox

Baffin Bay

GREENLAND

Banks Island

Snow goose

Somerset Island

Prince of Wales Island

Davis Strait

Arctic hare

Inuit building igloo

Baffin Island

Victoria Island

Prince Charles Island

Traditional church

Inuit fishing through ice

Kittiwake

Harp seals

Great Bear Lake

Silver

NUNAVUT

Wolf

Igloo-shaped houses

Southampton Island

IQALUIT

Seaplane

Hudson Strait

NORTHWEST TERRITORIES

YELLOWKNIFE

QUÉBEC

LOCATION

Great Slave Lake

Gold

Gray jay

CANADA

Moose

Hudson Bay

Slave

ⒺⒷ Beluga whale

N

Zinc and lead

Lake Athabasca

ALBERTA

Uranium

Reindeer Lake

Belcher Islands

W   E

Edmontonia dinosaur fossils

Beaver

Churchill

Nelson

Nickel and copper

S

Mountie

MANITOBA

EDMONTON

SASKATCHEWAN

Gold

ONTARIO

SCALE

MILES

0   100   200   300

Oil

Natural gas

Wheat

Saskatchewan

Lake Winnipeg

0   100   200   300   400   500

KILOMETERS

Calgary

Saskatoon

REGINA

Grain elevators

WINNIPEG

Calgary Stampede

Legislative Building

UNITED STATES OF AMERICA

ROYAL CANADIAN MOUNTED POLICE (MOUNTIES)
Canada's national police force was founded in 1873 to prevent disputes between native tribes and European traders.

◆ PROJECT: *Inuit Finger Masks* ◆

In ceremonies and rituals, the Inuit (Eskimos) use tiny finger masks to represent their spirit ancestors. The masks are often carved from wood or stone, but you can make yours out of cardboard.

❶ Cut out a circle about four inches (10 cm) in diameter. Cut two small holes at the bottom of the circle large enough for your fingers to poke through.

❷ Draw a face in the center of the circle and color it. Cut a fringe in the cardboard or glue feathers or beads around the face.

❸ To perform with the mask, move your hand slowly from side to side to the beat of a drum.

Eastern Canada

ABOUT 60 PERCENT OF THE POPULATION of Canada live along the shores of the St. Lawrence River and the Great Lakes, an area that occupies only 2 percent of the country's land area. From the early 17th century onward, European immigrants settled here because the land was fertile and the waterways provided transportation routes. Today, the region is home to many of Canada's biggest cities, including the two largest, Toronto and Montréal. Canada has two main languages—English and French. The majority of French speakers live in the province of Québec, which was once a French territory. The forests, lakes and rivers that cover most of Québec and Ontario provide a wealth of resources. Québec's forestry industry produces about 12 percent of the world's pulp and paper. Hydroelectric power stations create so much electricity that Québec and Ontario can export energy. The climate of eastern Canada ranges from temperate in the south to arctic in the north. For nine months of the year, Hudson Bay remains frozen, allowing polar bears to prowl the pack ice in search of food. Off Newfoundland's north shore float huge icebergs measuring up to 150 feet (45 m) high. Farther south, enormous tides surge in and out of the bays. In the Bay of Fundy, the sea can rise 50 feet (15 m) at high tide—high enough to cover a four-story building!

NEW BRUNSWICK
POPULATION: 757,100 ✳ CAPITAL: FREDERICTON

NEWFOUNDLAND
POPULATION: 533,800 ✳ CAPITAL: ST. JOHN'S

NOVA SCOTIA
POPULATION: 942,700 ✳ CAPITAL: HALIFAX

ONTARIO
POPULATION: 11,874,400 ✳ CAPITAL: TORONTO

PRINCE EDWARD ISLAND
POPULATION: 138,500 ✳ CAPITAL: CHARLOTTETOWN

QUÉBEC
POPULATION: 7,410,500 ✳ CAPITAL: QUÉBEC

✦ LOOK AGAIN ✦

- Which city is Canada's national capital?
- Which endangered sea mammal swims off the east coast of Newfoundland?
- What kind of mineral is mined in Newfoundland?

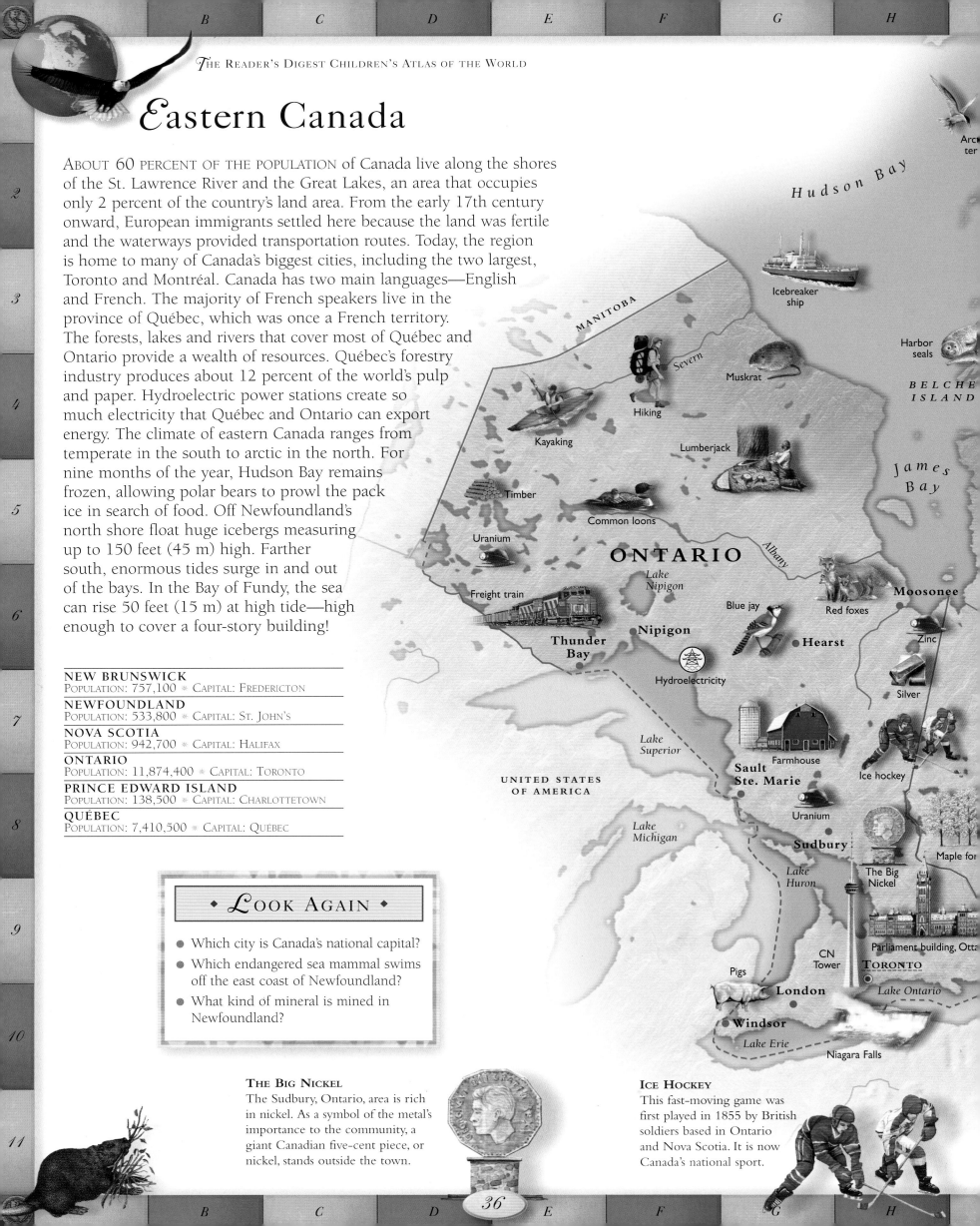

THE BIG NICKEL
The Sudbury, Ontario, area is rich in nickel. As a symbol of the metal's importance to the community, a giant Canadian five-cent piece, or nickel, stands outside the town.

ICE HOCKEY
This fast-moving game was first played in 1855 by British soldiers based in Ontario and Nova Scotia. It is now Canada's national sport.

Ivujivik

Polar bears

PÉNINSULE D'UNGAVA
(UNGAVA PENINSULA)

Wolverine

Snowy owl

Hudson Strait

Furs

Iceberg

Orca
(killer
whale)

Puffins

Feuilles

Ungava Bay

Labrador Sea

ATLANTIC OCEAN

AMAZING FACT

The Canadian National (CN) Tower in Toronto is the tallest freestanding structure in the world. Completed in 1976, it stands 1,816 feet (553 m) high—the equivalent of a 150-story building! On a clear day, you can see for more than 75 miles (120 km) from the top of the tower.

Moose

Hooded seal

QUÉBEC

Nain

Hydroelectricity

Beaver

Cross-country
skiing

Gannet

LABRADOR

Réservoir de la
Grande Deux

Smallwood
Reservoir

NEWFOUNDLAND

Black bear

Iron
ore

Churchill

Happy Valley–
Goose Bay

Lac
akami

Cross-country
skiing

Raccoon

Canada
geese

Blue whales

old

Timber

Camping

Harp seals

LOCATION

Lac
Mistassini

Paper

inc and
copper

Hydroelectricity

Cap-des-Rosiers
Lighthouse

Île d'Anticosti
(Anticosti Island)

Zinc

Lac
Saint-Jean

Saguenay

Statue of
De Maisonneuve,
founder of
Montréal

Château
Frontenac

PÉNINSULE
DE LA GASPÉSIE
(GASPÉ PENINSULA)

Gulf of St. Lawrence

Beaver

Traditional church

Newfoundland

St. Lawrence

QUÉBEC

Food processing

NEW
BRUNSWICK

PRINCE
EDWARD
ISLAND

Anne of Green
Gables's House

ST. JOHN'S

ST-PIERRE AND
MIQUELON (FRANCE)

TAWA

Montréal

FREDERICTON

CHARLOTTETOWN

Saint John

NOVA
SCOTIA

N

Hydroelectricity

HALIFAX

W E

UNITED STATES
OF AMERICA

Bay of Fundy

Fishing
port

Lobster

S

HARP SEALS
Each year in March, more than a quarter of a million of these seals travel to the islands in the Gulf of St. Lawrence to give birth to their young.

SCALE
MILES

0   50   100   150   200

0   100   200   300   400

KILOMETERS

Northeastern United States

THE NORTHEAST is home to 70 million people—more than one-quarter of the population of the United States. From Boston in the north to Washington, D.C. in the south, a line of great cities stretches for over 400 miles (640 km) along the Atlantic shore. Including its suburbs, New York City is home to almost 20 million people. It is the largest city in the U.S.A. and the third largest in the world. New York is one of the world's leading centers of trade, industry and culture. The heart of the city is the island of Manhattan, where giant skyscrapers, including some of the world's tallest, tower over long, straight streets packed with people and traffic.

The Appalachian Mountains separate the cities of the coast from the Great Lakes and the plains of the interior. They stretch for more than 1,600 miles (2,600 km) from northern Alabama, in the southern United States, to northern Maine. In the south, these mountains are rich in minerals—Kentucky produces more coal than any other state. Farms occupy many Appalachian valleys, but large areas of the mountains are covered by deciduous forests where black bears forage for blueberries and otters swim in the streams. In fall, these forests provide spectacular displays of color, as their leaves change from green to brilliant shades of orange, red and gold.

CONNECTICUT
POPULATION: 3,425,000 * CAPITAL: HARTFORD

DELAWARE
POPULATION: 796,200 * CAPITAL: DOVER

DISTRICT OF COLUMBIA
POPULATION: 571,800 * CAPITAL: WASHINGTON, D.C.

KENTUCKY
POPULATION: 4,065,600 * CAPITAL: FRANKFORT

MAINE
POPULATION: 1,286,700 * CAPITAL: AUGUSTA

MARYLAND
POPULATION: 5,375,200 * CAPITAL: ANNAPOLIS

MASSACHUSETTS
POPULATION: 6,379,300 * CAPITAL: BOSTON

NEW HAMPSHIRE
POPULATION: 1,259,200 * CAPITAL: CONCORD

NEW JERSEY
POPULATION: 8,484,400 * CAPITAL: TRENTON

NEW YORK
POPULATION: 19,011,400 * CAPITAL: ALBANY

PENNSYLVANIA
POPULATION: 12,287,200 * CAPITAL: HARRISBURG

RHODE ISLAND
POPULATION: 1,058,900 * CAPITAL: PROVIDENCE

VERMONT
POPULATION: 613,100 * CAPITAL: MONTPELIER

VIRGINIA
POPULATION: 7,187,700 * CAPITAL: RICHMOND

WEST VIRGINIA
POPULATION: 1,801,900 * CAPITAL: CHARLESTON

◆ PROJECT: *Iroquois Beads* ◆

According to the custom of the native Iroquois people, a person saying something important must give the listener a gift to confirm the truth of the statement. This gift is often a string of white and purple shell beads known as wampum. Try making your own Iroquois friendship beads. Thread some colored beads onto pieces of string and attach the strings to a length of yarn. Remember to explain the meaning of your gift to the receiver.

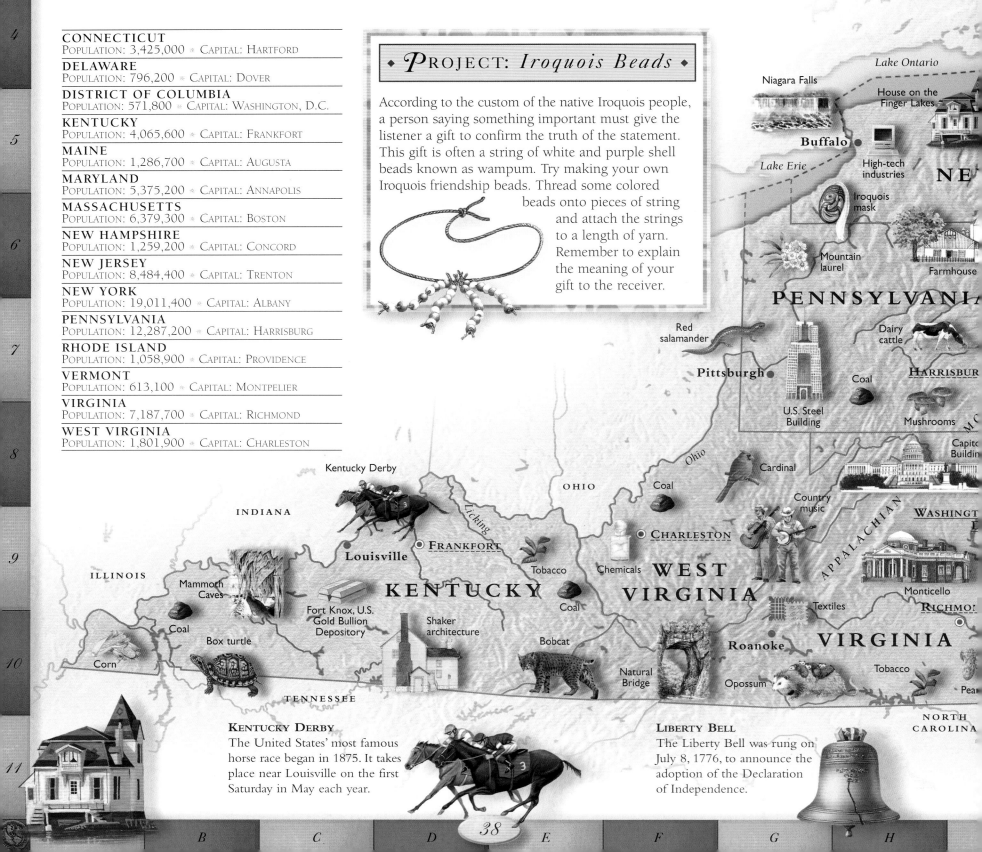

Lake Ontario
Niagara Falls
House on the Finger Lakes
Buffalo
Lake Erie
High-tech industries
Iroquois mask
NE
Mountain laurel
Farmhouse
PENNSYLVANIA
Red salamander
Dairy cattle
HARRISBUR
Pittsburgh
Coal
U.S. Steel Building
Mushrooms
Ohio
Cardinal
Capito Building
OHIO
Coal
Country music
Kentucky Derby
CHARLESTON
WASHINGT
INDIANA
Licking
APPALACHIAN
Louisville
FRANKFORT
Tobacco
Chemicals
WEST VIRGINIA
Monticello
ILLINOIS
Mammoth Caves
Coal
Bobcat
Roanoke
RICHMO
Coal
Fort Knox, U.S. Gold Bullion Depository
Shaker architecture
VIRGINIA
Box turtle
KENTUCKY
Corn
Natural Bridge
Opossum
Tobacco
TENNESSEE
Pea
NORTH CAROLINA

KENTUCKY DERBY
The United States' most famous horse race began in 1875. It takes place near Louisville on the first Saturday in May each year.

LIBERTY BELL
The Liberty Bell was rung on July 8, 1776, to announce the adoption of the Declaration of Independence.

Fort Kent

Potatoes

Chipmunk

Chickadee

Timber

Blueberries

MAINE

Mt. Washington Cog Railway

Paper

Lighthouse

CANADA

VERMONT

Zinc   Apples

MONTPELIER

Skiing

AUGUSTA

Poultry

Portland

Dairy cattle

Maple syrup

NEW HAMPSHIRE

Bluebird

Fort Ticonderoga

CONCORD

Manchester

Salmon

Timber

ORK

Baseball Hall of Fame

Albany

Basketball Hall of Fame

Connecticut

MASSACHUSETTS

High-tech industries

BOSTON

Cranberries

Mayflower

Amish people

Chrysler Building

Hudson

CONNECTICUT

HARTFORD

PROVIDENCE

RHODE ISLAND

Chocolate

New York

NEW JERSEY

Liberty Bell

Statue of Liberty

Tourism

Rhode Island Red

Minke whale

hiladelphia

TRENTON

Aircraft carrier

Poultry

Tourism

altimore

Atlantic City

NNAPOLIS

DOVER

DELAWARE

Blue marlin

MARYLAND

Crab

Norfolk

• AMAZING FACT •

The Statue of Liberty was a gift from the people of France to the people of the United States. It was designed by Frédéric-Auguste Bartholdi and engineered by Alexandre Gustave Eiffel, who built the Eiffel Tower in Paris, France. The statue took nine years to build and was unveiled in 1886. It is made up of 300 copper sheets and stands 151 feet (46 m) tall on a base 154 feet (47 m) high.

LOCATION

ATLANTIC OCEAN

N
W   E
S

SCALE

MILES

0   25   50   75   100   125

0   50   100   150   200

KILOMETERS

CHRYSLER BUILDING
This skyscraper was built by Walter Chrysler, founder of the Chrysler car empire. The steel arches at the top are modeled on car hubcaps.

MAYFLOWER
In 1620 the Mayflower carried the Pilgrims from England to America to establish one of the first permanent colonies.

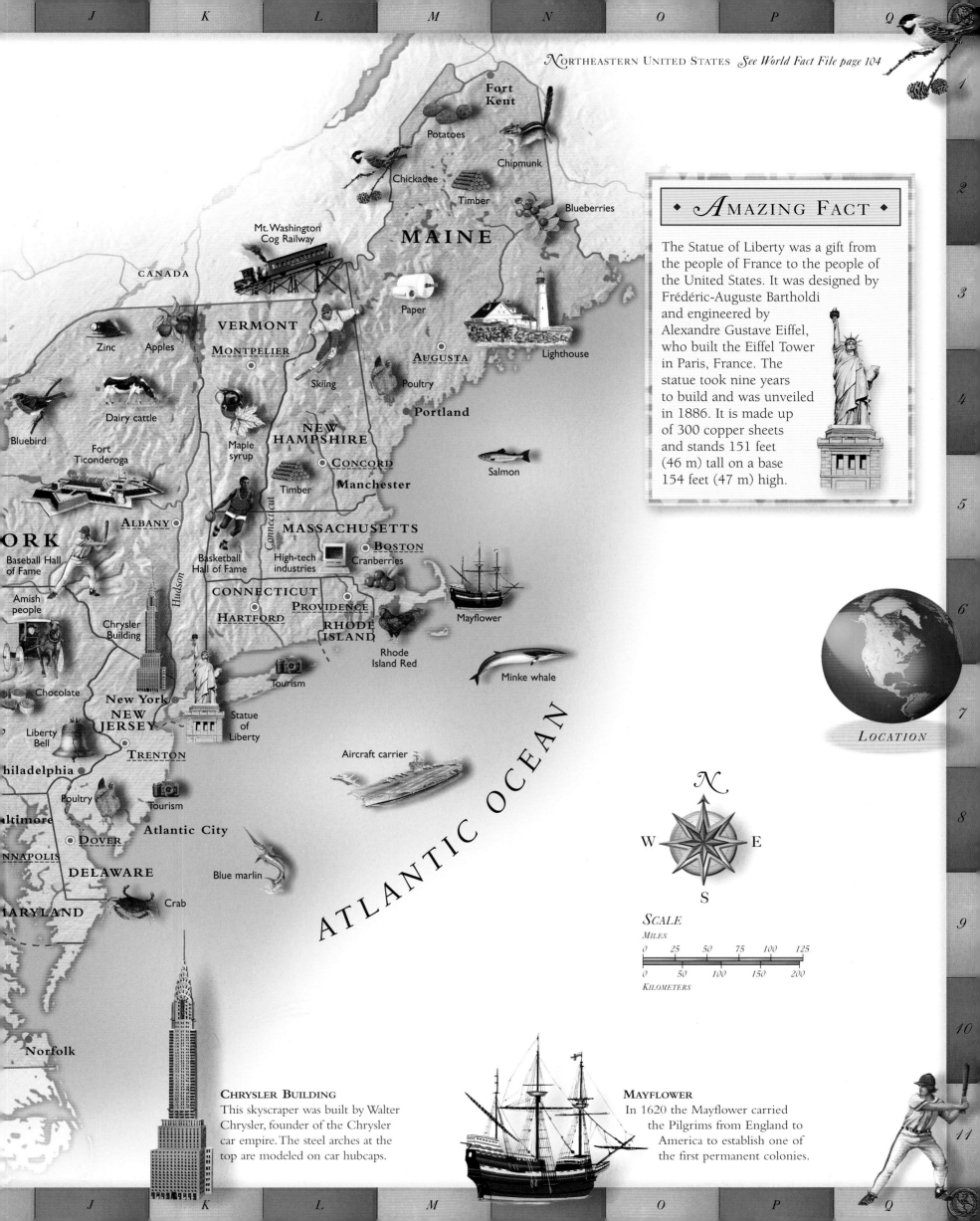

Southern United States

THE SOUTHERN UNITED STATES is a warm, humid region of plains, rivers, swamps and coastal lagoons. From southern Texas, a broad belt of lowland stretches around the Gulf of Mexico, across Florida and along the shores of the Atlantic Ocean. In the north and west, the coastal plains rise to plateaus and mountain ranges, including the Appalachian Mountains, which formed about 400 million years ago and are North America's oldest mountains. Mixed crop and livestock farms cover the fertile eastern and southern plains. In the west, on the dry Texas grasslands, ranch hands tend huge herds of cattle. Texas is the second-biggest American state after Alaska, and its beef industry and large oil reserves have made it one of the richest parts of the country. Numerous rivers cross the southern United States, including the Mississippi, one of North America's longest rivers and busiest inland waterways. Along the Gulf Coast and in northern Florida, these rivers have formed shallow lakes, muddy deltas and steamy swamps that are home to snakes, turtles and alligators. Florida's sunny climate and sandy beaches make it a popular vacation spot. The Walt Disney World theme park near Orlando is the world's number one tourist attraction, with more than 25 million visitors each year.

Many of the first Europeans to settle in this region came from France and Spain in the 17th century, and their descendants are called Creoles. Other French-speakers known as Cajuns arrived soon afterward from Canada. Florida's large Spanish-speaking population includes immigrants from the island of Cuba, which lies just 135 miles (217 km) south of Key West, the southernmost tip of Florida and the United States.

ALABAMA
POPULATION: 4,464,400 ∗ CAPITAL: MONTGOMERY

ARKANSAS
POPULATION: 2,692,100 ∗ CAPITAL: LITTLE ROCK

FLORIDA
POPULATION: 16,396,500 ∗ CAPITAL: TALLAHASSEE

GEORGIA
POPULATION: 8,383,900 ∗ CAPITAL: ATLANTA

LOUISIANA
POPULATION: 4,465,400 ∗ CAPITAL: BATON ROUGE

MISSISSIPPI
POPULATION: 2,858,000 ∗ CAPITAL: JACKSON

NORTH CAROLINA
POPULATION: 8,186,300 ∗ CAPITAL: RALEIGH

OKLAHOMA
POPULATION: 3,460,100 ∗ CAPITAL: OKLAHOMA CITY

SOUTH CAROLINA
POPULATION: 4,063,000 ∗ CAPITAL: COLUMBIA

TENNESSEE
POPULATION: 5,740,000 ∗ CAPITAL: NASHVILLE

TEXAS
POPULATION: 21,325,000 ∗ CAPITAL: AUSTIN

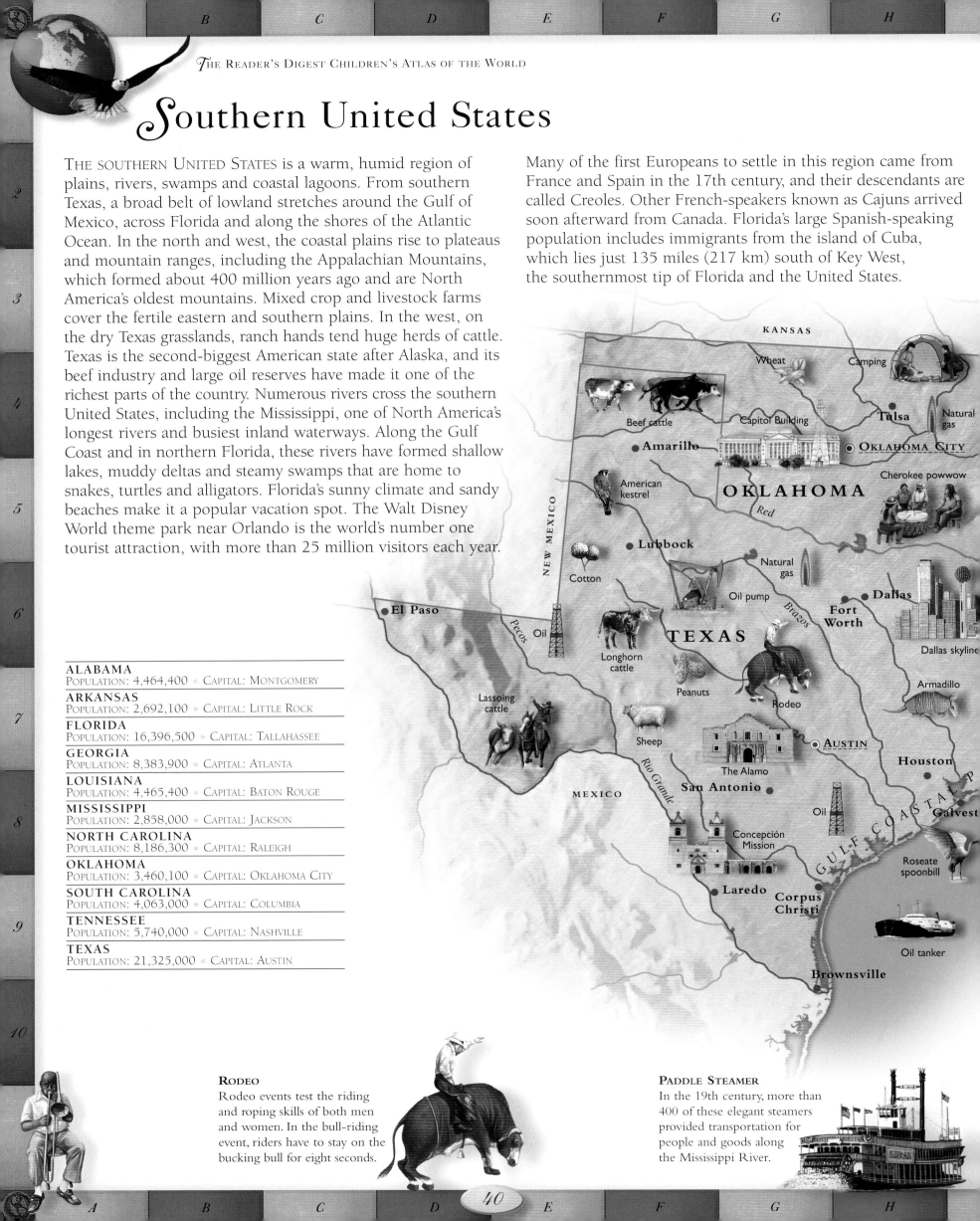

KANSAS

Wheat
Camping
Beef cattle
Capitol Building
Tulsa
Natural gas
Amarillo
OKLAHOMA CITY
Cherokee powwow
American kestrel
OKLAHOMA
Red
Lubbock
Natural gas
Cotton
Oil pump
Dallas
NEW MEXICO
El Paso
Brazos
Fort Worth
Pecos
Oil
Dallas skyline
Longhorn cattle
TEXAS
Armadillo
Peanuts
Rodeo
Lassoing cattle
Sheep
Austin
Houston
The Alamo
MEXICO
Rio Grande
San Antonio
Oil
GULF COASTAL PLAIN
Galvest
Concepción Mission
Roseate spoonbill
Laredo
Corpus Christi
Oil tanker
Brownsville

RODEO
Rodeo events test the riding and roping skills of both men and women. In the bull-riding event, riders have to stay on the bucking bull for eight seconds.

PADDLE STEAMER
In the 19th century, more than 400 of these elegant steamers provided transportation for people and goods along the Mississippi River.

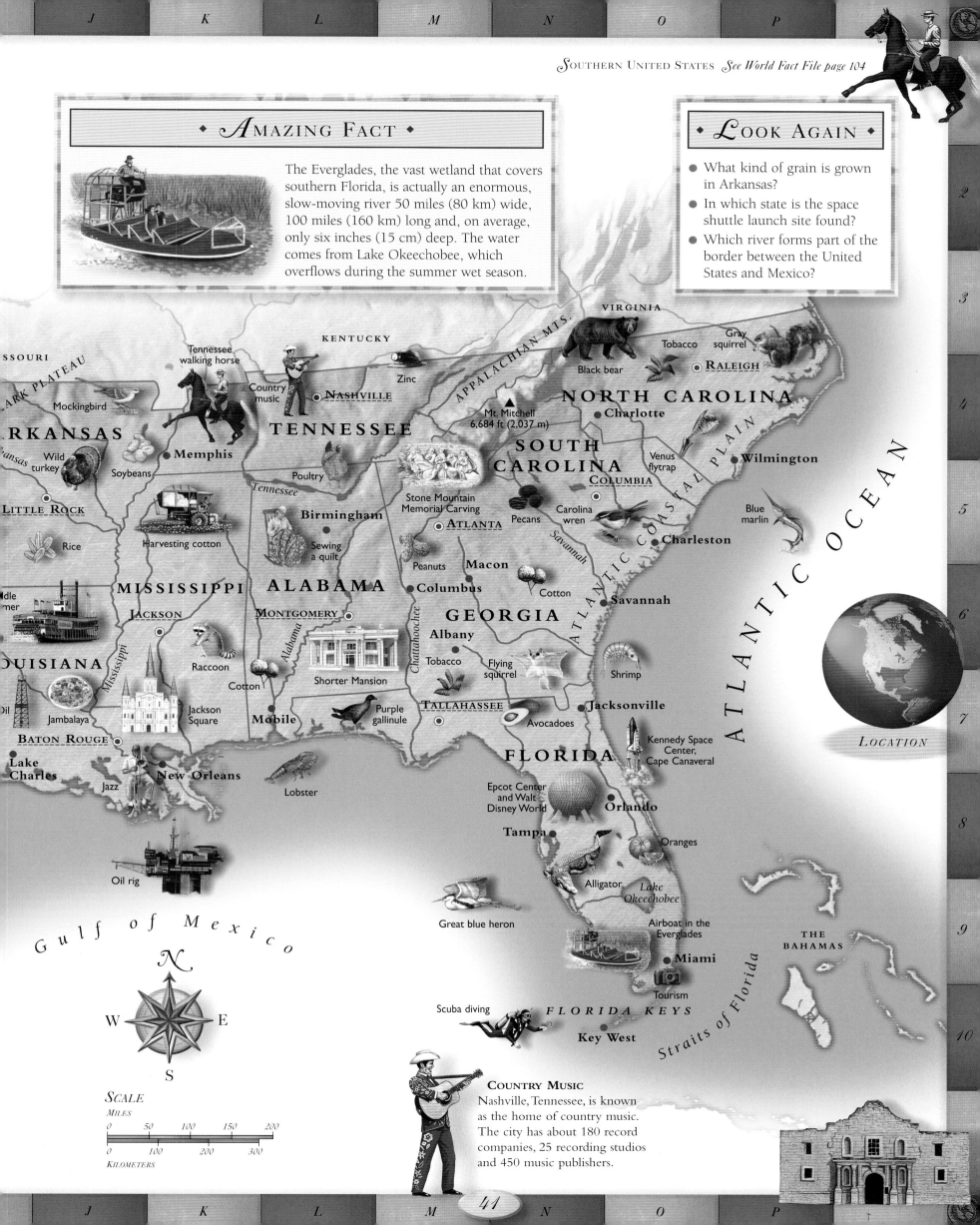

2

3

◆ Amazing Fact ◆

The Everglades, the vast wetland that covers southern Florida, is actually an enormous, slow-moving river 50 miles (80 km) wide, 100 miles (160 km) long and, on average, only six inches (15 cm) deep. The water comes from Lake Okeechobee, which overflows during the summer wet season.

◆ Look Again ◆

- What kind of grain is grown in Arkansas?
- In which state is the space shuttle launch site found?
- Which river forms part of the border between the United States and Mexico?

VIRGINIA

KENTUCKY

SSOURI

OZARK PLATEAU

Tennessee walking horse

Mockingbird

Country music

NASHVILLE

Zinc

APPALACHIAN MTS.

Black bear

Tobacco

Gray squirrel

RALEIGH

NORTH CAROLINA

Charlotte

ARKANSAS

Wild turkey

Arkansas

Soybeans

Memphis

Poultry

Tennessee

TENNESSEE

Mt. Mitchell 6,684 ft (2,037 m)

SOUTH CAROLINA

Venus flytrap

Wilmington

ATLANTIC COASTAL PLAIN

LITTLE ROCK

Rice

Harvesting cotton

Birmingham

Sewing a quilt

Stone Mountain Memorial Carving

ATLANTA

Pecans

Carolina wren

COLUMBIA

Charleston

Blue marlin

MISSISSIPPI

ALABAMA

Peanuts

Macon

ATLANTIC OCEAN

ddle mer

JACKSON

Raccoon

MONTGOMERY

Alabama

Chattahoochee

Columbus

Cotton

Savannah

Savannah

LOUISIANA

Mississippi

Cotton

Shorter Mansion

GEORGIA

Albany

Tobacco

Flying squirrel

Shrimp

Oil

Jambalaya

Jackson Square

Mobile

Purple gallinule

TALLAHASSEE

Avocadoes

Jacksonville

BATON ROUGE

Lake Charles

New Orleans

Jazz

Lobster

FLORIDA

Kennedy Space Center, Cape Canaveral

LOCATION

Epcot Center and Walt Disney World

Orlando

Tampa

Oranges

Oil rig

Alligator

Lake Okeechobee

THE BAHAMAS

Gulf of Mexico

Great blue heron

Airboat in the Everglades

Miami

Tourism

Scuba diving

FLORIDA KEYS

Straits of Florida

Key West

N

W   E

S

Scale

MILES

0   50   100   150   200

0   100   200   300

KILOMETERS

Country Music

Nashville, Tennessee, is known as the home of country music. The city has about 180 record companies, 25 recording studios and 450 music publishers.

Central United States

THE CENTRAL UNITED STATES consists of a vast area of lowland known as the Midwest or prairies. In the northeastern part of this region lie the Great Lakes, the largest group of freshwater lakes in the world. Rivers and canals connect the lakes to the Atlantic Ocean and the Gulf of Mexico, forming a major transportation network. This network and the area's many natural resources (including coal and iron ore) have helped turn the Great Lakes region into the industrial heart of the United States. Factories now line the southern shores of Lake Michigan and Lake Erie, and supply most of the country's iron, steel and cars. Unfortunately, these industries create a great deal of waste, and the Great Lakes are now badly polluted. The area south and west of the lakes was once an enormous natural grassland, roamed by millions of bison and deer, and home to Native American tribes such as the Sioux and the Comanche. Now it is one of the world's most important farming regions. Iowa lies at the center of an area known as the Corn Belt because it produces half of the world's corn. Almost all of this corn is used to fatten the region's pigs and cattle, which provide most of the United States' meat. Farther west, on the Great Plains, is a "wheat belt." Here, immense fields of wheat stretch as far as the eye can see.

ILLINOIS
POPULATION: 12,482,300 ＊ CAPITAL: SPRINGFIELD

INDIANA
POPULATION: 6,114,700 ＊ CAPITAL: INDIANAPOLIS

IOWA
POPULATION: 2,923,200 ＊ CAPITAL: DES MOINES

KANSAS
POPULATION: 2,694,600 ＊ CAPITAL: TOPEKA

MICHIGAN
POPULATION: 9,990,800 ＊ CAPITAL: LANSING

MINNESOTA
POPULATION: 4,972,300 ＊ CAPITAL: ST. PAUL

MISSOURI
POPULATION: 5,629,700 ＊ CAPITAL: JEFFERSON CITY

NEBRASKA
POPULATION: 1,713,200 ＊ CAPITAL: LINCOLN

NORTH DAKOTA
POPULATION: 634,400 ＊ CAPITAL: BISMARCK

OHIO
POPULATION: 11,373,500 ＊ CAPITAL: COLUMBUS

SOUTH DAKOTA
POPULATION: 756,600 ＊ CAPITAL: PIERRE

WISCONSIN
POPULATION: 5,401,900 ＊ CAPITAL: MADISON

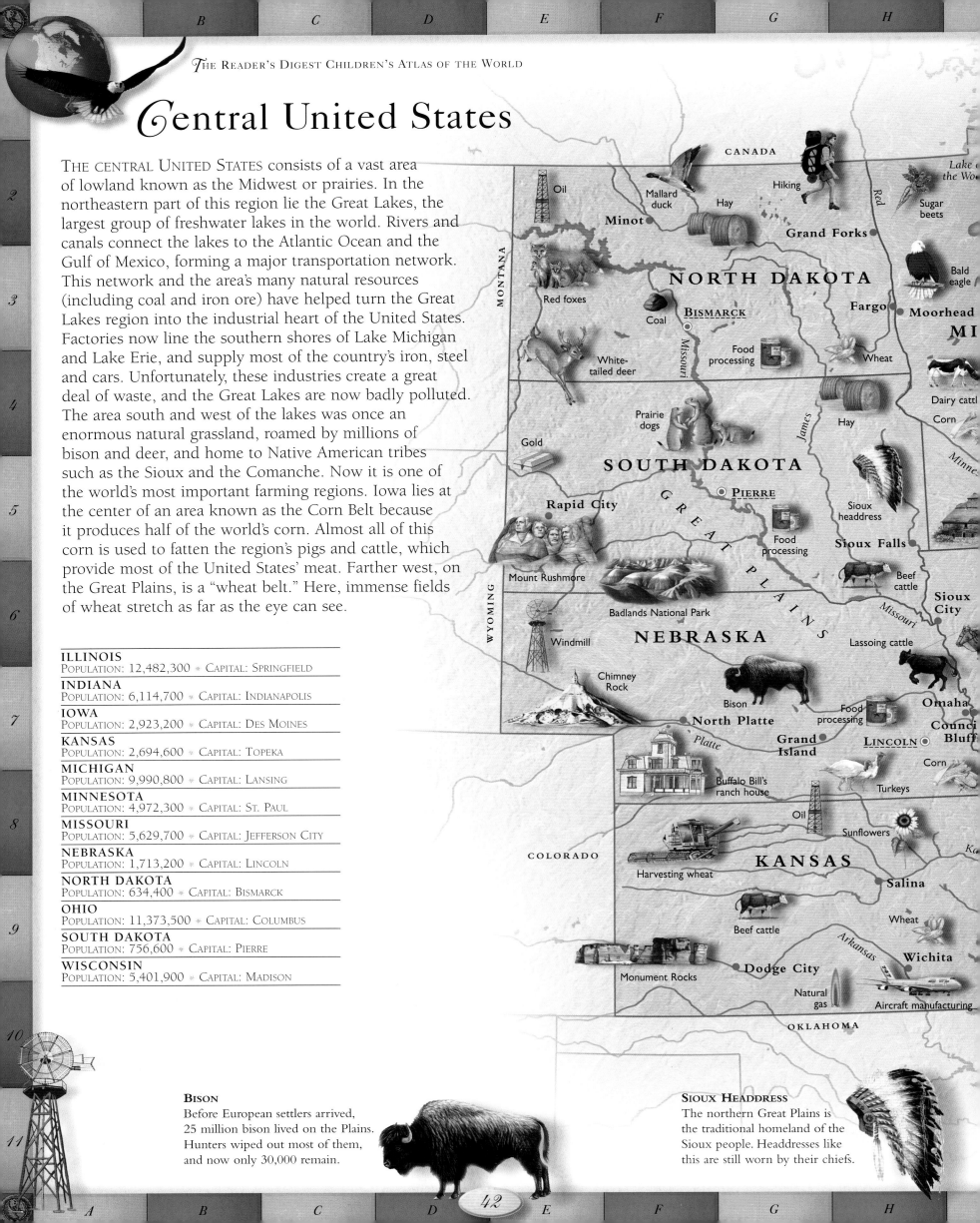

BISON
Before European settlers arrived, 25 million bison lived on the Plains. Hunters wiped out most of them, and now only 30,000 remain.

SIOUX HEADDRESS
The northern Great Plains is the traditional homeland of the Sioux people. Headdresses like this are still worn by their chiefs.

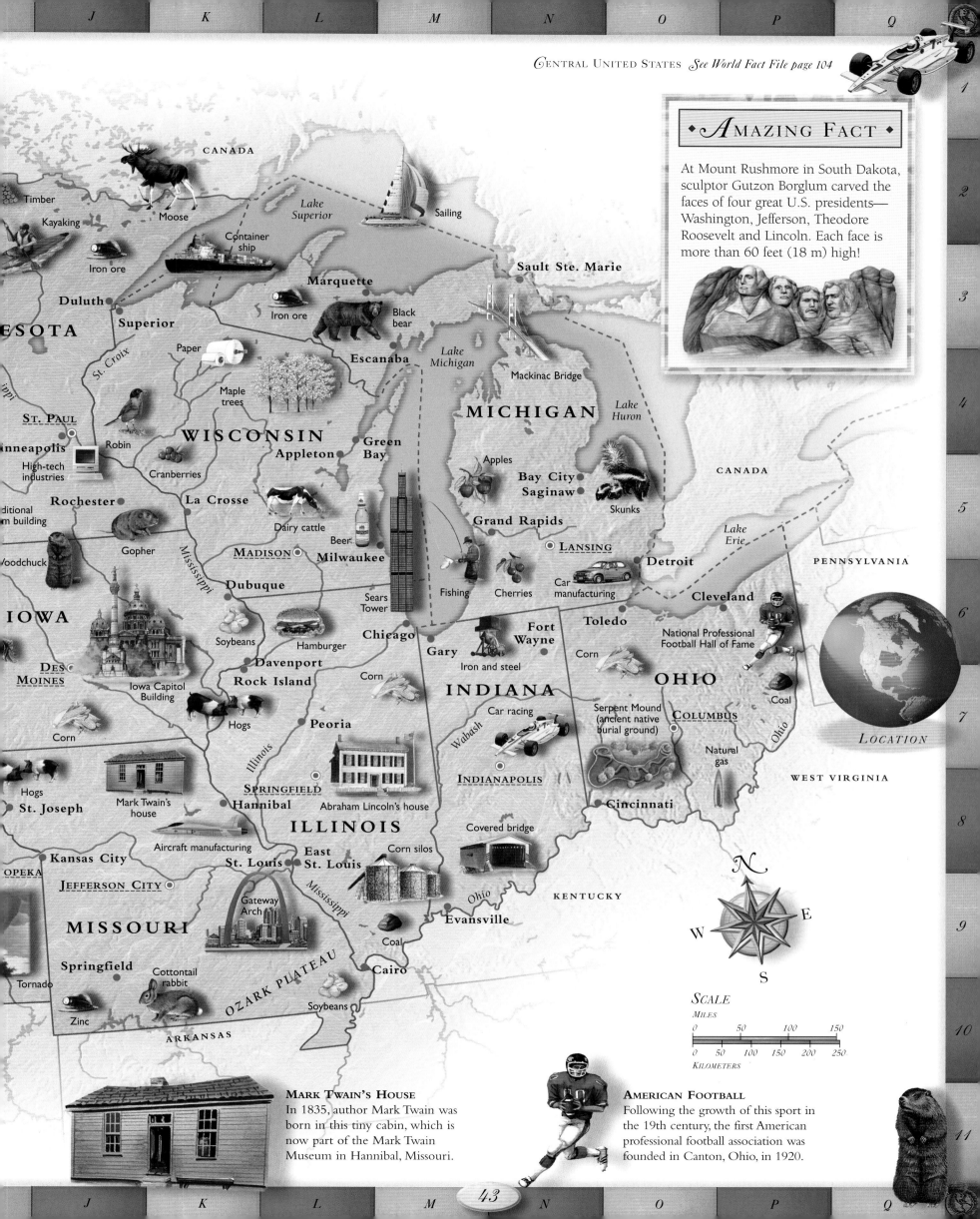

◆ AMAZING FACT ◆

At Mount Rushmore in South Dakota, sculptor Gutzon Borglum carved the faces of four great U.S. presidents— Washington, Jefferson, Theodore Roosevelt and Lincoln. Each face is more than 60 feet (18 m) high!

CANADA

Timber

Kayaking

Moose

Lake Superior

Sailing

Container ship

Iron ore

Duluth

Superior

Marquette

Iron ore

Black bear

Sault Ste. Marie

Paper

Escanaba

Lake Michigan

Mackinac Bridge

ESOTA

St. Croix

Maple trees

Lake Huron

CANADA

ippi

ST. PAUL

MICHIGAN

nneapolis

Robin

WISCONSIN

Appleton

Green Bay

Apples

Bay City

High-tech industries

Cranberries

La Crosse

Saginaw

Skunks

Lake Erie

Rochester

ditional m building

Gopher

Dairy cattle

Beer

Grand Rapids

LANSING

PENNSYLVANIA

oodchuck

MADISON

Milwaukee

Fishing

Cherries

Car manufacturing

Detroit

IOWA

Mississippi

Dubuque

Sears Tower

Cleveland

National Professional Football Hall of Fame

Toledo

DES MOINES

Soybeans

Hamburger

Chicago

Gary

Fort Wayne

Corn

OHIO

Coal

Iowa Capitol Building

Davenport

Rock Island

Corn

Iron and steel

INDIANA

Serpent Mound (ancient native burial ground)

COLUMBUS

Ohio

Natural gas

Hogs

Peoria

Car racing

Corn

Illinois

Wabash

WEST VIRGINIA

Hogs

St. Joseph

Mark Twain's house

SPRINGFIELD

Hannibal

Abraham Lincoln's house

INDIANAPOLIS

Cincinnati

Kansas City

ILLINOIS

Covered bridge

OPEKA

St. Louis

East St. Louis

Corn silos

JEFFERSON CITY

Aircraft manufacturing

Ohio

KENTUCKY

Gateway Arch

Mississippi

MISSOURI

Evansville

Springfield

Cottontail rabbit

Coal

Cairo

Tornado

OZARK PLATEAU

Zinc

Soybeans

ARKANSAS

LOCATION

N

W · E

S

SCALE

MILES

0 · 50 · 100 · 150

0 · 50 · 100 · 150 · 200 · 250

KILOMETERS

MARK TWAIN'S HOUSE

In 1835, author Mark Twain was born in this tiny cabin, which is now part of the Mark Twain Museum in Hannibal, Missouri.

AMERICAN FOOTBALL

Following the growth of this sport in the 19th century, the first American professional football association was founded in Canton, Ohio, in 1920.

Western United States

THE COLOSSAL ROCKY MOUNTAINS separate the western United States from the plains of the Midwest. Among the valleys and peaks of this spectacular range, mountain goats bound up steep rock faces and elk feed beside fast-flowing streams. There is little agriculture here, but herds of cattle graze the mountain meadows. West of the Rockies lies a series of dry plateaus, valleys and ranges. The Colorado Plateau has some of the continent's most spectacular scenery, including the world's largest gorge, the Grand Canyon. The states of Washington, Oregon and Idaho are known as the Pacific Northwest. The wet, densely forested western part of this area provides 40 percent of the United States' timber. The largest state in the region, California, is home to more people than any other American state. Most of the population lives in or near the coastal cities of Los Angeles and San Francisco. Inland, between the mountains of the Coast Ranges and the Sierra Nevada, farms form a patchwork of fields across the fertile, irrigated Central Valley. The most westerly state, Hawaii, lies 2,500 miles (4,000 km) off the coast, in the middle of the Pacific Ocean. Hawaii consists of 132 islands, which were formed by undersea volcanoes. Several Hawaiian volcanoes still erupt, including Mauna Loa, the largest active volcano in the world.

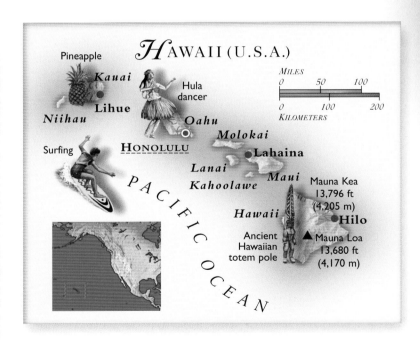

HAWAII (U.S.A.)

Pineapple
Kauai
Hula dancer
Lihue
Niihau
Oahu
Surfing
Molokai
HONOLULU
Lahaina
Lanai
Maui
Kahoolawe
Hawaii
Mauna Kea 13,796 ft (4,205 m)
Hilo
Ancient Hawaiian totem pole
Mauna Loa 13,680 ft (4,170 m)

MILES
0   50   100
0   100   200
KILOMETERS

PACIFIC OCEAN

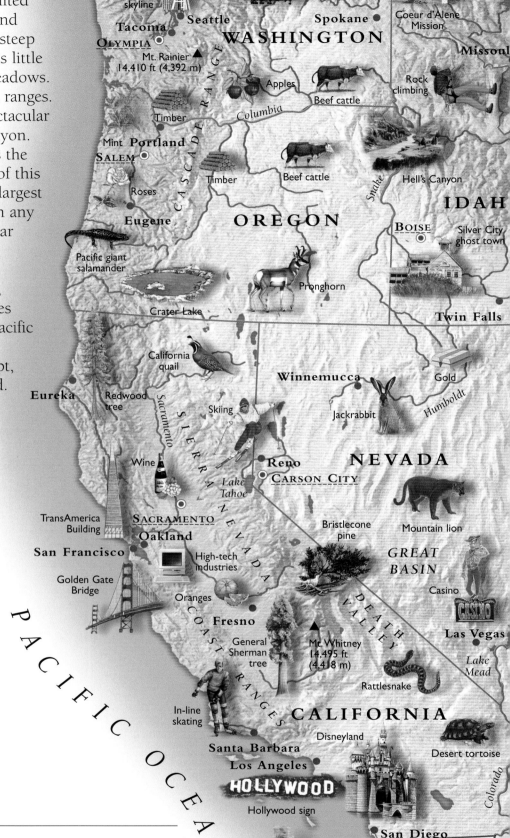

CANADA

Aircraft manufacturing
Seattle skyline
Tacoma   Seattle
OLYMPIA
Mt. Rainier 14,410 ft (4,392 m)
WASHINGTON
Spokane
Coeur d'Alene Mission
Missoul
Apples
Rock climbing
Beef cattle
Timber
Columbia
Mint Portland
SALEM
Timber
Beef cattle
Snake
Hell's Canyon
IDAH
Roses
OREGON
BOISE
Silver City ghost town
Eugene
Pacific giant salamander
Pronghorn
Twin Falls
Crater Lake
California quail
Winnemucca
Gold
Eureka
Redwood tree
Jackrabbit
Humboldt
Skiing
NEVADA
Wine
Reno
CARSON CITY
Lake Tahoe
Bristlecone pine
Mountain lion
TransAmerica Building
SACRAMENTO
Oakland
San Francisco
High-tech industries
GREAT BASIN
Golden Gate Bridge
Oranges
Casino
Fresno
General Sherman tree
Mt. Whitney 14,495 ft (4,418 m)
Las Vegas
Lake Mead
Rattlesnake
In-line skating
CALIFORNIA
Disneyland
Santa Barbara
Desert tortoise
Los Angeles
HOLLYWOOD
Hollywood sign
San Diego
MEXICO
Colorado

CASCADE RANGE
SIERRA NEVADA
COAST RANGES
DEATH VALLEY
PACIFIC OCEAN

ARIZONA
POPULATION: 5,307,300 * CAPITAL: PHOENIX

CALIFORNIA
POPULATION: 34,501,100 * CAPITAL: SACRAMENTO

COLORADO
POPULATION: 4,417,700 * CAPITAL: DENVER

HAWAII
POPULATION: 1,224,400 * CAPITAL: HONOLULU

IDAHO
POPULATION: 1,321,000 * CAPITAL: BOISE

MONTANA
POPULATION: 904,400 * CAPITAL: HELENA

NEVADA
POPULATION: 2,106,100 * CAPITAL: CARSON CITY

NEW MEXICO
POPULATION: 1,829,100 * CAPITAL: SANTA FE

OREGON
POPULATION: 3,472,900 * CAPITAL: SALEM

UTAH
POPULATION: 2,269,800 * CAPITAL: SALT LAKE CITY

WASHINGTON
POPULATION: 5,988,000 * CAPITAL: OLYMPIA

WYOMING
POPULATION: 494,400 * CAPITAL: CHEYENNE

GENERAL SHERMAN TREE
This giant sequoia is the world's largest living thing. It is as tall as a 23-story building and is at least 2,300 years old.

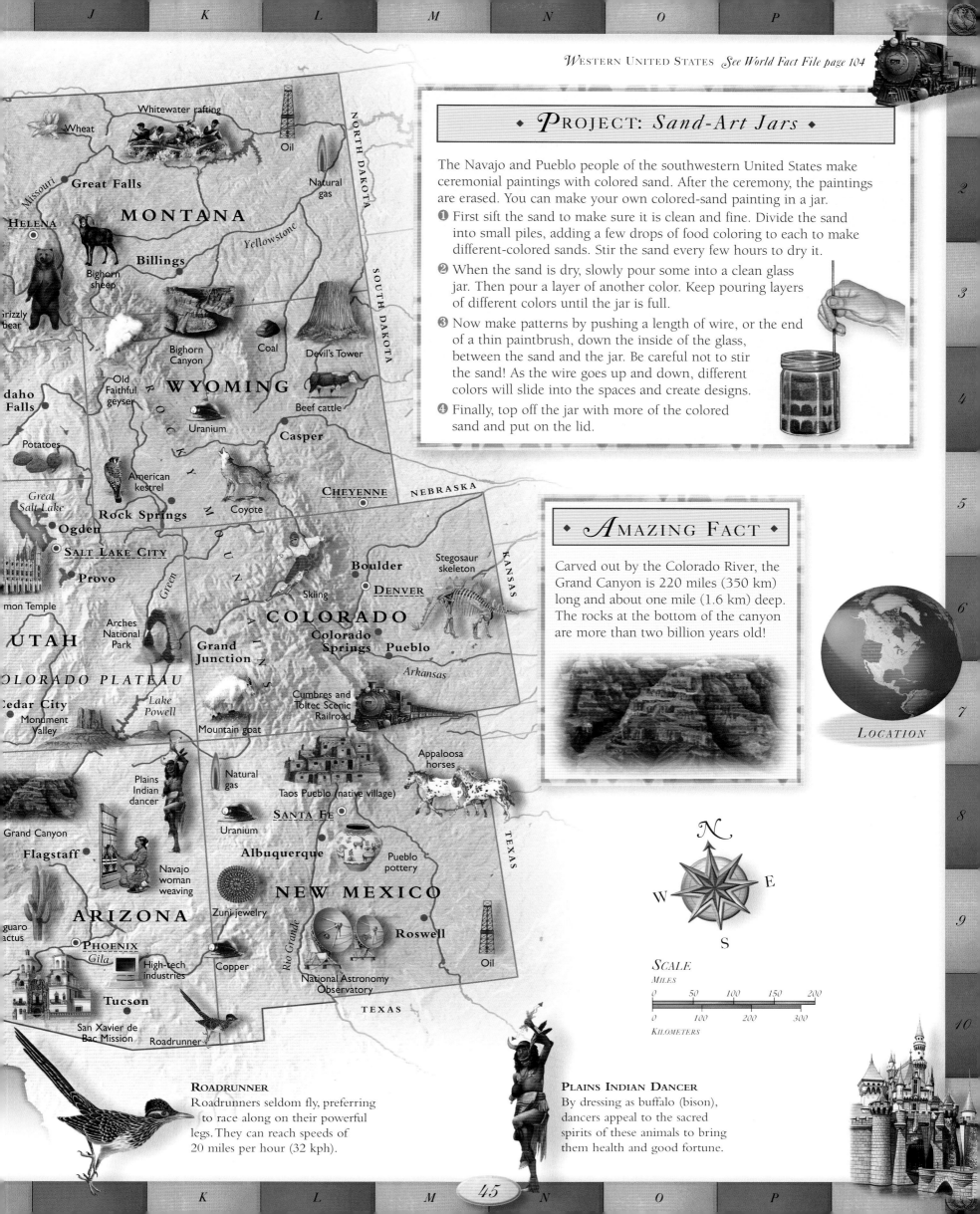

J K L M N O P

Whitewater rafting

Wheat

Oil

Natural gas

NORTH DAKOTA

Missouri

Great Falls

MONTANA

Yellowstone

○ **HELENA**

Grizzly bear

Bighorn sheep

Billings

SOUTH DAKOTA

Bighorn Canyon

Coal

Devil's Tower

Old Faithful geyser

WYOMING

Idaho Falls

Uranium

Beef cattle

Potatoes

American kestrel

Casper

Great Salt Lake

Coyote

CHEYENNE

NEBRASKA

Rock Springs

Ogden

SALT LAKE CITY

Green

Skiing

Stegosaur skeleton

KANSAS

Provo

mon Temple

Boulder

DENVER

COLORADO

Arches National Park

Colorado Springs

Pueblo

UTAH

Grand Junction

Arkansas

OLORADO PLATEAU

Lake Powell

Cumbres and Toltec Scenic Railroad

edar City

Monument Valley

Mountain goat

Appaloosa horses

Plains Indian dancer

Natural gas

Taos Pueblo (native village)

Grand Canyon

Navajo woman weaving

SANTA FE

Uranium

TEXAS

Flagstaff

Albuquerque

Pueblo pottery

guaro actus

ARIZONA

Zuni jewelry

NEW MEXICO

PHOENIX

Gila

High-tech industries

Copper

Rio Grande

Roswell

Tucson

National Astronomy Observatory

Oil

San Xavier de Bac Mission

Roadrunner

TEXAS

• PROJECT: *Sand-Art Jars* •

The Navajo and Pueblo people of the southwestern United States make ceremonial paintings with colored sand. After the ceremony, the paintings are erased. You can make your own colored-sand painting in a jar.

❶ First sift the sand to make sure it is clean and fine. Divide the sand into small piles, adding a few drops of food coloring to each to make different-colored sands. Stir the sand every few hours to dry it.

❷ When the sand is dry, slowly pour some into a clean glass jar. Then pour a layer of another color. Keep pouring layers of different colors until the jar is full.

❸ Now make patterns by pushing a length of wire, or the end of a thin paintbrush, down the inside of the glass, between the sand and the jar. Be careful not to stir the sand! As the wire goes up and down, different colors will slide into the spaces and create designs.

❹ Finally, top off the jar with more of the colored sand and put on the lid.

• AMAZING FACT •

Carved out by the Colorado River, the Grand Canyon is 220 miles (350 km) long and about one mile (1.6 km) deep. The rocks at the bottom of the canyon are more than two billion years old!

LOCATION

N

W E

S

SCALE

MILES

0   50   100   150   200

0   100   200   300

KILOMETERS

ROADRUNNER
Roadrunners seldom fly, preferring to race along on their powerful legs. They can reach speeds of 20 miles per hour (32 kph).

PLAINS INDIAN DANCER
By dressing as buffalo (bison), dancers appeal to the sacred spirits of these animals to bring them health and good fortune.

Mexico, Central America and the Caribbean

MEXICO AND CENTRAL AMERICA form a land bridge between the United States and South America. At its narrowest point, this strip of land is only 50 miles (80 km) wide and is split by the Panama Canal, an artificial waterway that links the Atlantic and Pacific oceans. Mexico is more than twice the size of the seven Central American countries combined. It is dominated by a large dry plateau, and only 18 percent of the land can be farmed. The narrow plains on the east coast are warm and humid, and contain large oil reserves. Three-quarters of Mexicans live in cities and towns, and Mexico City is one of the largest and fastest-growing cities in the world. Most of Central America is mountainous, and much of the land is covered in rain forests where colorful parrots shriek from the treetops and chattering monkeys swing among branches. Although only a small proportion of Central America can be farmed, about half of the people live in rural areas and many grow their own food on small plots of land. To the east lie the Caribbean Islands, which are surrounded by sandy beaches, and are among the most heavily populated places on Earth. Spain ruled much of Mexico, Central America and the Caribbean for centuries, and today most of the people speak Spanish. Their ancestors may be settlers from Europe, Native American peoples or Africans who were first brought to the region as slaves.

ANTIGUA AND BARBUDA
POPULATION: 67,448 * CAPITAL: ST. JOHN'S

THE BAHAMAS
POPULATION: 300,529 * CAPITAL: NASSAU

BARBADOS
POPULATION: 276,607 * CAPITAL: BRIDGETOWN

BELIZE
POPULATION: 262,999 * CAPITAL: BELMOPAN

COSTA RICA
POPULATION: 3,834,934 * CAPITAL: SAN JOSÉ

CUBA
POPULATION: 11,224,321 * CAPITAL: HAVANA

DOMINICA
POPULATION: 70,158 * CAPITAL: ROSEAU

DOMINICAN REPUBLIC
POPULATION: 8,721,594 * CAPITAL: SANTO DOMINGO

EL SALVADOR
POPULATION: 6,353,681 * CAPITAL: SAN SALVADOR

GRENADA
POPULATION: 89,211 * CAPITAL: ST. GEORGE'S

GUATEMALA
POPULATION: 13,314,079 * CAPITAL: GUATEMALA

HAITI
POPULATION: 7,063,722 * CAPITAL: PORT-AU-PRINCE

HONDURAS
POPULATION: 6,560,608 * CAPITAL: TEGUCIGALPA

JAMAICA
POPULATION: 2,680,029 * CAPITAL: KINGSTON

MEXICO
POPULATION: 103,400,165 * CAPITAL: MEXICO CITY

NICARAGUA
POPULATION: 5,023,818 * CAPITAL: MANAGUA

PANAMA
POPULATION: 2,882,329 * CAPITAL: PANAMA

ST. KITTS–NEVIS
POPULATION: 38,736 * CAPITAL: BASSETERRE

ST. LUCIA
POPULATION: 160,145 * CAPITAL: CASTRIES

ST. VINCENT AND THE GRENADINES
POPULATION: 116,394 * CAPITAL: KINGSTOWN

TRINIDAD AND TOBAGO
POPULATION: 1,163,724 * CAPITAL: PORT-OF-SPAIN

SINGING GRASSHOPPER MOUSE
This mouse is named for its habit of squeaking or "singing" to warn off rivals. Grasshoppers are its favorite food.

Map labels:
Tijuana
Mexicali
Gila monster
Tourism
Ciudad Juárez
Saguaro cactus
Beef cattle
Mexican cowboy
UNITED STATES OF AMERICA
BAJA CALIFORNIA
Great white shark
Hermosillo
Chihuahua
Singing grasshopper mouse
Vampire bat
Silver
Natural gas
SIERRA MADRE OCCIDENTAL
Rio Grande
Leatherback turtle
Elephant seals
Culiacán
Monarch butterfly
Monterrey
Cotton
Matamoros
Gulf of Mexico
La Paz
Torreón
Ancient Toltec stone statue
Mariachi musicians
Snapper
Lobster
Gold
Iron ore
MEXICO
Tampico
El Castillo, Chichen Itza, Maya city ruins
Folk dancer
Corn
Metropolitan Cathedral
Oil
Oil
Bay of Campeche
YUCATAN PENINSULA
Common dolphins
Guadalajara
MEXICO CITY
Veracruz
Jaguar
Aztec snake carving
Soccer
Orizaba 18,700 ft (5,700 m)
Great Plaza, Tikal
Belize
BELMOPAN
Tourism
Olmec stone carving
Scarlet macaw
Folk costume
GUATEMALA
Acapulco
Thatched corncrib
PACIFIC OCEAN
Eagle ray
GUATEMALA
SAN SALVADOR
EL SALVADOR

J K L M N O P

◆ PROJECT: *Make a Mexican Piñata* ◆

A piñata is a pot made from papier-mâché and filled with toys and candy, often shaped like a star or animal. It is a popular part of many celebrations and festivals in Mexico and Central America. Children hang the piñata from the ceiling or a tree branch and take turns trying to break it open. You can make a Mexican piñata for your next party.

❶ Cover a large balloon with strips of newspaper dipped in flour-and-water paste or white glue. Wait for this papier-mâché to dry and then repeat with at least two more layers of newspaper.

❷ When the papier-mâché is completely dry, cut a small hole in the top and fill the piñata with all sorts of goodies. Re-cover the hole with more papier-mâché.

❸ Make star points out of cardboard as shown. Tape them onto the ball using the tabs. Decorate the star with paint and colored tissue paper.

Step 3A   Step 3B

❹ Make two small holes next to each other at the top of the piñata. Thread curved wire through one hole and out the other. Hang up the piñata and have guests take turns hitting it with a stick to open it.

◆ AMAZING FACT ◆

The saguaro cactus is found only in the deserts of northwestern Mexico and the southwestern United States. It grows incredibly slowly, taking 25 years to reach a height of one foot (30 cm). But it can live for 200 years and grow as high as a four-story house. Like other cacti, the saguaro survives on water stored in its stem. A fully grown saguaro may contain enough water to fill 100 bathtubs!

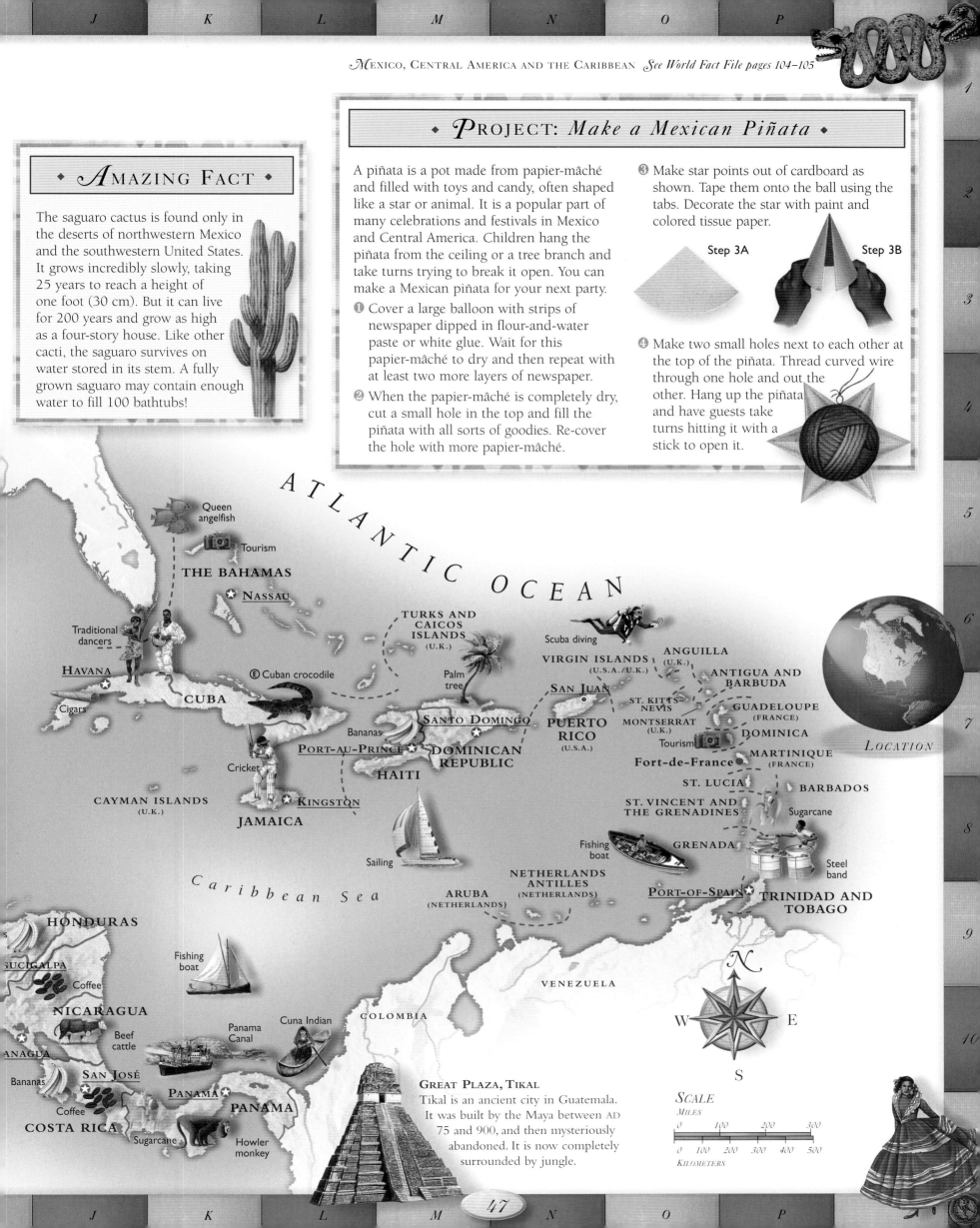

ATLANTIC OCEAN

Queen angelfish

Tourism

THE BAHAMAS

Nassau

Traditional dancers

Havana

Cigars

CUBA

Ⓔ Cuban crocodile

Bananas

PORT-AU-PRINCE

Cricket

CAYMAN ISLANDS (U.K.)

Kingston

JAMAICA

Sailing

TURKS AND CAICOS ISLANDS (U.K.)

Palm tree

Scuba diving

VIRGIN ISLANDS (U.S.A./U.K.)

ANGUILLA (U.K.)

ANTIGUA AND BARBUDA

St. Kitts-Nevis

MONTSERRAT (U.K.)

Santo Domingo

PUERTO RICO (U.S.A.)

San Juan

GUADELOUPE (FRANCE)

DOMINICA

Tourism

MARTINIQUE (FRANCE)

Fort-de-France

LOCATION

DOMINICAN REPUBLIC

HAITI

ST. LUCIA

BARBADOS

ST. VINCENT AND THE GRENADINES

GRENADA

Sugarcane

Steel band

Fishing boat

NETHERLANDS ANTILLES (NETHERLANDS)

ARUBA (NETHERLANDS)

Caribbean Sea

PORT-OF-SPAIN

TRINIDAD AND TOBAGO

HONDURAS

Fishing boat

UCIGALPA

Coffee

NICARAGUA

Beef cattle

ANAGUA

Bananas

San José

Coffee

COSTA RICA

Panama Canal

Cuna Indian

PANAMA

PANAMA

Sugarcane

Howler monkey

COLOMBIA

VENEZUELA

N
W   E
S

GREAT PLAZA, TIKAL

Tikal is an ancient city in Guatemala. It was built by the Maya between AD 75 and 900, and then mysteriously abandoned. It is now completely surrounded by jungle.

SCALE

MILES
0   100   200   300

0   100   200   300   400   500
KILOMETERS

J K L M N O P

South America

From its tropical northern shore, South America stretches 4,500 miles (7,240 km) southward to the chilly, storm-battered peninsula of Cape Horn, just 600 miles (1,000 km) from Antarctica. The Andes run the entire length of the continent's west coast, forming the longest mountain chain in the world. In the north, the Amazon River (the world's second-longest river) snakes eastward from the Andes to the Atlantic Ocean, through vast rain forests that once covered more than one-third of the continent. To the south, the forests give way to the grasslands of the Gran Chaco and the Pampas. The southern tip of South America is a dry, windswept plateau known as Patagonia. South America's inhabitants include people of European, native Indian and African origin. Most people speak Spanish, but Portuguese is the official language in Brazil.

Major Mountains and Rivers

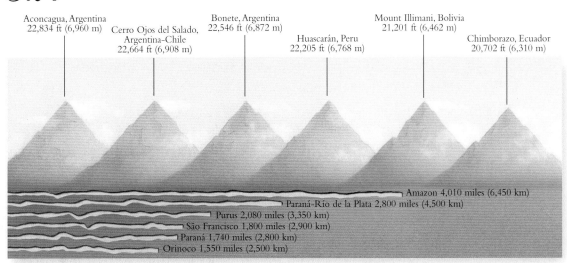

Aconcagua, Argentina 22,834 ft (6,960 m)

Cerro Ojos del Salado, Argentina-Chile 22,664 ft (6,908 m)

Bonete, Argentina 22,546 ft (6,872 m)

Huascarán, Peru 22,205 ft (6,768 m)

Mount Illimani, Bolivia 21,201 ft (6,462 m)

Chimborazo, Ecuador 20,702 ft (6,310 m)

Amazon 4,010 miles (6,450 km)
Paraná-Río de la Plata 2,800 miles (4,500 km)
Purus 2,080 miles (3,350 km)
São Francisco 1,800 miles (2,900 km)
Paraná 1,740 miles (2,800 km)
Orinoco 1,550 miles (2,500 km)

Political Map

VENEZUELA
GUYANA
SURINAME
FRENCH GUIANA (FRANCE)
COLOMBIA
GALÁPAGOS ISLANDS (ECUADOR)
ECUADOR
BRAZIL
PERU
BOLIVIA
EASTER ISLAND (CHILE)
MARTIN VAZ ISLANDS (BRAZIL)
PARAGUAY
JUAN FERNANDEZ ISLANDS (CHILE)
CHILE
URUGUAY
ARGENTINA
FALKLAND ISLANDS (U.K.)
SOUTH GEORGIA (U.K.)

Continent Facts

Regional land area: 6,877,943 sq. miles (17,818,505 sq. km)
Regional population: 354,885,240
Independent countries: Argentina, Bolivia, Brazil, Chile, Colombia, Ecuador, Guyana, Paraguay, Peru, Suriname, Uruguay, Venezuela

World Records

WORLD'S LONGEST MOUNTAIN CHAIN
Andes, western South America 4,700 miles (7,600 km)

WORLD'S DRIEST PLACE
Atacama Desert, Chile, average annual rainfall less than 1/250 in (0.1 mm)

WORLD'S HIGHEST WATERFALL
Angel Falls, Venezuela, 3,212 ft (979 m)

WORLD'S HIGHEST CAPITAL CITY
La Paz, Bolivia, 11,913 ft (3,631 m)

WORLD'S HIGHEST NAVIGABLE LAKE
Lake Titicaca, Peru-Bolivia, 12,500 ft (3,810 m)

WORLD'S LARGEST RIVER BY VOLUME
Amazon, Peru-Brazil, discharges 7,100,000 cubic feet (200,000 cubic m) per second into Atlantic Ocean

WORLD'S LARGEST RIVER BASIN
Amazon Basin, northern South America, 2,720,000 sq. miles (7,045,000 sq. km)

WORLD'S LARGEST LAGOON
Lagoa dos Patos, Brazil, 3,803 sq. miles (9,850 sq. km)

Continent Records

HIGHEST MOUNTAIN
Aconcagua, Argentina, 22,834 ft (6,960 m)

LOWEST POINT
Valdés Peninsula, Argentina, 131 ft (40 m) below sea level

LARGEST LAKE
Lake Titicaca, Peru-Bolivia, 3,200 sq. miles (8,288 sq. km)

LONGEST RIVER
Amazon River, Peru-Brazil, 4,010 miles (6,450 km)

LARGEST COUNTRY BY AREA
Brazil, 3,286,470 sq. miles (8,511,965 sq. km)

LARGEST COUNTRY BY POPULATION
Brazil, population 176,029,560

LARGEST CITY BY POPULATION
São Paulo, Brazil, population 18,119,000

◆ Amazing Fact ◆

The Atacama Desert in northern Chile is the driest place in the world. Rain showers occur only once or twice a century, and in some parts of the desert rain has never been recorded!

PHYSICAL MAP

NORTH AMERICA

Tropic of Cancer

Caribbean Sea

AFRICA

ATLANTIC OCEAN

Lake Maracaibo

Orinoco

GUIANA HIGHLANDS

Amazon Delta

Gulf of Panama

LLANOS

Rio Negro

Rio Branco

GALÁPAGOS ISLANDS

Chimborazo

Marañón

AMAZON BASIN

Amazon

Gulf of Guayaquil

SELVAS

Purus

Tapajos

Xingu

Tocantins

São Francisco

Equator

Madeira

Huascarán

BRAZILIAN HIGHLANDS

MATO GROSSO PLATEAU

PACIFIC OCEAN

Lake Titicaca

Mt. Illimani

Lake Poopó

ATACAMA DESERT

GRAN CHACO

Paraguay

Paraná

SERRA DO MAR

Tropic of Capricorn

Cerro Ojos del Salado

Bonete

Uruguay

Lagoa dos Patos

Easter Island

Aconcagua

PAMPAS

Rio de la Plata

ANDES

Colorado

Blanca Bay

San Matias Gulf

VALDÉS PENINSULA

PATAGONIA

San Jorge Gulf

FALKLAND ISLANDS

South Georgia

Tierra del Fuego

CAPE HORN

Drake Passage

Antarctic Circle

ANTARCTICA

Northern South America

MOST OF NORTHERN SOUTH AMERICA is drained by the world's second-longest river, the Amazon, and its more than 200 tributaries. These waterways flow through lush tropical rain forests that are home to up to one third of all the plants and animals on Earth. Sadly, the rain forests are rapidly disappearing as a growing population clears the land for farming. More than one fifth of the rain forest, an area the size of France, has been cut down in the last twenty years. More than a quarter of the world's rain forests lie within Brazil, the largest country in South America. Brazil has many resources, including iron ore, oil and gold. It is the continent's most industrialized country and the world's leading producer of coffee, bananas and sugarcane. Northwest of Brazil lies Venezuela, a tropical country that is South America's top oil producer. From Venezuela, the Andes curve southward through Colombia, Ecuador and Peru. At the northern end of this mountain range, the climate is wet, and large coffee and banana plantations cover the hillsides. Farther south, little rain falls and crops can only be grown by using water from mountain streams. On the upper slopes of the Peruvian Andes, farmers grow potatoes and wheat and raise animals, including llamas and alpacas. Six hundred miles (1,000 km) off the coast of Ecuador lie the Galápagos Islands, which are famous for their unusual wildlife, which includes marine iguanas and giant tortoises.

BRAZIL
POPULATION: 176,029,560 ⁕ CAPITAL: BRASÍLIA

COLOMBIA
POPULATION: 41,008,227 ⁕ CAPITAL: BOGOTÁ

ECUADOR
POPULATION: 13,447,494 ⁕ CAPITAL: QUITO

GUYANA
POPULATION: 698,209 ⁕ CAPITAL: GEORGETOWN

PERU
POPULATION: 27,949,639 ⁕ CAPITAL: LIMA

SURINAME
POPULATION: 436,494 ⁕ CAPITAL: PARAMARIBO

VENEZUELA
POPULATION: 24,287,670 ⁕ CAPITAL: CARACAS

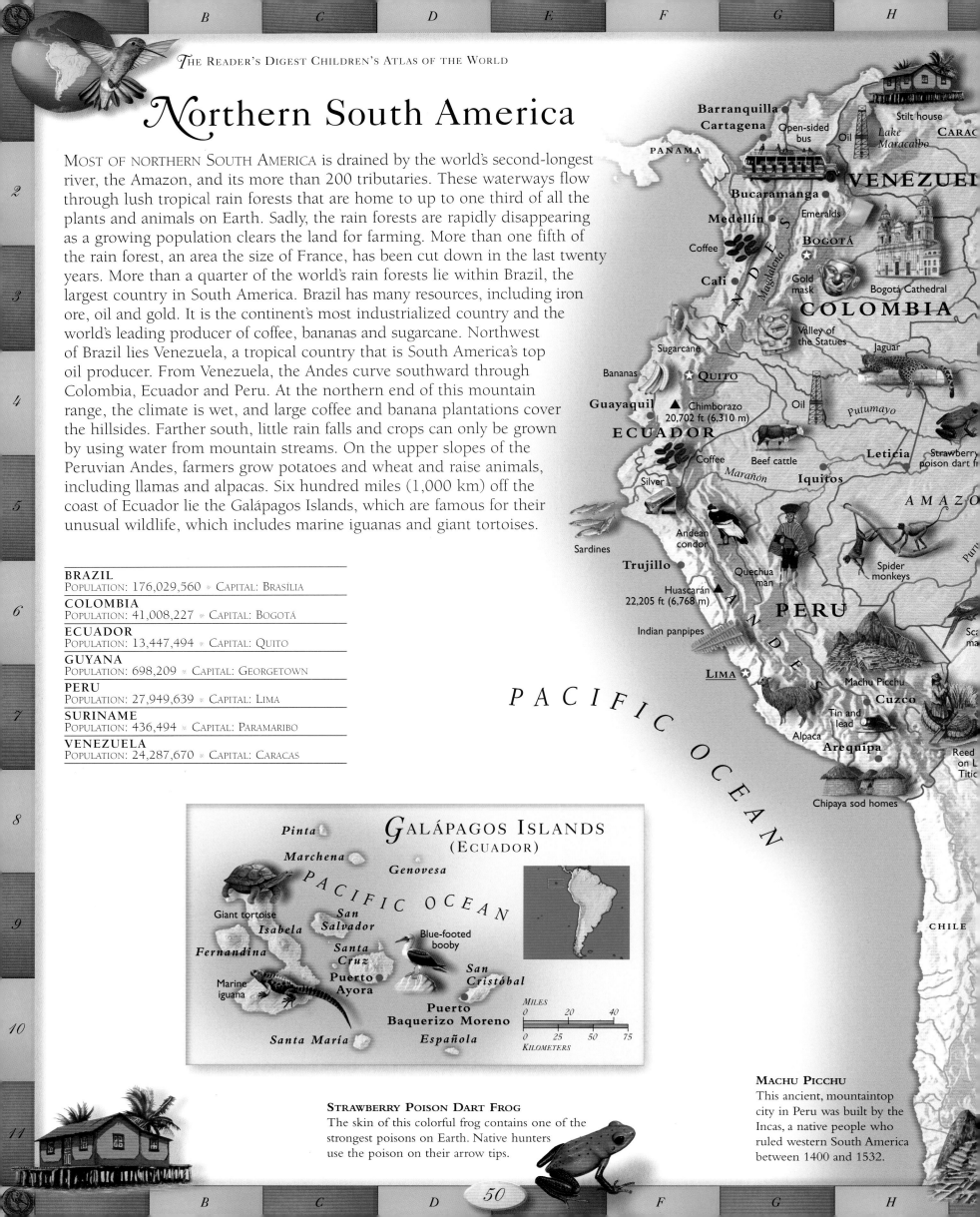

GALÁPAGOS ISLANDS
(ECUADOR)

Pinta
Marchena
Genovesa
PACIFIC OCEAN
Giant tortoise
Isabela
San Salvador
Blue-footed booby
Fernandina
Santa Cruz
Puerto Ayora
San Cristóbal
Marine iguana
Puerto Baquerizo Moreno
Santa María
Española

MILES
0   20   40
0 25 50 75
KILOMETERS

STRAWBERRY POISON DART FROG
The skin of this colorful frog contains one of the strongest poisons on Earth. Native hunters use the poison on their arrow tips.

MACHU PICCHU
This ancient, mountaintop city in Peru was built by the Incas, a native people who ruled western South America between 1400 and 1532.

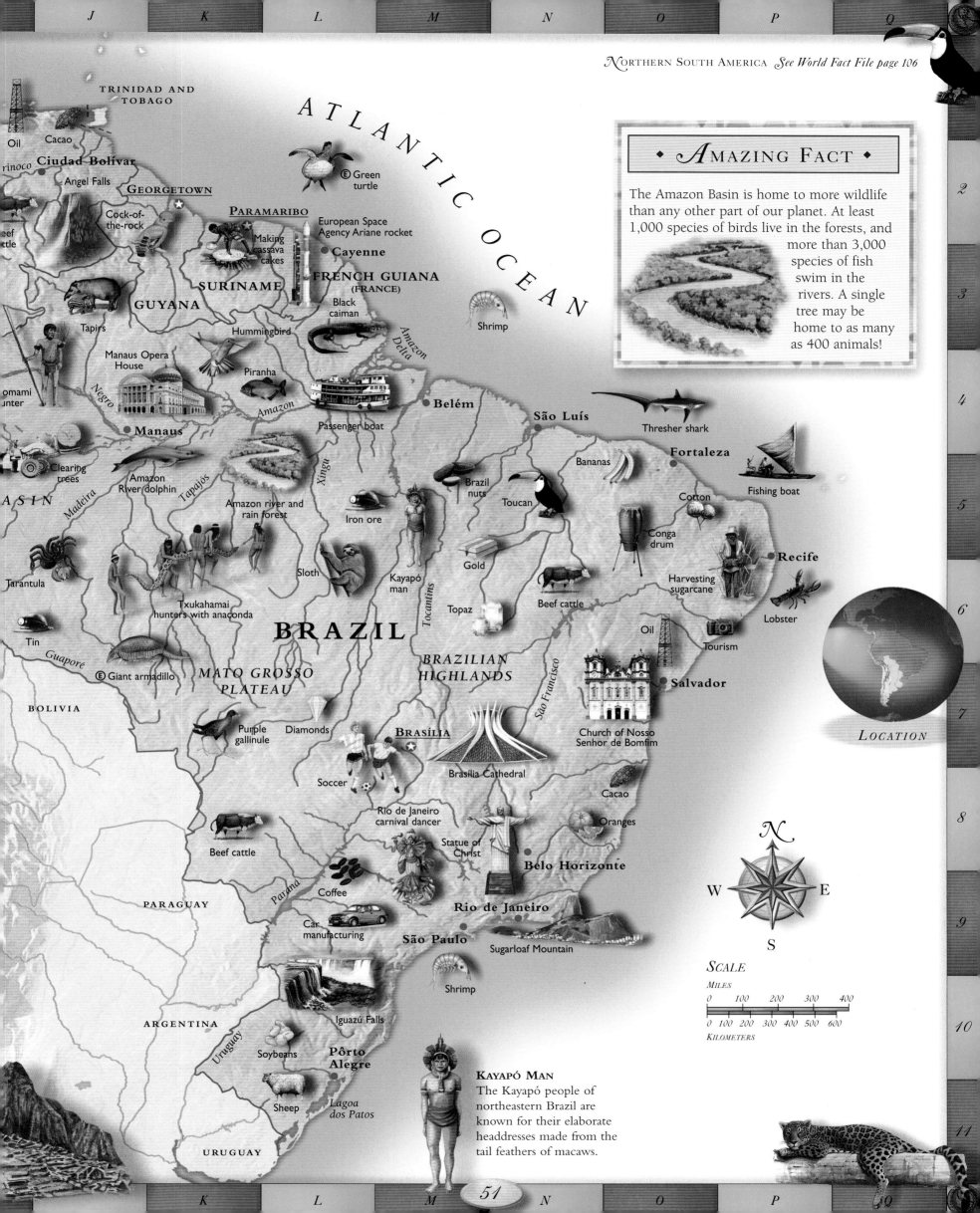

J K L M N O P Q

TRINIDAD AND
TOBAGO

Oil
Cacao

rinoco
Ciudad Bolívar

Angel Falls

eef
ttle

Cock-of-
the-rock

GEORGETOWN

GUYANA

Tapirs

omami
unter

Manaus Opera
House

SURINAME

PARAMARIBO

Making
cassava
cakes

Ⓔ Green
turtle

ATLANTIC OCEAN

European Space
Agency Ariane rocket

Cayenne

FRENCH GUIANA
(FRANCE)

Black
caiman

Hummingbird

Shrimp

Amazon
Delta

• AMAZING FACT •

The Amazon Basin is home to more wildlife
than any other part of our planet. At least
1,000 species of birds live in the forests, and
more than 3,000
species of fish
swim in the
rivers. A single
tree may be
home to as many
as 400 animals!

ASIN

Clearing
trees

Amazon
River dolphin

Negro

Manaus

Piranha

Amazon

Madeira

Tapajós

Amazon river and
rain forest

Xingu

Passenger boat

Belém

São Luís

Thresher shark

Fortaleza

Bananas

Brazil
nuts

Toucan

Cotton

Fishing boat

Conga
drum

Iron ore

Recife

Tarantula

Sloth

Kayapó
man

Gold

Harvesting
sugarcane

Tin

Guaporé

Txukahamai
hunters with anaconda

BRAZIL

Tocantins

Topaz

Beef cattle

Lobster

Ⓔ Giant armadillo

MATO GROSSO
PLATEAU

BRAZILIAN
HIGHLANDS

Oil

São Francisco

Tourism

BOLIVIA

Salvador

LOCATION

Purple
gallinule

Diamonds

BRASÍLIA

Brasília Cathedral

Church of Nosso
Senhor de Bomfim

Soccer

Cacao

Rio de Janeiro
carnival dancer

Oranges

Beef cattle

Statue of
Christ

Belo Horizonte

N

PARAGUAY

Paraná

Coffee

Rio de Janeiro

W   E

Car
manufacturing

São Paulo

Sugarloaf Mountain

S

Shrimp

SCALE

MILES

0 100 200 300 400

0 100 200 300 400 500 600

KILOMETERS

ARGENTINA

Iguazú Falls

Uruguay

Soybeans

Pôrto
Alegre

KAYAPÓ MAN

The Kayapó people of
northeastern Brazil are
known for their elaborate
headdresses made from the
tail feathers of macaws.

Sheep

Lagoa
dos Patos

URUGUAY

J K L M N O P Q

Southern South America

SOUTHERN SOUTH AMERICA IS SHAPED like a long, narrow triangle that tapers to a point on the southern island of Tierra del Fuego. The Andes run down the western side of the region, separating the country of Chile from its neighbors. Twenty times as long as it is wide, Chile has a variety of climates and landscapes. In the cold, wet, sparsely populated south, mountains rise steeply from the ocean, and glaciers snake through valleys. Central Chile has milder weather and many farms, vineyards and orchards. The north is very arid and includes the driest place in the world, the Atacama Desert. East of the Atacama, the Andes spread into Bolivia, one of the poorest countries in South America. From eastern Bolivia, wide plains stretch southward through Paraguay; Uruguay and northern Argentina. Enormous herds of cattle and sheep roam the eastern and southern parts of these plains, tended by ranch hands called gauchos. Argentina has more than 50 million cattle, and beef production is one of its most important industries. The country's most fertile grasslands, the Pampas, surround the capital, Buenos Aires. This city is home to one-third of the Argentinian population. Few people live in southern Argentina, a cold, barren plateau known as Patagonia, but the area is rich in minerals. The seas around Tierra del Fuego in the far south are often stormy. Hundreds of ships have been wrecked attempting to round Cape Horn or navigate the Strait of Magellan.

ARGENTINA
POPULATION: 37,812,817 • CAPITAL: BUENOS AIRES

BOLIVIA
POPULATION: 8,445,134 • CAPITALS: LA PAZ, SUCRE

CHILE
POPULATION: 15,498,930 • CAPITAL: SANTIAGO

PARAGUAY
POPULATION: 5,884,491 • CAPITAL: ASUNCIÓN

URUGUAY
POPULATION: 3,386,575 • CAPITAL: MONTEVIDEO

◆ PROJECT: *Easter Island Moai* ◆

Easter Island is covered with huge statues called "moai." Some are more than 30 ft (9 m) high! The early inhabitants of Easter Island may have built the statues to honor their ancestors. You can make an Easter Island statue, too.

❶ Mix equal parts of plaster and vermiculite (both available at hardware stores). Stir as you add enough water to make a thick plaster. Pour the mixture into an old shoe box.

❷ When the mixture hardens, tear away the cardboard. Carve the stone using tools such as a plastic knife or an ice pop stick.

❸ Alternatively, make your carving out of a block of modeling clay, plaster of Paris or any other modeling material.

LLAMA
A common domestic animal in South America, the llama is a relative of the camel. It is kept for its wool and is also used for carrying goods through mountainous terrain.

Hydroelectricity

BRAZIL

BRAZIL

BRAZIL

PARAGUAY

Streetcar

ASUNCIÓN

Paraguay

Maté (tea)

Presidential palace

Corrientes

Paraná

Greater rhea

Beef cattle

Cotton

Polo

Pilcomayo

Chacoan peccary

GRAN CHACO

Maned wolf

Sugarcane

San Miguel de Tucumán

Río Salado

Oil

Natural gas

Corn

Motmot

BOLIVIA

Trinidad

Timber

Bolivian folk costume

Santa Cruz

Cochabamba

SUCRE

Tin

Giant bromelia

Guaporé

Giant anteater

Mamoré

Spectacled bear

Zinc

Lake Poopó

Village musicians

Gold

La Paz

Mt. Illimani 21,201 ft (6,462 m)

Silver

Andean condor

ANDES

Llamas

Cerro Ojos del Salado 22,664 ft (6,908 m)

Bonete 22,546 ft (6,872 m)

PERU

Lake Titicaca

Arica

Iquique

ATACAMA DESERT

Antofagasta

Copper

Copiapó

Iron

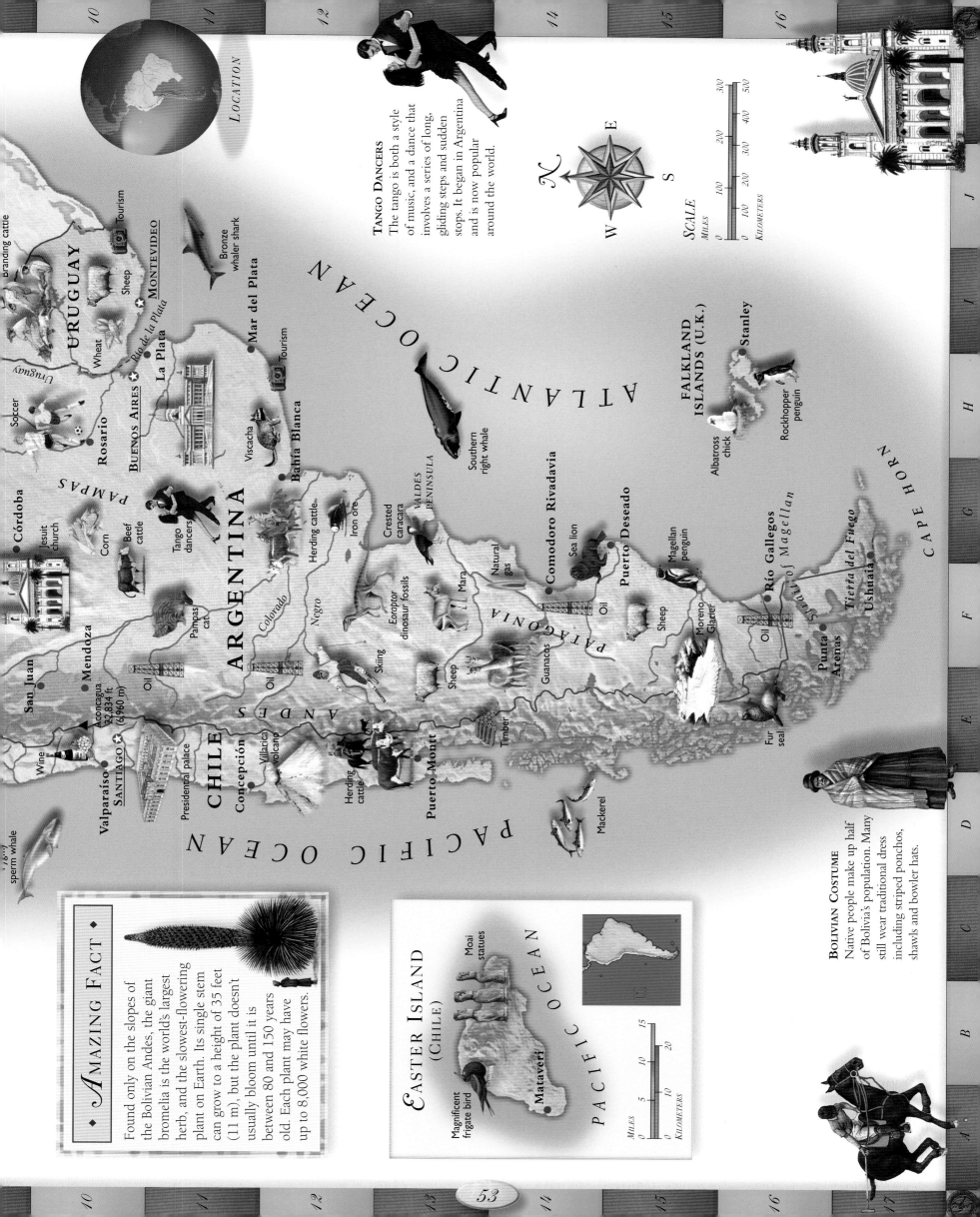

LOCATION

TANGO DANCERS
The tango is both a style of music, and a dance that involves a series of long, gliding steps and sudden stops. It began in Argentina and is now popular around the world.

N
W E
S

SCALE
MILES
0   100   200   300
0   100   200   300   400   500
KILOMETERS

URUGUAY
branching cattle
Soccer
Córdoba
Jesuit church
Wheat
Rosario
Sheep
MONTEVIDEO
Tourism
Río de la Plata
Bronze whaler shark
Mar del Plata
La Plata
Tourism
BUENOS AIRES
Uruguay
Uruguay

ATLANTIC OCEAN

Southern right whale

FALKLAND ISLANDS (U.K.)
Stanley
Albatross chick
Rockhopper penguin

PAMPAS
ARGENTINA
Corn
Beef cattle
Tango dancers
Pampas cat
Viscacha
Bahía Blanca
Crested caracara
VALDÉS PENINSULA
Herding cattle
Iron ore
Eoraptor dinosaur fossils
Mara
Natural gas
Sea lion
Comodoro Rivadavia
Puerto Deseado
Magellan penguin
PATAGONIA
Oil
Sheep
Río Gallegos
Moreno Glacier
Oil
Strait of Magellan
Tierra del Fuego
Punta Arenas
Ushuaia

CAPE HORN

San Juan
Aconcagua 22,834 ft (6,960 m)
Mendoza
Wine
Colorado
Negro
Oil
Skiing
Oil
Sheep
Guanacos
Timber
Fur seal

ANDES

CHILE
Valparaíso
SANTIAGO
Presidential palace
Concepción
Villarica volcano
Herding cattle
Puerto Montt
Mackerel

PACIFIC OCEAN

sperm whale

◆ **AMAZING FACT** ◆
Found only on the slopes of the Bolivian Andes, the giant bromelia is the world's largest herb, and the slowest-flowering plant on Earth. Its single stem can grow to a height of 35 feet (11 m), but the plant doesn't usually bloom until it is between 80 and 150 years old. Each plant may have up to 8,000 white flowers.

EASTER ISLAND
(CHILE)
Moai statues
Magnificent frigate bird
Mataveri
PACIFIC OCEAN
MILES
0   5   10   15
0   10   20
KILOMETERS

BOLIVIAN COSTUME
Native people make up half of Bolivia's population. Many still wear traditional dress including striped ponchos, shawls and bowler hats.

53

Europe

EUROPE IS A SMALL, DENSELY POPULATED CONTINENT made up of many countries, each of which has its own culture and, in most cases, its own language. It is bounded by the Arctic and Atlantic oceans in the north and west, and the Mediterranean Sea in the south. In the east, Russia's Ural Mountains separate Europe from Asia. A series of mountain ranges, including the Pyrenees, the Alps and the Carpathian Mountains, crosses Europe from east to west. South of these ranges, the land is rugged and the climate is warm and dry in summer and mild and wet in winter. To the north, a broad band of flat land known as the European Plain extends from the Atlantic coast to western Russia. Northwestern Europe has a mild, wet climate, but in the east and far north winters can be bitterly cold. At one time, most of Europe was covered in forest, but the trees were gradually cleared to make way for cities, farms and industries.

Major Mountains and Rivers

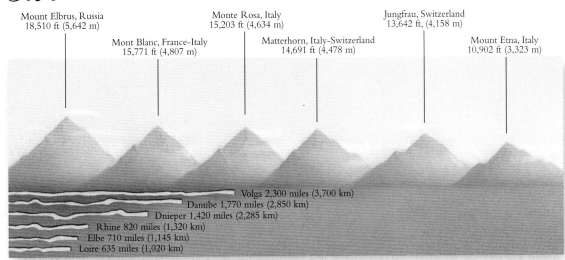

Mount Elbrus, Russia
18,510 ft (5,642 m)

Mont Blanc, France-Italy
15,771 ft (4,807 m)

Monte Rosa, Italy
15,203 ft (4,634 m)

Matterhorn, Italy-Switzerland
14,691 ft (4,478 m)

Jungfrau, Switzerland
13,642 ft, (4,158 m)

Mount Etna, Italy
10,902 ft (3,323 m)

Volga 2,300 miles (3,700 km)
Danube 1,770 miles (2,850 km)
Dnieper 1,420 miles (2,285 km)
Rhine 820 miles (1,320 km)
Elbe 710 miles (1,145 km)
Loire 635 miles (1,020 km)

Continent Facts

Regional land area: 3,997,929 sq. miles (10,354,636 sq. km) (including European Russia)
Regional population: 695,812,202 (including European Russia)
Independent countries: Albania, Andorra, Austria, Belarus, Belgium, Bosnia and Herzegovina, Bulgaria, Croatia, Czech Republic, Denmark, Estonia, Finland, France, Germany, Greece, Hungary, Iceland, Ireland, Italy, Latvia, Liechtenstein, Lithuania, Luxembourg, Macedonia, Malta, Moldova, Monaco, The Netherlands, Norway, Poland, Portugal, Romania, Russia, San Marino, Slovakia, Slovenia, Spain, Sweden, Switzerland, Ukraine, United Kingdom, Vatican City, Yugoslavia

World Records

WORLD'S SMALLEST COUNTRY
VATICAN CITY, 0.17 SQ. MILES (0.44 SQ. KM)

WORLD'S TALLEST STALAGMITE
KRÁSNOHORSKÁ CAVE, SLOVAKIA, 105 FT (32 M)

Continent Records

HIGHEST MOUNTAIN
MOUNT ELBRUS, RUSSIA, 18,510 FT (5,642 M)

LOWEST POINT
VOLGA RIVER DELTA, 92 FT (28 M) BELOW SEA LEVEL

LARGEST LAKE
LAKE LADOGA, RUSSIA, 6,835 SQ. MILES (17,703 SQ. KM)

LONGEST RIVER
VOLGA RIVER, RUSSIA, 2,300 MILES (3,700 KM)

LARGEST COUNTRY BY AREA
EUROPEAN RUSSIA, 233,089 SQ. MILES (603,701 SQ. KM)

LARGEST COUNTRY BY POPULATION
EUROPEAN RUSSIA, population 113,083,287

LARGEST CITY BY POPULATION
PARIS, FRANCE, population 11,174,743

Political Map

ICELAND

FAEROE ISLANDS
(DENMARK)

SWEDEN

FINLAND

NORWAY

ESTONIA

UNITED
KINGDOM

LATVIA

RUSSIA

DENMARK

KALININGRAD
OBLAST
(RUSSIA)

LITHUANIA

IRELAND

THE
NETHERLANDS

POLAND

BELARUS

GERMANY

BELGIUM

CZECH
REPUBLIC

LUXEMBOURG

SLOVAKIA

UKRAINE

FRANCE

1

AUSTRIA

SWITZERLAND

HUNGARY

MOLDOVA

SLOVENIA

CROATIA

ROMANIA

3

YUGOSLAVIA

4

BOSNIA and
HERZEGOVINA

BULGARIA

2

5

ALBANIA

MACEDONIA

SPAIN

ITALY

PORTUGAL

GREECE

MALTA

Key to Numbered Countries

- 1 LIECHTENSTEIN
- 2 ANDORRA
- 3 MONACO
- 4 SAN MARINO
- 5 VATICAN CITY

EUROPE

PHYSICAL MAP

NORTH AMERICA

ARCTIC OCEAN

× NORTH POLE

Greenland

Norwegian Sea

Barents Sea

FAEROE ISLANDS

Iceland

Arctic Circle

ASIA

ATLANTIC OCEAN

URAL MOUNTAINS

SCANDINAVIA

Lake Onega

Gulf of Bothnia

Lake Vänern

Lake Ladoga

Volga

Ireland

North Sea

Baltic Sea

EUROPEAN PLAIN

Great Britain

Channel

Elbe

English

Rhine

Seine

CARPATHIAN MTS.

Dnieper

Don

Bay of Biscay

Loire

Jungfrau

A L P S

Caspian Sea

Matterhorn

Mont Blanc

Monte Rosa

Mt. Elbrus

CAUCASUS MTS.

PYRENEES

Danube

Black Sea

IBERIAN PENINSULA

Corsica

APENNINES

Adriatic Sea

BALKAN PENINSULA

BALEARIC IS.

Strait of Gibraltar

Sardinia

Sicily

Mediterranean Sea

Ionian Sea

Aegean Sea

Mt. Etna

Crete

Tropic of Cancer

AFRICA

Equator

The United Kingdom and the Republic of Ireland

THE UNITED KINGDOM AND THE REPUBLIC OF IRELAND occupy islands known as the British Isles. The United Kingdom is made up of the countries of England, Wales, Scotland and Northern Ireland, which are ruled by one government based in London but have their own cultures. Scotland and Wales also have their own parliaments, and Scotland has its own legal and educational systems, churches and bank notes. England is a crowded country with many large cities. Almost eight million people live in London, the capital city. London is one of the world's most important centers of trade and finance and is famous for its many historic buildings. Southeastern England is flat and fertile and its farms provide most of the United Kingdom's crops. The country's most important industries are located in central England, an area known as the Midlands, and around the coalfields of the Pennine hills. To the west and north, the countryside is wet and mountainous and is used mainly for grazing animals. In the rugged, sparsely populated Scottish Highlands, red deer and sheep roam the hills and eagles soar overhead.

The Republic of Ireland occupies about 85 percent of the island of Ireland. It is a land of green plains surrounded by coastal mountains. Most of the country's industries are located in the capital, Dublin, and the southern city of Cork.

IRELAND
POPULATION: 3,883,159 ★ CAPITAL: DUBLIN

UNITED KINGDOM
POPULATION: 58,836,700 ★ CAPITAL: LONDON

ENGLAND
POPULATION: 49,181,300 ★ CAPITAL: LONDON

NORTHERN IRELAND
POPULATION: 1,689,300 ★ CAPITAL: BELFAST

SCOTLAND
POPULATION: 5,064,200 ★ CAPITAL: EDINBURGH

WALES
POPULATION: 2,903,200 ★ CAPITAL: CARDIFF

◆ AMAZING FACT ◆

In the 19th century, as a hoax, the name of the Welsh village Llanfairpwllgwyngyll was lengthened to the tongue-twisting Llanfairpwllgwyngyllgogerychwyrn-drobwllllantysiliogogogoch. The name means "St. Mary's church by the pool of white hazel trees, near the rapid whirlpool, by the red cave of the Church of St. Tysilio." In 1988 the village officially returned to using the shorter name. However, the railway station is still called by the 58-letter version.

LLANFAIRPWLLGWYNGYLLGOGERYCHWYRNDROBWLLLLANTYSILIOGOGOGOCH

◆ LOOK AGAIN ◆

- Which famous railway bridge is located near the capital of Scotland?
- Name a sport that is played in Ireland.
- What is the name of the group of islands near Land's End?

Shetland pony

SHETLAND ISLANDS

Lerwick

Cod

ORKNEY ISLANDS

Kirkwall

John o'Groats

Thurso

Highland piper

Highland cattle

Aberdeen

Hammer throwing, Highland Games

Oil rig

Haddock

North Sea

Forth railway bridge

Coal

Glamis Castle

Dundee

Golf

EDINBURGH

Tweed

Beef cattle

Hadrian's Wall

Inverness

SCOTLAND

Urquhart Castle and Loch Ness

Dee

Tay

GRAMPIAN MTS.

Forth

Clyde

Capercaillie

Ben Nevis 4,406 ft (1,343 m)

Coal

Glasgow

Arran

Oban

Otter

Salmon

Mull

Skye

Sheep

Islay

Iona Abbey

SOUTH HEBRIDES

South Uist

North Uist

Lewis with Harris

Textiles

Stornoway

Giant's Causeway rock formation

Fishing trawler

STONEHENGE
This prehistoric stone monument, or megalith, was a religious and ceremonial site for thousands of years.

BLARNEY CASTLE
It is said that if you kiss the Blarney Stone in the tower of this castle you will become a clever and persuasive talker.

Spain and Portugal

SPAIN AND PORTUGAL OCCUPY the Iberian Peninsula, a wide, square-shaped piece of land in southwestern Europe. This peninsula is separated from the rest of the continent by the Pyrenees, a mountain range that contains the tiny country of Andorra. Most of the Iberian Peninsula consists of a huge plateau known as the Meseta, which is covered with dry grasslands, olive groves and forested hills. At the center of the Meseta, 2,120 feet (646 m) above sea level, lies Madrid—the largest city in Spain and the highest capital city in Europe. Spain's second-largest city, Barcelona, lies on the narrow plains of the east coast. This coastline and the nearby Balearic Islands are warm and sunny for much of the year, and in summer, crowds of vacationers from all over Europe sunbathe on the sandy beaches. The southern tip of Spain lies only nine miles (15 km) from Africa. Between AD 711 and the 12th century, most of Spain was ruled by the Moors, an Arabic people from North Africa, and towns such as Granada and Seville have many ornate Moorish buildings. West of Spain lies Portugal. Once the heart of a vast, worldwide empire, Portugal is now one of the poorest countries in western Europe. Olive groves and cork oak forests cover the dry, southern plains. In the many river valleys that cross the country, farmers grow grapes for winemaking. Among the best-known Portuguese wines is port, which is named after the country's second-largest city, Porto.

ANDORRA
POPULATION: 68,403 ＊ CAPITAL: ANDORRA

PORTUGAL
POPULATION: 10,084,245 ＊ CAPITAL: LISBON

SPAIN
POPULATION: 40,077,100 ＊ CAPITAL: MADRID

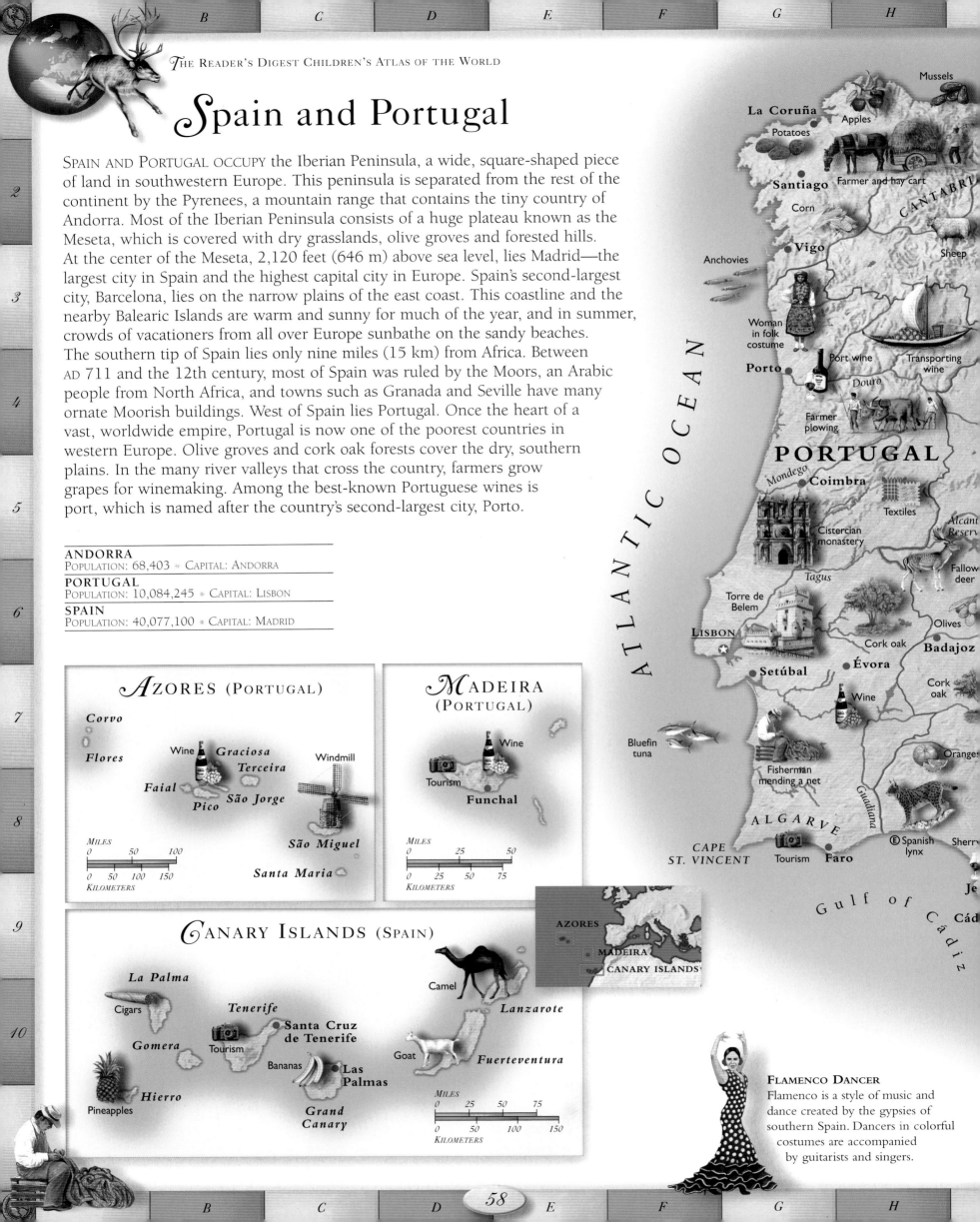

AZORES (PORTUGAL)

Corvo
Flores
Wine
Graciosa
Terceira
Faial
Pico
São Jorge
Windmill
São Miguel
Santa Maria

MILES
0   50   100
0   50   100   150
KILOMETERS

MADEIRA (PORTUGAL)

Wine
Tourism
Funchal

MILES
0   25   50
0   25   50   75
KILOMETERS

CANARY ISLANDS (SPAIN)

La Palma
Cigars
Gomera
Tenerife
Tourism
Santa Cruz de Tenerife
Bananas
Hierro
Pineapples
Camel
Lanzarote
Goat
Las Palmas
Fuerteventura
Grand Canary

MILES
0   25   50   75
0   50   100   150
KILOMETERS

AZORES
MADEIRA
CANARY ISLANDS

La Coruña
Apples
Mussels
Potatoes
Santiago
Farmer and hay cart
Corn
CANTABRI
Vigo
Sheep
Anchovies
Woman in folk costume
Porto
Port wine
Transporting wine
Douro
Farmer plowing

ATLANTIC OCEAN

PORTUGAL

Mondego
Coimbra
Textiles
Cistercian monastery
Alcánt Reserv
Tagus
Torre de Belem
Fallow deer
LISBON
Cork oak
Olives
Badajoz
Setúbal
Évora
Cork oak
Wine
Bluefin tuna
Fisherman mending a net
Guadiana
ALGARVE
CAPE ST. VINCENT
Tourism
Faro
Ⓔ Spanish lynx
Sherry
Oranges
Spanish lynx
Gulf of   Cádiz
Je

FLAMENCO DANCER
Flamenco is a style of music and dance created by the gypsies of southern Spain. Dancers in colorful costumes are accompanied by guitarists and singers.

Bay of Biscay

Gijón

Oviedo

Santander

OUNTAINS

FRANCE

Basque folk dancer

Brown bear

Altamira cave paintings

Wheat

Potatoes

Bilbao

Donostia-San Sebastián

P Y R E N E E S

Iron and steel

Running of the bulls

Pamplona

Bearded vulture

Pico de Aneto 11,168 ft (3,404 m)

ANDORRA

ANDORRA

Vacationer

Valladolid

Douro

Holy Week procession

Wild boars

Saragossa

Ebro

Torre de Aragón

Beef cattle

Barley

Sagrada Familia church

Textiles

COSTA BRAVA

Barcelona

Segovia

Alcazar

Wine

Salamanca

heat

High-tech industries

El Escorial

MADRID

Spanish guitarist

Olives

Oil

BALEARIC ISLANDS

Minorca

Mahón

Statue of Don Quixote and Sancho Panza

Toledo

Paella

Jara Gate

Olives

Majorca

Palma

SPAIN

M E S E T A

Tagus

Bullfighting

Oranges

Car manufacturing

Valencia

Sardines

Tourism

Ibiza

Ibiza

Guadiana

Farmhouse

Windmills of La Mancha

Collecting saffron

Tourism

Mezquita Mosque

Wine

Sunflowers

Alicante

Mediterranean Sea

ERRA MORENA

Guadalquivir

Córdoba

Olives

Alhambra Palace

Flamenco dancer

Citrus fruit

Murcia

Fishing boat

Granada

Mulhacén 11,407 ft ▲ (3,477 m)

Cartagena

eville

Málaga

Tajo Bridge

Tourism

Almería

Andalucian ranch hand

COSTA DEL SOL

Sailing

GIBRALTAR (U.K.)

Sardines

Algeciras

Ceuta (SPAIN)

N

W   E

S

MOROCCO

Melilla (SPAIN)

ALGERIA

LOCATION

SAGRADA FAMILIA CHURCH
The spires of this Barcelona church are covered with shells and ceramics, and stand 350 foot (110 m) high. The building was begun in 1884. More than 100 years later, it is still being built.

SCALE

MILES

0   25   50   75   100

0   50   100   150

KILOMETERS

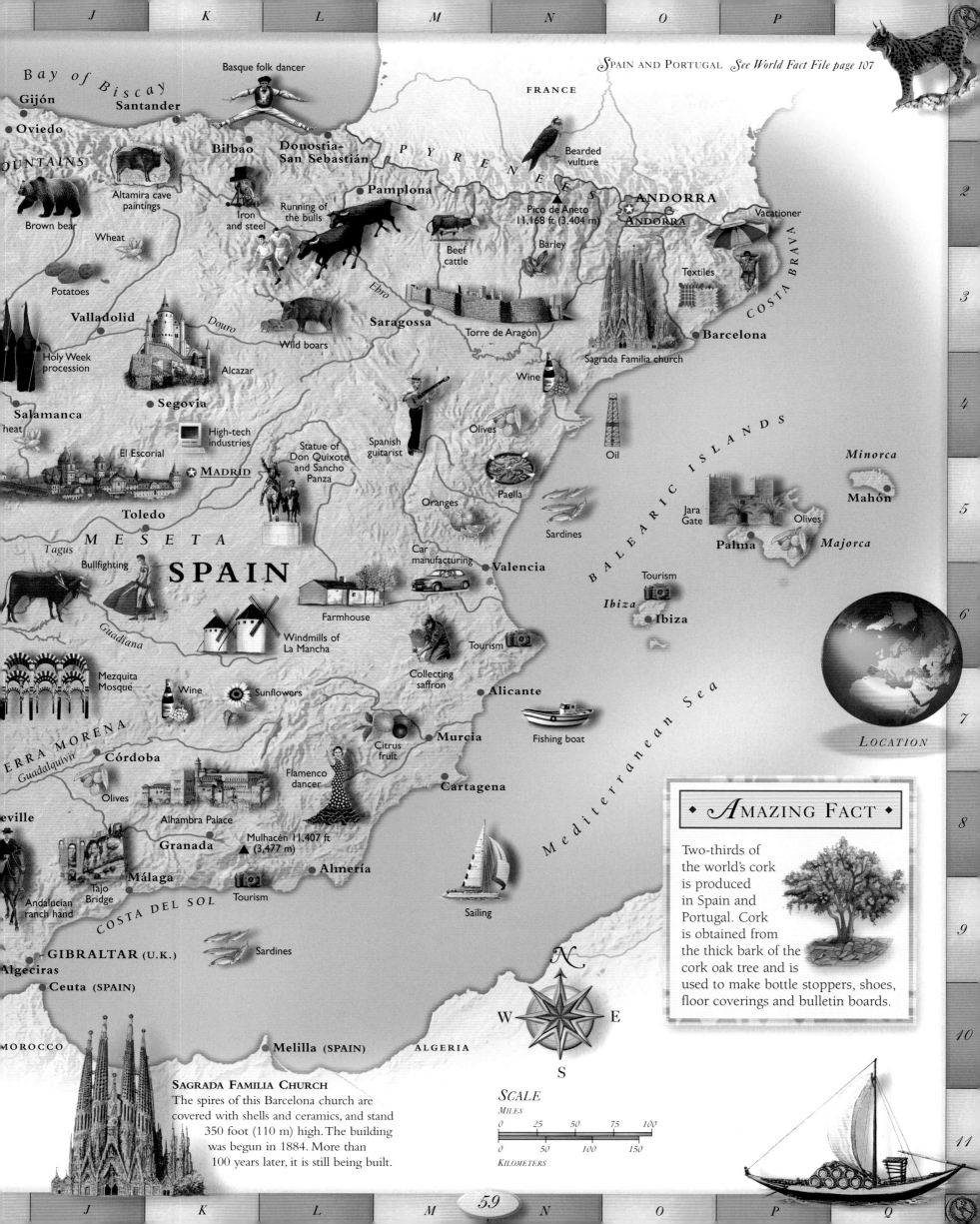

France

FRANCE, THE LARGEST COUNTRY in western Europe, has a varied climate and landscape. In the north, the weather is mild and wet, and much of the land is flat. As you travel south, the climate becomes warmer and the land more mountainous. Three-quarters of the population live in towns and cities, but most of the country is farmland, and France is Europe's leading farming country. The northern plains are covered in fields of wheat and sugar beets, and in central and southern France vineyards dot the hillsides—more wine is produced in France than in any other country except Italy. The area around Paris, the capital, is the most densely populated region. It is home to one-fifth of the country's population and most of its industries. Several great rivers, including the Seine and the Loire, cross France's northern and western plains. These waterways were once the country's main transportation routes, and their banks are lined with historic villages and magnificent castles known as châteaus. In the south, the mountains of the Pyrenees and the Alps separate France from Spain and Italy. Among their snow-capped peaks lie popular ski resorts and national parks that are home to eagles, marmots and goatlike antelopes called chamois. Along the Mediterranean coast there are many busy beach resorts. Near the Italian border lies Monaco, the second-smallest country in the world. Monaco is famous for its casinos and its annual Grand Prix motor race.

FRANCE
POPULATION: 59,765,983 ⁕ CAPITAL: PARIS
MONACO
POPULATION: 31,987 ⁕ CAPITAL: MONACO

◆ AMAZING FACT ◆

France is now connected to Great Britain by an undersea rail link known as the Channel Tunnel. The tunnel took seven years to build and includes two rail tracks. Trains take 35 minutes to pass through the tunnel. Travelers can journey from London to Paris in about three hours.

BOULES
Boules is a bowling game that is popular in France. It is played with metal balls on a hard dirt surface.

EIFFEL TOWER
Once the tallest structure in the world, the Eiffel Tower was erected for the Paris Exposition of 1889 by engineer Alexandre-Gustave Eiffel.

ENGLAND

English Channel

Cross-channel ferry
Channel Tunnel
Tourism
Cherbourg
Le Havre
Mont-St-Michel
Bayeux Tapestry
Vers
Medieval houses
Brest
Camembert cheese
Quimper
Apples
Rennes
Tourism
Car racing, Le Mans
Standing stones
Dairy cattle
St-Nazaire
Tou
Nantes
Fishing boat
Tourism
Château Chenonceau
Beef cattle
La Rochelle
Sh
ATLANTIC OCEAN
Tourism
Limo china
Mackerel
Château de la Brède
Oysters
Bordeaux
Lascaux paintin
Bay of Biscay
Wine
French breads
Ga
Windsurfing
Boules
Biarritz
Natural gas
Ⓔ Pyrenean ibex
P Y R E N
SPAIN

J K L M N O P Q

Dunkerque
Calais
ulogne
Nuclear energy
Lille
sels
Potatoes
Sugar beets
Dieppe
Amiens
Wheat
Rouen
Car manufacturing
PARIS
Fashion
Chartres Cathedral
Eiffel Tower
Seine
Château de Chambord
Loire
Bourges

BELGIUM

Cafe

Reims
Champagne
Troyes
Tour de France
Gaul fort
Meuse

LUXEMBOURG

Metz
Iron ore
Iron and steel
Nancy
Wine
Moselle

GERMANY

Coal
Strasbourg
Nuclear energy
Folk costume

Chapel of Notre Dame du Haut

Dijon
Mustard
T.G.V. high-speed train
Doubs
Saône
Dairy cattle
Besançon
Mountain climbing

SWITZERLAND

FRANCE

Snail
Tungsten
Playing the cabrette
Farmer with goats
Coal
Lyon
St-Étienne
Chapel of St-Michel D'Aiguilhe
French breads
Wine
Textiles
Marmot
A L P S
Mont Blanc 15,771 ft (4,807 m)
Chamois
Grenoble
Skiing
Rhône
Saône

ITALY

Geese
Hunting for truffles
Nuclear energy
Avignon
Harvesting lavender
Perfume
Rhône
Durance

Casino, Monte Carlo
MONACO
Mackerel
Nice
Cannes
Cannes Film Festival
Marseille
Tourism
Aircraft manufacturing
Toulouse
Montpellier
Pont du Gard
Sailing
Flamingo
Waterskiing
Walled town of Carcassonne
ORRA
Perpignan
Solar furnace

Mediterranean Sea

Osprey
Corsica
Tourism
Ajaccio
Statue of Napoleon

TOUR DE FRANCE
France's most famous sporting event, this cycle race around the entire country covers about 2,500 miles (4,000 km).

LOCATION

N
W — E
S
SCALE
MILES
0 25 50 75 100
0 50 100 150
KILOMETERS

◆ **PROJECT:** *Cave Painting* ◆

The cave paintings at Lascaux were created about 15,000 years ago. Here's how you can create your own painting that will look thousands of years old.

❶ Stuff a strong paper bag with crumpled newspaper and then staple the bag closed.

❷ Mix some glue and sand and use this to paint the whole bag. When it dries it will look like a rock.

❸ Collect three or four different-colored soils. Sift out the lumps and then mix each color with glue to make earth paints (add water if the paints are too thick). Now you are ready to paint. Like the artists who created the Lascaux cave paintings, you can paint animals living in your area.

◆ **LOOK AGAIN** ◆

● Which cathedral lies southwest of Paris?

● Name a horned animal found in the Pyrenees.

● What kind of food is produced in Dijon?

● Which small country is located east of Nice?

The Low Countries

THE DENSELY POPULATED COUNTRIES of the Netherlands (also called Holland), Belgium and Luxembourg are known as the Low Countries because they have no high mountains and few hills. Much of the land, including one-third of the Netherlands, actually lies below sea level. Over the centuries, local people have built large barriers known as dikes to keep the sea out, pumped water out of the marshes behind the dikes to create areas of new land called polders, and constructed thousands of miles of canals. Throughout the region, barges chug along these waterways, past windmills, dairy farms and colorful fields of tulips—both Belgium and the Netherlands export flowers and bulbs all over the world. The capital of the Netherlands, Amsterdam, has more than 150 canals, many of which are lined with tall, narrow, 17th-century buildings. In Belgium, canals link the country's ports to the historic cities of Bruges and Ghent, and to Brussels, the capital. Brussels is often referred to as the capital of Europe because it is the headquarters of the European Union (EU). Southeast of Brussels lies the only high part of the Low Countries, the Ardennes. This range of forest-covered hills spreads across the northern half of Luxembourg, one of Europe's smallest countries but also one of its most important financial centers.

BELGIUM
POPULATION: 10,274,595 * CAPITAL: BRUSSELS

LUXEMBOURG
POPULATION: 448,569 * CAPITAL: LUXEMBOURG

THE NETHERLANDS
POPULATION: 16,067,754 * CAPITALS: AMSTERDAM, THE HAGUE

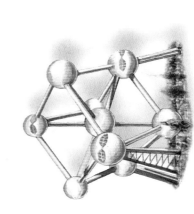

THE ATOMIUM
The Atomium represents an iron molecule and is one of the rare remains of the World Exhibition held in Brussels in 1958.

◆ AMAZING FACT ◆

The Low Countries have more than 5,000 miles (8,000 km) of canals, which are used for transportation and for draining the land. Because much of the region lies below sea level, water has to be pumped into canals built high above ground level. You could be standing in a field in the Low Countries and see a ship pass by above your head!

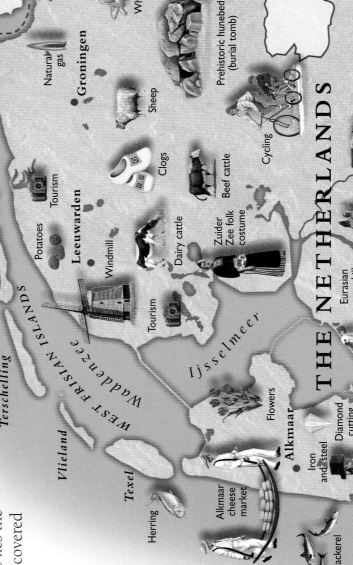

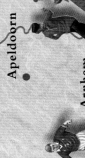

Map labels

THE NETHERLANDS

Wheat
Natural gas
Prehistoric hunebed (burial tomb)
Dairy cattle
Pigs
Groningen
Sheep
Folk dancers
Cycling
Beef cattle
Apeldoorn
Tourism
Leeuwarden
Poultry
Arnhem
Potatoes
Clogs
Beef cattle
Rhine
Ameland
Windmill
Dairy cattle
Zuider Zee folk costume
Tourism
Ijsselmeer
Dom Cathedral tower
Lek
Harbor seals
Terschelling
WEST FRISIAN ISLANDS
Eurasian spoonbill
Soccer
Waddenzee
Tourism
Amsterdam
Utrecht
Vlieland
Flowers
AMSTERDAM
Texel
Diamond cutting
Tulips
Iron and steel
Alkmaar
Herring
Alkmaar cheese market
Haarlem
Peace Palace
THE HAGUE
Mackerel
Rotterdam
Container ship

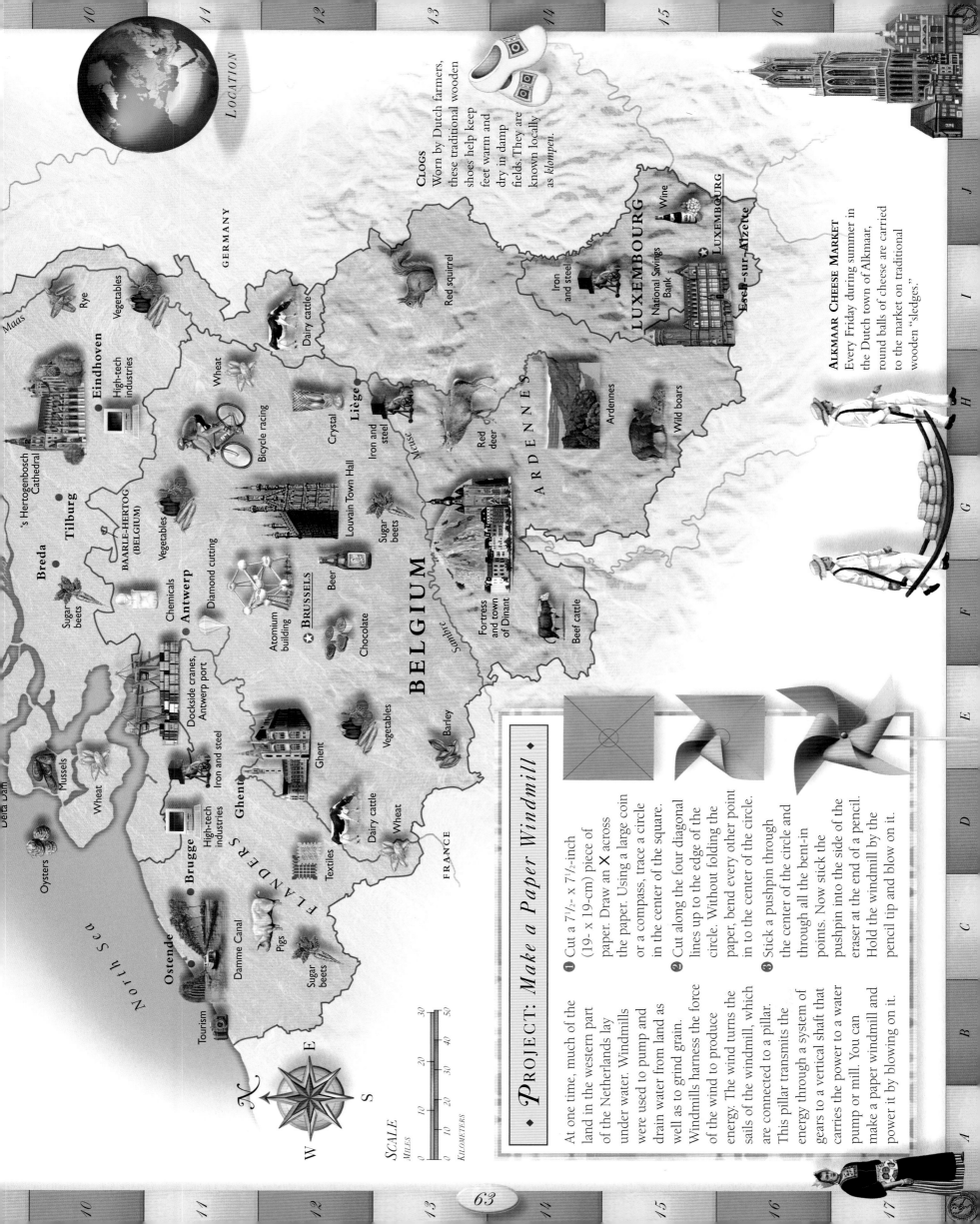

LOCATION

CLOGS
Worn by Dutch farmers, these traditional wooden shoes help keep feet warm and dry in damp fields. They are known locally as *klompen*.

Maas

GERMANY

Rye

Vegetables

's Hertogenbosch Cathedral

● Eindhoven   High-tech industries

Dairy cattle

Wheat

Breda

Tilburg

Sugar beets

BAARLE-HERTOG (BELGIUM)

Bicycle racing

Vegetables

Crystal

● Liège

Iron and steel

Meuse

Louvain Town Hall

Sugar beets

Red deer

A R D E N N E S

Ardennes

Wild boars

Red squirrel

Iron and steel

LUXEMBOURG

National Savings Bank

★ LUXEMBOURG

Wine

Esch-sur-Alzette

Chemicals

Antwerp

Diamond cutting

Atomium building

★ BRUSSELS

Beer

Chocolate

BELGIUM

Sambre

Fortress and town of Dinant

Beef cattle

Delta Dam

Mussels

Wheat

Oysters

Dockside cranes, Antwerp port

Iron and steel

Ghent

Ghent

Barley

Vegetables

Dairy cattle

Wheat

N o r t h   S e a

● **Brugge**

High-tech industries

F L A N D E R S

Textiles

Tourism

Damme Canal

Pigs

Sugar beets

Ostende

FRANCE

ALKMAAR CHEESE MARKET
Every Friday during summer in the Dutch town of Alkmaar, round balls of cheese are carried to the market on traditional wooden "sledges."

SCALE
MILES
0   10   20   30
0   10   20   30   40   50
KILOMETERS

N
W   E
S

◆ **PROJECT:** *Make a Paper Windmill* ◆

At one time, much of the land in the western part of the Netherlands lay under water. Windmills were used to pump and drain water from land as well as to grind grain. Windmills harness the force of the wind to produce energy. The wind turns the sails of the windmill, which are connected to a pillar. This pillar transmits the energy through a system of gears to a vertical shaft that carries the power to a water pump or mill. You can make a paper windmill and power it by blowing on it.

❶ Cut a 7½- x 7½-inch (19- x 19-cm) piece of paper. Draw an **X** across the paper. Using a large coin or a compass, trace a circle in the center of the square.

❷ Cut along the four diagonal lines up to the edge of the circle. Without folding the paper, bend every other point in to the center of the circle.

❸ Stick a pushpin through the center of the circle and through all the bent-in points. Now stick the pushpin into the side of the eraser at the end of a pencil. Hold the windmill by the pencil tip and blow on it.

A   B   C   D   E   F   G   H   I   J

Western Central Europe

AFTER WORLD WAR II, GERMANY was divided into two countries: East Germany and West Germany. They were reunited in 1990 and Germany is now home to more than 80 million people, the largest population of any European country except Russia. Many of Germany's cities lie on rivers. The Rhine River connects the country's most important industrial region, the Ruhr Valley, to the ports of the Netherlands and the Swiss city of Basel. On its journey northward, the Rhine meanders past forests of spruce and fir, steep hillsides covered with vineyards, and cliffs crowned by medieval castles. From southern Germany, the spectacular Alps mountain range stretches across the countries of Switzerland and Austria, where it covers about two-thirds of the land. Throughout these mountains, roads and railways wind through narrow river valleys and cross steep passes. In summer, cows graze in the alpine meadows; in winter, skiers hurtle down the slopes. Switzerland is a peaceful country which hasn't been involved in a war since 1814. This has encouraged people from all over the world to deposit money in Swiss banks, and the country is now a leading financial center. In Austria, many farms and industries lie on the northeastern lowlands. This area is crossed by the Danube, Europe's second-longest river. The Danube passes through Austria's capital, Vienna—home to one-fifth of Austria's population and one of Europe's grandest cities.

AUSTRIA
POPULATION: 8,169,929 ■ CAPITAL: VIENNA

GERMANY
POPULATION: 83,251,851 ■ CAPITAL: BERLIN

LIECHTENSTEIN
POPULATION: 32,842 ■ CAPITAL: VADUZ

SWITZERLAND
POPULATION: 7,301,994 ■ CAPITAL: BERN

◆ PROJECT: *Swiss Chocolate Fondue* ◆

The Swiss eat a dish called fondue, which is often made from cheese. Pieces of bread are dipped in a mixture of hot melted cheese and white wine. This fondue is different—it's made with chocolate!

1 Place 8 oz (250 g) semisweet chocolate pieces into a saucepan with 1 cup (8 oz/250 ml) whipping cream.

2 Ask an adult to help you warm the ingredients gently until the chocolate has melted. Beat the mixture until it becomes glossy.

3 Let the mixture cool a little. Then spear a piece of fruit (strawberries or grapes are good) on a fork, dip it in the fondue and have a taste. Yum!

◆ AMAZING FACT ◆

The country of Liechtenstein is home to only 32,842 people and is just four miles (6 km) wide. That means you could walk across it in less than two hours! The prince of Liechtenstein lives in this castle at Vaduz, the capital.

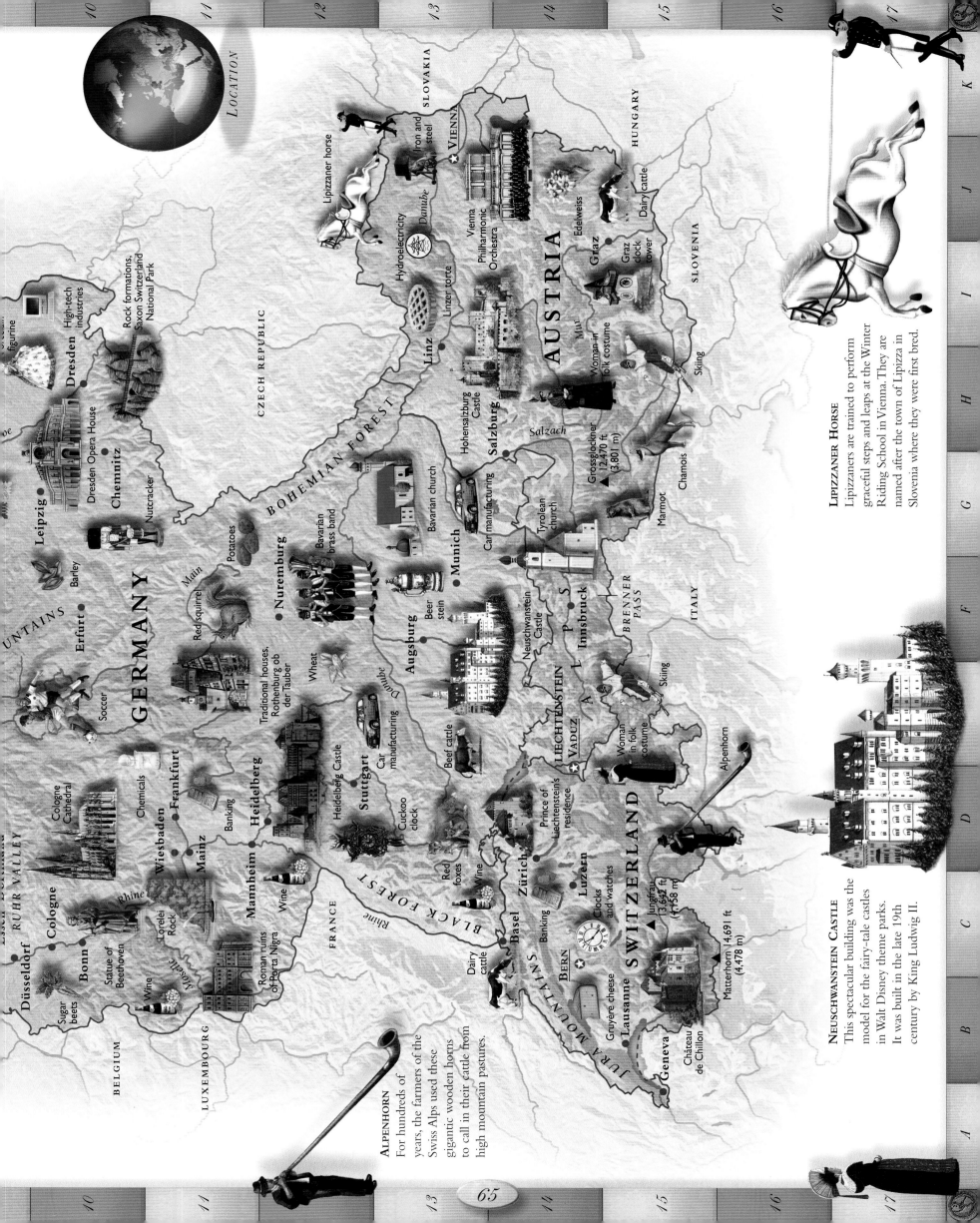

LIPIZZANER HORSE
Lipizzaners are trained to perform graceful steps and leaps at the Winter Riding School in Vienna. They are named after the town of Lipizza in Slovenia where they were first bred.

NEUSCHWANSTEIN CASTLE
This spectacular building was the model for the fairy-tale castles in Walt Disney theme parks. It was built in the late 19th century by King Ludwig II.

ALPENHORN
For hundreds of years, the farmers of the Swiss Alps used these gigantic wooden horns to call in their cattle from high mountain pastures.

Italy

ITALY CONSISTS OF A LONG, boot-shaped peninsula, the large islands of Sicily and Sardinia, and about 70 smaller islands. Within Italy lie two other countries: San Marino in the east, and the Vatican City (the world's smallest country) in the city of Rome. The Vatican City is the home of the Pope, the head of the Roman Catholic Church. Most of mainland Italy is mountainous. The Alps form a great arc around the northern border, and the Apennines stretch almost the entire length of the peninsula. Between these two mountain ranges lies the Northern Plain, a flat, fertile region drained by the Po River. This plain has Italy's richest farmland and is home to the country's most important industries, including the car factories of Turin, and Milan's fashion and design houses.

Each year, more than 50 million tourists travel to Italy to visit its ancient ruins, historic cities and museums, and to enjoy the sunny summer weather. The country's mild climate allows farmers to grow large quantities of wheat, citrus fruit, olives and grapes—Italy is the world's leading producer of olive oil and wine. Parts of Italy are regularly rocked by earthquakes, and the country has the only active volcanoes on mainland Europe. On the island of Sicily, Mount Etna has erupted at least 260 times since the first recorded eruption in 70 BC. About 60 miles (95 km) south of Sicily lie the islands of Malta. At various times in its history, Malta was ruled by the Romans, Arabs, Turks, French and British. It is now an independent republic.

COLOSSEUM
This Roman stadium was built in the first century AD and used for events such as gladiator contests. It was even flooded for mock sea battles.

◆ AMAZING FACT ◆

The Leaning Tower of Pisa was constructed as a bell tower between AD 1173 and 1370. Unfortunately, it was built on unstable ground, and it began to sink and tilt to one side after completion of the first three stories. Although the tower leans about 15 feet (4.5 m) out of line, it has recently been stabilized so that it will not fall over.

ITALY
POPULATION: 57,715,625 ◆ CAPITAL: ROME
MALTA
POPULATION: 397,499 ◆ CAPITAL: VALLETTA
SAN MARINO
POPULATION: 27,730 ◆ CAPITAL: SAN MARINO
VATICAN CITY
POPULATION: 900 ◆ CAPITAL: VATICAN CITY

MOUNT VESUVIUS AND POMPEII
In AD 79, Mount Vesuvius erupted, burying the town of Pompeii under stone and ash. The ruins were not discovered until the 18th century.

Strait of Otranto

Adriatic Sea

Tyrrhenian Sea

Ionian Sea

Gulf of Taranto

Mediterranean Sea

ITALY

Trulli houses
Winemaking
Brindisi
Bari
Crabs
Octopus
Oysters
Taranto
Appian Way (Roman road)
Vesuvius and the ruins of Pompeii Forum
Goats
Olives
Wall lizard
Great barracuda
Cosenza
Reggio di Calabria
Sheep
Oranges
Sea horse
Potatoes
Foggia
Red mullet
Oil
Wine
Anchovies
Stromboli
LIPARI ISLANDS
Pescara
Abbey of Monte Cassino
Soccer
Pizza maker
Naples
Tourism
Ischia
Mt. Vesuvius 4,190 ft (1,277m)
Capri
Salerno
Garfish
Olives
Wolf
Basilica, Vatican City
Tiber
Vatican guard
Colosseum
VATICAN CITY ★ **ROME**
Container ship
Sunflowers
Sunflowers
Giglio
Scuba diving
Bluefin tuna
Sardines
CORSICA (FRANCE)
Iron ore
Sardinia
Goats
Olives
Sheep
Sassari
Cagliari
Woman in folk costume
Tourism
Sardines

Swordfish
Ustica
Wheat
Temple of Concordia
Palermo
Wine
Sardines
Oil
Mt. Etna 10,902 ft (3,323 m)
Cirrus fruit
Sicily
Messina
Tourism
Syracuse
Tourism
Great barracuda

SAN MARINO
The smallest republic in Europe and the oldest republic in the world, San Marino was founded around AD 300 by Christians fleeing religious persecution.

MALTA ★ **VALLETTA**
Tourism

MILES
0   25   50   75   100   150
KILOMETERS
0   50   100   150

◆ PROJECT: *Making a Mosaic* ◆

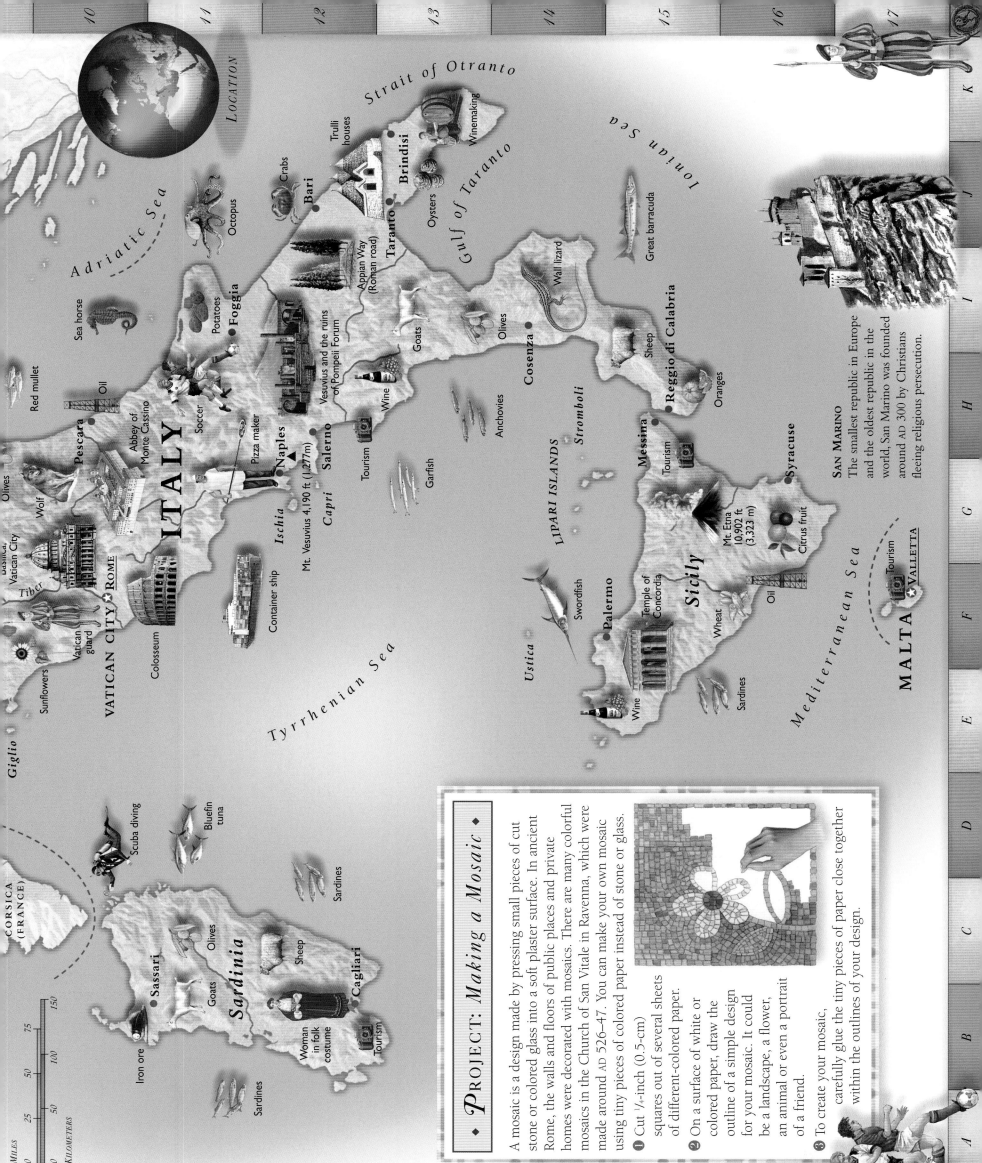

A mosaic is a design made by pressing small pieces of cut stone or colored glass into a soft plaster surface. In ancient Rome, the walls and floors of public places and private homes were decorated with mosaics. There are many colorful mosaics in the Church of San Vitale in Ravenna, which were made around AD 526–47. You can make your own mosaic using tiny pieces of colored paper instead of stone or glass.

① Cut ¼-inch (0.5-cm) squares out of several sheets of different-colored paper.

② On a surface of white or colored paper, draw the outline of a simple design for your mosaic. It could be a landscape, a flower, an animal or even a portrait of a friend.

③ To create your mosaic, carefully glue the tiny pieces of paper close together within the outlines of your design.

Southeastern Europe

THIS REGION IS OFTEN REFERRED TO as the Balkans. It lies at the edge of Europe, close to Asia, and is home to many peoples from both continents. Throughout history, many peoples and ethnic groups have disputes between countries and ethnic groups have occurred here regularly. In 1991, the republics of Slovenia, Croatia, Bosnia and Herzegovina, and Macedonia declared their independence from Yugoslavia. This led to a war that destroyed cities, farms and industries, and left thousands of people homeless. Most of southeastern Europe is rugged and mountainous. Along the coast of Croatia, rocky slopes rise steeply from the water. Inland, forests and farms surround the peaks that spread eastward through Yugoslavia and into Romania and Bulgaria. In Bulgaria's Balkan

Mountains, an area known as the Valley of the Roses produces more than two-thirds of the world's rose oil, an essential ingredient in most perfumes. Southeastern Europe's best farmland lies along the Danube River, which connects many of the region's towns to the ports of the Black Sea. In Greece, overgrazing by sheep and goats has stripped some of the land of trees and shrubs, but the warm climate allows farmers to grow olives, grapes, citrus fruit and wheat. Greece's sunny weather and scenic attractions bring tourists from all over the world. In Athens, home to one-third of Greece's population, rush-hour traffic roars past 2,000-year-old temples. On the Greek islands, clusters of white buildings cling to cliffs, and fishing boats drift across clear turquoise bays.

ALBANIA
POPULATION: 3,544,841 • CAPITAL: TIRANË

BOSNIA AND HERZEGOVINA
POPULATION: 3,964,388 • CAPITAL: SARAJEVO

BULGARIA
POPULATION: 7,621,337 • CAPITAL: SOFIA

CROATIA
POPULATION: 4,390,751 • CAPITAL: ZAGREB

GREECE
POPULATION: 10,645,343 • CAPITAL: ATHENS

MACEDONIA
POPULATION: 2,054,800 • CAPITAL: SKOPJE

ROMANIA
POPULATION: 22,317,730 • CAPITAL: BUCHAREST

SLOVENIA
POPULATION: 1,932,917 • CAPITAL: LJUBLJANA

YUGOSLAVIA
POPULATION: 10,656,929 • CAPITAL: BELGRADE

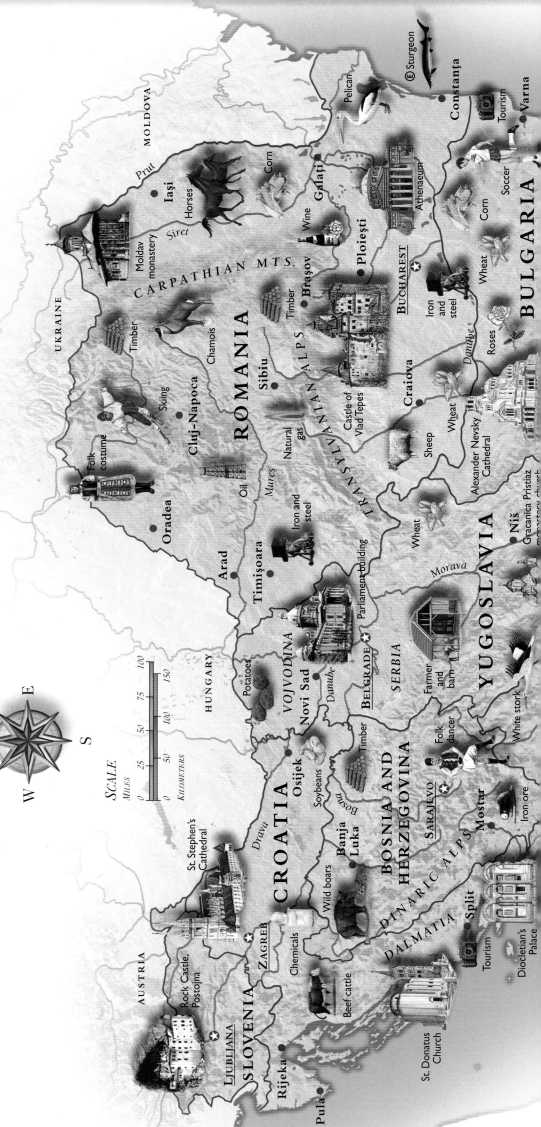

SCALE

MILES

KILOMETERS

N E S W

LOCATION

Black Sea

Adriatic Sea

ITALY

KOSOVO

Shkodër
Copper
ALBANIA
Durrës
TIRANË
Black kite
Vlorë
Inspecting carpets
Korçë
Bitola
Corn

MACEDONIA
SKOPJE
Vardar
Struma
RHODOPE MTS.
Mt Musala
9,596 ft
(2,925 m)
Skiing
Greek Orthodox monk
Iron/ steel
Goats

Shipka Memorial Church
Plovdiv
Food processing
Tobacco
Wheat
TURKEY

Thessaloníki
Eastern Orthodox Church
Monastery Meteora
Cotton
Mt. Olympus
9,570 ft
(2,917 m)
Tourism

GREECE
Ruins of Delphi
Wine
Bouzouki
Corfu
Levkás
Olives
IONIAN ISLANDS
Cephalonia
Zákinthos
Volos
NORTHERN SPORADES
Skyros
Euboea
Khalkís
Lignite
Sardines

Alexandroúpolis
Thásos
Samothráki
Lemnos
Olives
Sailing
Lesbos
Chíos
Sámos
Mackerel
Aegean Sea

TURKEY

ATHENS
Parthenon
Piraeus
Evzones guards
Andros
Tinos
Mykonos
CYCLADES
Naxos
Páros
Tourism

Patras
PELOPONNESE
Tripolis
King Agamemnon's gold death mask
Ruins of Olympia
Kithira

Ionian Sea

Sea of Crete
Iráklion
Canea
Wine
Crete
Bull's head sculpture, Knossos
Thíra
Traditional church
DODECANESE
Windmill
Rhodes
Kárpathos

Mediterranean Sea

◆ PROJECT: *Make a Cave* ◆

The Postojna Caves in Slovenia are famous for their stalactites and stalagmites. These formations took thousands of years to develop, but you can make your own cave with stalactites and stalagmites in just a few days.

① Draw a cave scene on the inside bottom of a shoe box. Line the outside and inside walls of the box with aluminum foil. Turn the box on its side so that the scene becomes the cave's back wall. Ask an adult to help you punch two holes close together at each end of the top of the box. Place a glass outside each end of the box.

② Thread a length of string in through one hole at one end and out through one hole at the other end. Repeat with the other two holes. Make sure the strings reach the bottom of each glass and hang down a little inside the cave.

③ Fill the glasses with hot water and stir in washing soda until no more will dissolve. Make sure you wash your hands well after using the washing soda. Over the next few days, as the water soaks into the strings and then starts to evaporate, small salt formations will appear where the strings sag. At the same time, small mounds of salt will form where the water drips onto the cave floor. Gradually, these formations will grow into stalactites and stalagmites.

EVZONES GUARDS
Wearing their traditional skirts and tasseled hats and shoes, the evzones stand guard outside the parliament in Athens.

CASTLE OF VLAD TEPES
Vlad Tepes, a 15th-century Romanian prince known as Vlad the Impaler, is said to have inspired the legend of Dracula the vampire.

BLACK KITE
These birds of prey are found throughout southeastern Europe. At night, they roost in trees in huge flocks as many as 100 birds.

Eastern Europe

IN RECENT YEARS, MANY POLITICAL CHANGES have occurred within this vast region. During 1990 and 1991, the republics of Latvia, Estonia, Lithuania, Belarus, Moldova and the Ukraine, all formerly part of the Soviet Union, became independent countries. In 1993, Czechoslovakia divided into two countries, the Czech Republic and Slovakia. Mountains line the borders of the Czech Republic and cover most of Slovakia, but elsewhere eastern Europe is generally flat. Wide grasslands cover central Hungary and most of the Ukraine. In Poland, rivers that rise in the southern mountains meander northward across a wide plain of rich farmland toward coastal swamps and sand dunes. The Baltic States of Lithuania, Latvia and Estonia are covered with meadows, marshes and more than 9,000 lakes. Around the Baltic Sea, winters can be bitterly cold, and icebreaker ships often have to clear a path between the region's ports. About two-thirds of eastern Europe's people live in cities, and many work in heavy industries such as mining, steelmaking and shipbuilding. These industries have created serious pollution problems. Acid rain has destroyed forests in Poland and the Czech Republic, and people are no longer allowed to swim in some polluted lakes in Hungary. In the Ukraine and Belarus, large areas of land can no longer be farmed because they were contaminated by radioactivity after an accident at the Chernobyl nuclear power plant near Kiev in 1986. Despite this, the Ukraine remains one of the largest producers of wheat in the world.

◆ LOOK AGAIN ◆

- What kind of glassware is produced in the Czech Republic?
- Name a mineral that is mined in eastern Hungary.
- Ukrainians eat a soup called borscht. What is it made of?

BELARUS
POPULATION: 10,335,382 ◆ CAPITAL: MINSK

CZECH REPUBLIC
POPULATION: 10,256,760 ◆ CAPITAL: PRAGUE

ESTONIA
POPULATION: 1,415,681 ◆ CAPITAL: TALLINN

HUNGARY
POPULATION: 10,075,034 ◆ CAPITAL: BUDAPEST

LATVIA
POPULATION: 2,366,515 ◆ CAPITAL: RIGA

LITHUANIA
POPULATION: 3,601,138 ◆ CAPITAL: VILNIUS

MOLDOVA
POPULATION: 4,434,547 ◆ CAPITAL: CHIŞINĂU

POLAND
POPULATION: 38,625,478 ◆ CAPITAL: WARSAW

SLOVAKIA
POPULATION: 5,422,366 ◆ CAPITAL: BRATISLAVA

UKRAINE
POPULATION: 48,396,470 ◆ CAPITAL: KIEV

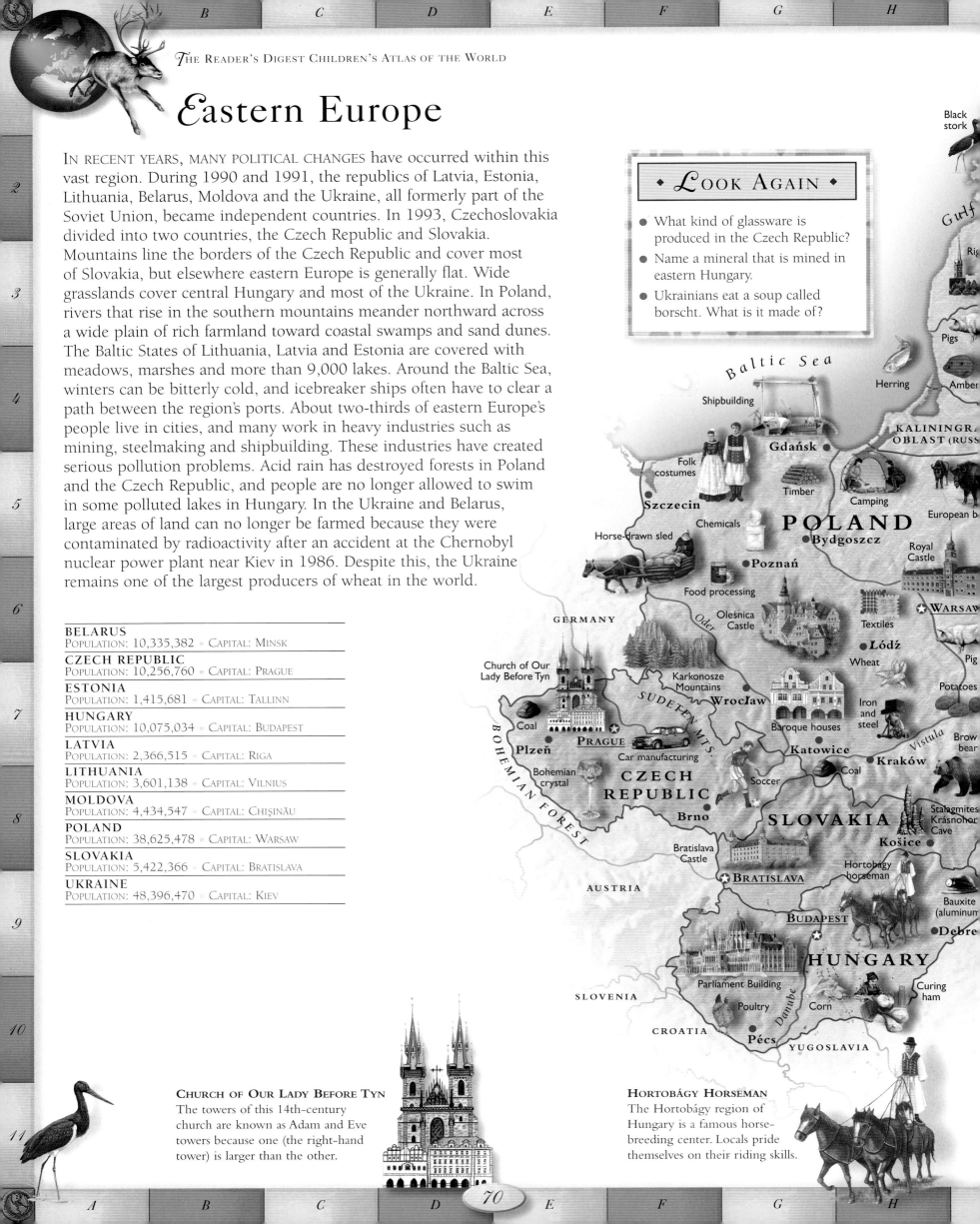

Black stork

Gulf

Rig

Pigs

Amber

Baltic Sea

Herring

Shipbuilding

KALININGRA OBLAST (RUSS

Folk costumes

Gdańsk

Timber

Camping

European b

Szczecin

Chemicals

POLAND

Horse-drawn sled

●Bydgoszcz

Royal Castle

●Poznań

Food processing

GERMANY

Oder

Oleśnica Castle

Textiles

●WARSAW

Church of Our Lady Before Tyn

Karkonosze Mountains

●Łódź

Wheat

Pig

SUDETEN MTS.

Wrocław

Potatoes

Coal

Baroque houses

Iron and steel

BOHEMIAN FOREST

Plzeň

PRAGUE

Car manufacturing

Bohemian crystal

CZECH REPUBLIC

Soccer

Coal

Katowice

Kraków

Brow bear

Vistula

Brno

SLOVAKIA

Stalagmites Krásnohor Cave

Bratislava Castle

Košice

Hortobágy horseman

BRATISLAVA

AUSTRIA

Bauxite (aluminum

BUDAPEST

●Debre

SLOVENIA

Parliament Building

HUNGARY

Curing ham

CROATIA

Poultry

Corn

Danube

●Pécs

YUGOSLAVIA

CHURCH OF OUR LADY BEFORE TYN
The towers of this 14th-century church are known as Adam and Eve towers because one (the right-hand tower) is larger than the other.

HORTOBÁGY HORSEMAN
The Hortobágy region of Hungary is a famous horse-breeding center. Locals pride themselves on their riding skills.

J K L M N O P Q

Gulf of Finland

Old Town, Tallinn

TALLINN

Lake Peipus

Tourism

ESTONIA

Riga

Fallow deer

Beef cattle

LATVIA

RIGA

Food processing

Folk dancers

Daugava

LITHUANIA

Island Castle, Trakai

Red foxes

Timber

Rye

Vitsyebsk

VILNIUS

Chemicals

Dnieper

Station Square

RUSSIA

Neman

Flax

MINSK

High-tech industries

Mahilyow

Clocks and watches

BELARUS

Dairy cattle

Barley

Potatoes

Osprey

Brest Fortress

Pripyat'

Folk costume

Homyel'

Cossack dancer

Dairy cattle

Chernobyl nuclear reactor

Tobacco

Kharkiv

Wolf

Sugar beets

Porcelain manufacturing

KIEV

High-tech industries

St. Sophia's Cathedral

Borscht (beet soup)

Natural gas

L'viv

Car manufacturing

Painted eggs

Textiles

Hydroelectricity

Collecting corn

Manganese

Sugar beets

Wild boars

Natural gas

UKRAINE

Lynx

Geese

Wheat

Dnieper

Dnipropetrovs'k

Coal

Wine

Bug

Folk dancers

Wheat

Iron and steel

Donets'k

Wildcat

Dniester

Prut

Hydroelectricity

Kakhovka Reservoir

Corn

ROMANIA

MOLDOVA

Sunflowers

CHIŞINĂU

Odessa

Tourism

Caviar

RUSSIA

Harvesting hay

Wheat

Fishing boat

Swallow's Nest Castle

Sturgeon

Wine

Sea of Azov

Food processing

CRIMEAN MTS.

Black Sea

Sevastapol'

CARPATHIAN MTS.

SCALE

MILES

0   50   100   150

0   50   100   150   200   250

KILOMETERS

N W E S

EUROPEAN BISON
Bison once roamed through the forests of Europe. They still live in their natural environment in parts of Poland.

Symbols of rebirth and a new beginning, decorated eggs are an Easter tradition in eastern Europe. It's easy to paint an egg—the tricky part is preparing the shell. Take the raw eggs out of the refrigerator a few hours before you start. If they are too cold, they will be hard to blow.

❶ Take an egg and gently prick the larger end of the shell with a pin. Chip the shell away until the hole is about ¼-inch (0.5 cm) across.

❷ Make a tiny hole in the smaller end. Put your fingers over both holes and gently shake the egg to break up the yolk. Hold the egg over a dish and blow through the small hole. The insides of the egg will slowly empty into the dish. Rinse the eggshell with water and let it dry.

❸ Now you are ready to paint. Carefully thread a piece of stiff wire through the holes in the shell. Hold the egg by the wire and paint your design on it.

❹ Lay the wire across a bowl so the painted egg can dry without being touched.

LOCATION

J K L M N O P Q

Northern Europe

THE COUNTRIES OF NORTHERN EUROPE are known as the Nordic countries. They are sometimes called Scandinavia, but strictly speaking this name refers only to the wide peninsula occupied by Norway and Sweden. On the western side of this peninsula, fjords—spectacular, steep-sided bays formed by glaciers—and more than 150,000 islands create a maze of waterways. Inland, mountain peaks and high plateaus cover most of Norway. To the east, the marshy plains of Sweden and Finland are studded with thousands of lakes and cloaked in coniferous forests that are home to moose, brown bears and wolves. The northern half of this region has a cold climate, with long, dark, snowy winters. In the far south, the climate is more temperate and the land more fertile.

Only one-twentieth of Norway can be farmed, but more than three-quarters of Denmark is used for agriculture. There is little farmland on Iceland, a volcanic island which lies 600 miles (1,000 km) west of Norway. The island's barren interior consists mainly of volcanoes, hot springs and lava fields. Parts of Iceland are so like the surface of the moon that astronauts trained there for moon landings. Some upland areas are covered by huge sheets of ice. Vatnajökull, an ice sheet in the southeast, is larger than all the glaciers in Europe combined.

DENMARK
POPULATION: 5,368,854 • CAPITAL: COPENHAGEN
FINLAND
POPULATION: 5,183,545 • CAPITAL: HELSINKI
ICELAND
POPULATION: 279,384 • CAPITAL: REYKJAVIK
NORWAY
POPULATION: 4,525,116 • CAPITAL: OSLO
SWEDEN
POPULATION: 8,876,744 • CAPITAL: STOCKHOLM

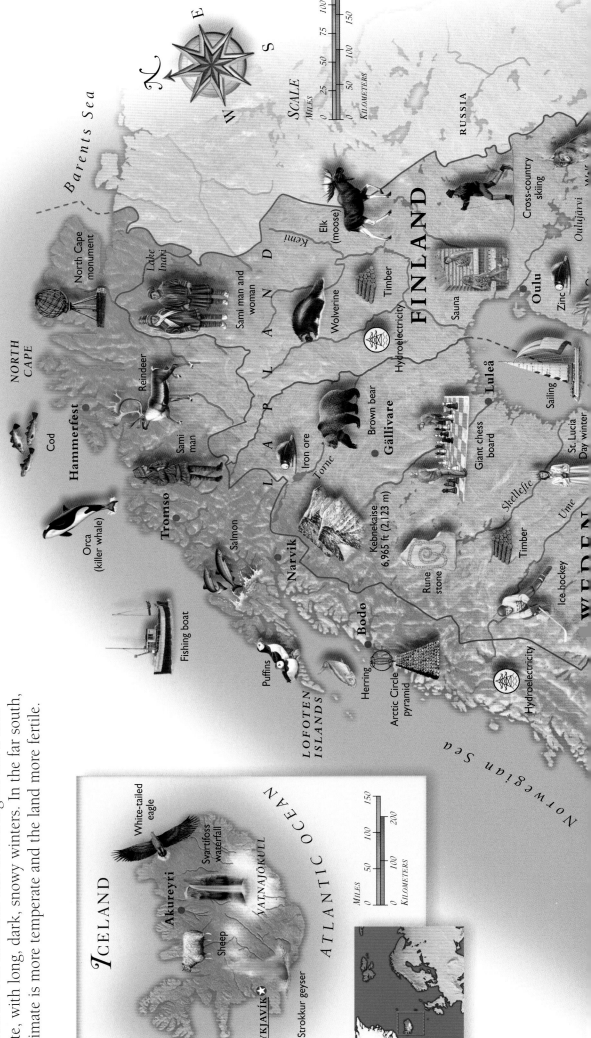

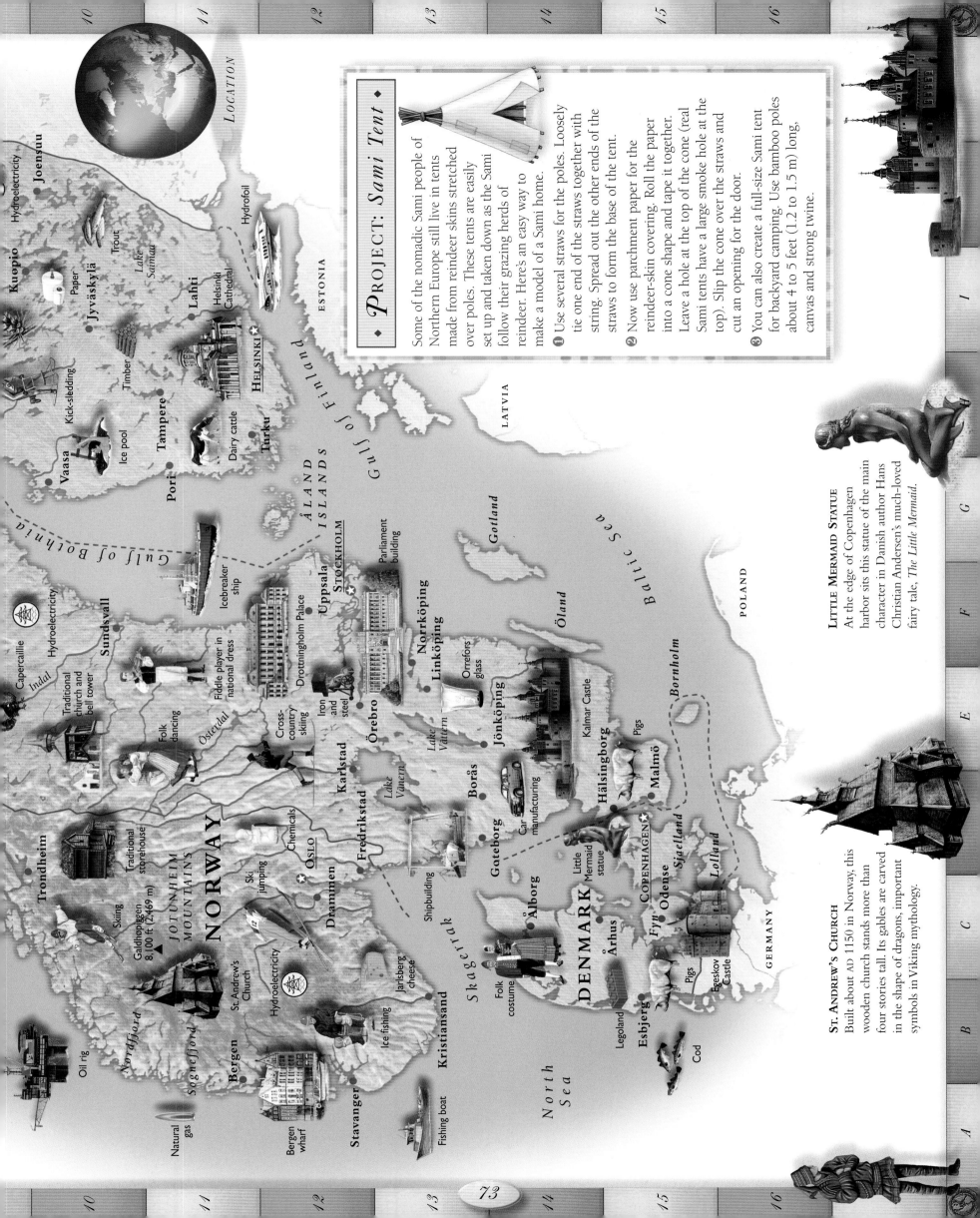

LOCATION

◆ PROJECT: *Sami Tent* ◆

Some of the nomadic Sami people of Northern Europe still live in tents made from reindeer skins stretched over poles. These tents are easily set up and taken down as the Sami follow their grazing herds of reindeer. Here's an easy way to make a model of a Sami home.

1. Use several straws for the poles. Loosely tie one end of the straws together with string. Spread out the other ends of the straws to form the base of the tent.

2. Now use parchment paper for the reindeer-skin covering. Roll the paper into a cone shape and tape it together. Leave a hole at the top of the cone (real Sami tents have a large smoke hole at the top). Slip the cone over the straws and cut an opening for the door.

3. You can also create a full-size Sami tent for backyard camping. Use bamboo poles about 4 to 5 feet (1.2 to 1.5 m) long, canvas and strong twine.

LITTLE MERMAID STATUE
At the edge of Copenhagen harbor sits this statue of the main character in Danish author Hans Christian Andersen's much-loved fairy tale, *The Little Mermaid.*

ST. ANDREW'S CHURCH
Built about AD 1150 in Norway, this wooden church stands more than four stories tall. Its gables are carved in the shape of dragons, important symbols in Viking mythology.

Joensuu
Hydroelectricity
Kuopio
Paper
Trout
Jyväskylä
Lake Saimaa
Lahti
Hydrofoil
Helsinki Cathedral
HELSINKI
Kick-sledding
Timber
Vaasa
Ice pool
Tampere
Dairy cattle
Turku
Pori

ESTONIA
LATVIA
LITHUANIA

ÅLAND ISLANDS
Gulf of Finland
Gulf of Bothnia

Icebreaker ship
Parliament building
Uppsala
STOCKHOLM
Drottningholm Palace
Fiddle player in national dress
Norrköping
Linköping
Örebro
Orrefors glass
Gotland
Lake Vättern
Jönköping
Öland
Kalmar Castle
Pigs
Hälsingborg
Malmö
Bornholm
Baltic Sea
POLAND

Capercaillie
Hydroelectricity
Indal
Sundsvall
Traditional church and bell tower
Folk dancing
Osterdal
Cross-country skiing
Karlstad
Iron and steel
Lake Vänern
Borås
Car manufacturing
Göteborg
Fredrikstad
Ålborg
Little Mermaid statue
COPENHAGEN
Odense
Fyn
Sjaelland
Lolland
Egeskov Castle
Pigs
Århus
DENMARK
Esbjerg
Legoland
Folk costume
Cod
GERMANY

Trondheim
Traditional storehouse
JOTUNHEIM MOUNTAINS
Galdhøpiggen 8,100 ft (2,469 m)
NORWAY
Skiing
Ski jumping
Chemicals
OSLO
Drammen
Shipbuilding
Jarlsberg cheese
Hydroelectricity
St. Andrew's Church
Bergen
Nordfjord
Sognefjord
Oil rig
Natural gas
Bergen wharf
Stavanger
Kristiansand
Skagerrak
Ice fishing
North Sea
Fishing boat

Asia

THE WORLD'S BIGGEST CONTINENT, Asia stretches almost halfway around the globe and covers one-third of Earth's landmass. It has the world's tallest mountains, the world's largest lake and the world's lowest point on land. It was the birthplace of many great religions and important civilizations, and is now home to 60 percent of the people on Earth. Most Asians live in the east and south, where the climate is warm and wet and there are large areas of forest, fertile plains and hundreds of tropical islands. Deserts and barren mountain ranges dominate the southwest and center of the continent. To the north, the grasslands, or steppes, of central Asia give way to the immense coniferous forests of Russia. A belt of freezing tundra extends along the continent's north coast. Russia is the world's largest country by area, but China has the world's largest population.

Continent Facts

Regional land area: 17,139,445 sq. miles (44,391,162 sq. km) (excluding European Russia)
Regional population: 3,806,418,195 (excluding European Russia)
Independent countries: Afghanistan, Armenia, Azerbaijan, Bahrain, Bangladesh, Bhutan, Brunei, Cambodia, China, Cyprus, East Timor, Georgia, India, Indonesia, Iran, Iraq, Israel, Japan, Jordan, Kazakstan, Kuwait, Kyrgyzstan, Laos, Lebanon, Malaysia, Maldives, Mongolia, Myanmar (Burma), Nepal, North Korea, Oman, Pakistan, Philippines, Qatar, Russia, Saudi Arabia, Singapore, South Korea, Sri Lanka, Syria, Taiwan, Tajikistan, Thailand, Turkey, Turkmenistan, United Arab Emirates, Uzbekistan, Vietnam, Yemen

Major Mountains and Rivers

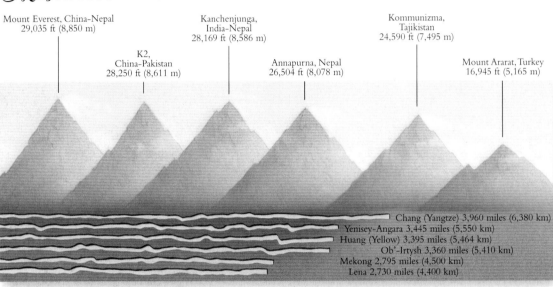

Mount Everest, China-Nepal 29,035 ft (8,850 m)
K2, China-Pakistan 28,250 ft (8,611 m)
Kanchenjunga, India-Nepal 28,169 ft (8,586 m)
Annapurna, Nepal 26,504 ft (8,078 m)
Kommunizma, Tajikistan 24,590 ft (7,495 m)
Mount Ararat, Turkey 16,945 ft (5,165 m)

Chang (Yangtze) 3,960 miles (6,380 km)
Yenisey-Angara 3,445 miles (5,550 km)
Huang (Yellow) 3,395 miles (5,464 km)
Ob'-Irtysh 3,360 miles (5,410 km)
Mekong 2,795 miles (4,500 km)
Lena 2,730 miles (4,400 km)

World Records

WORLD'S HIGHEST MOUNTAIN
MOUNT EVEREST, CHINA-NEPAL, 29,035 FT (8,850 M)

WORLD'S LOWEST POINT ON LAND
DEAD SEA, ISRAEL-JORDAN, 1,348 FT (411 M) BELOW SEA LEVEL

WORLD'S LARGEST LAKE BY AREA
CASPIAN SEA, WESTERN ASIA, 143,550 SQ. MILES (371,800 SQ. KM)

WORLD'S OLDEST, DEEPEST AND LARGEST (BY VOLUME) LAKE
LAKE BAIKAL, RUSSIA, 25 MILLION YEARS OLD; 5,371 FT (1,637 M) DEEP; 5,500 CUBIC MILES (23,000 CUBIC KM) OF WATER

WORLD'S LARGEST COUNTRY BY AREA
RUSSIA, 6,592,812 SQ. MILES (17,075,383 SQ. KM)

WORLD'S LARGEST COUNTRY BY POPULATION
CHINA, POPULATION 1,284,303,705

WORLD'S LARGEST CITY BY POPULATION
TOKYO, JAPAN, POPULATION 33,418,366

WORLD'S LONGEST WALL
GREAT WALL OF CHINA, 2,150 MILES (3,460 KM)

WORLD'S LONGEST RAILWAY LINE
TRANS-SIBERIAN, RUSSIA, 5,777 MILES (9,297 KM)

Continent Records

LONGEST RIVER
CHANG (YANGTZE), 3,960 MILES (6,380 KM)

Political Map

RUSSIA
KAZAKSTAN
MONGOLIA
GEORGIA
UZBEKISTAN KYRGYZSTAN
TURKEY
TURKMENISTAN
TAJIKISTAN
CHINA
NORTH KOREA
CYPRUS
SYRIA
AFGHANISTAN
SOUTH KOREA
JAPAN
IRAQ
JORDAN
IRAN
PAKISTAN
NEPAL
INDIA
TAIWAN
SAUDI ARABIA
OMAN
MYANMAR (BURMA)
LAOS
THAILAND
PHILIPPINES
YEMEN
CAMBODIA
VIETNAM
SRI LANKA
MALDIVES
MALAYSIA
INDONESIA
EAST TIMOR

Key to Numbered Countries

1 ARMENIA	7 QATAR
2 AZERBAIJAN	8 UNITED ARAB EMIRATES
3 LEBANON	9 BHUTAN
4 ISRAEL	10 BANGLADESH
5 KUWAIT	■ 11 SINGAPORE
■ 6 BAHRAIN	12 BRUNEI

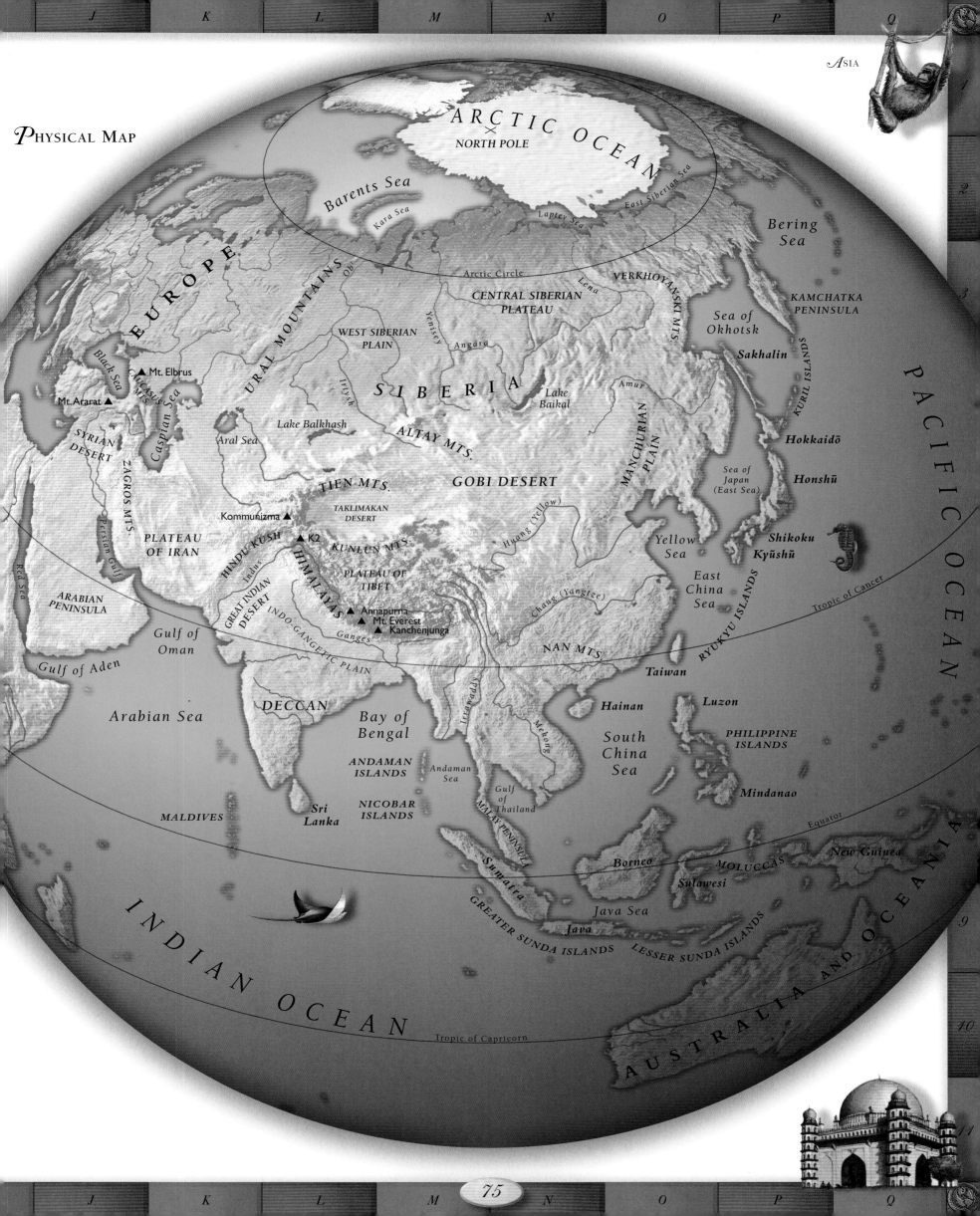

ARCTIC OCEAN
× NORTH POLE

Barents Sea

Kara Sea

Laptev Sea

East Siberian Sea

Bering Sea

EUROPE

Arctic Circle

Lena

VERKHOYANSKI MTS.

KAMCHATKA PENINSULA

CENTRAL SIBERIAN PLATEAU

Sea of Okhotsk

Ob

WEST SIBERIAN PLAIN

Yenisey

Angara

SIBERIA

Sakhalin

Amur

KURIL ISLANDS

URAL MOUNTAINS

Irtysh

Lake Baikal

MANCHURIAN PLAIN

Hokkaidō

Black Sea

▲ Mt. Elbrus

CAUCASUS MTS.

ALTAY MTS.

Sea of Japan (East Sea)

Honshū

Mt. Ararat ▲

Caspian Sea

Lake Balkhash

GOBI DESERT

SYRIAN DESERT

Aral Sea

TIEN MTS.

ZAGROS MTS.

Kommunizma ▲

TAKLIMAKAN DESERT

Huang (Yellow)

Shikoku

Yellow Sea

Kyūshū

PLATEAU OF IRAN

Persian Gulf

HINDU KUSH

▲ K2

KUNLUN MTS.

East China Sea

Red Sea

Indus

HIMALAYAS

PLATEAU OF TIBET

Chang (Yangtze)

RYUKYU ISLANDS

Tropic of Cancer

ARABIAN PENINSULA

GREAT INDIAN DESERT

▲ Annapurna
▲ Mt. Everest
▲ Kanchenjunga

INDO-GANGETIC PLAIN

Ganges

NAN MTS.

Gulf of Oman

Taiwan

Gulf of Aden

DECCAN

Bay of Bengal

Irrawaddy

Hainan

Luzon

Arabian Sea

South China Sea

PHILIPPINE ISLANDS

ANDAMAN ISLANDS

Andaman Sea

Mekong

MALDIVES

Sri Lanka

NICOBAR ISLANDS

Gulf of Thailand

Mindanao

MALAY PENINSULA

New Guinea

Sumatra

Borneo

MOLUCCAS

GREATER SUNDA ISLANDS

Sulawesi

Java Sea

LESSER SUNDA ISLANDS

Java

INDIAN OCEAN

PACIFIC OCEAN

AUSTRALIA AND OCEANIA

Equator

Tropic of Capricorn

Russia

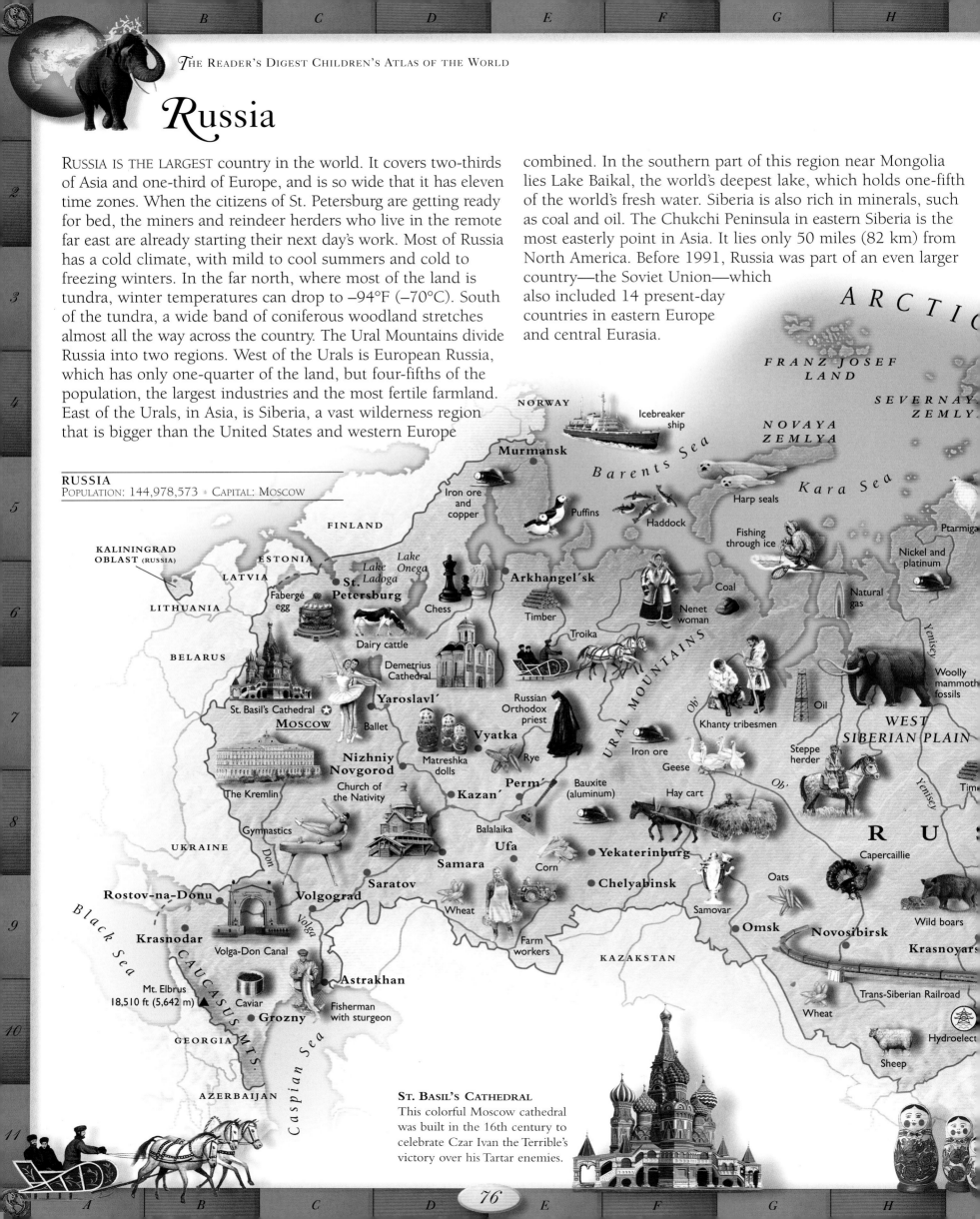

RUSSIA IS THE LARGEST country in the world. It covers two-thirds of Asia and one-third of Europe, and is so wide that it has eleven time zones. When the citizens of St. Petersburg are getting ready for bed, the miners and reindeer herders who live in the remote far east are already starting their next day's work. Most of Russia has a cold climate, with mild to cool summers and cold to freezing winters. In the far north, where most of the land is tundra, winter temperatures can drop to –94°F (–70°C). South of the tundra, a wide band of coniferous woodland stretches almost all the way across the country. The Ural Mountains divide Russia into two regions. West of the Urals is European Russia, which has only one-quarter of the land, but four-fifths of the population, the largest industries and the most fertile farmland. East of the Urals, in Asia, is Siberia, a vast wilderness region that is bigger than the United States and western Europe combined. In the southern part of this region near Mongolia lies Lake Baikal, the world's deepest lake, which holds one-fifth of the world's fresh water. Siberia is also rich in minerals, such as coal and oil. The Chukchi Peninsula in eastern Siberia is the most easterly point in Asia. It lies only 50 miles (82 km) from North America. Before 1991, Russia was part of an even larger country—the Soviet Union—which also included 14 present-day countries in eastern Europe and central Eurasia.

RUSSIA
POPULATION: 144,978,573 · CAPITAL: MOSCOW

ST. BASIL'S CATHEDRAL

This colorful Moscow cathedral was built in the 16th century to celebrate Czar Ivan the Terrible's victory over his Tartar enemies.

◆ AMAZING FACT ◆

Stretching almost one-quarter of the way around the globe, the Trans-Siberian Railroad is the longest railway in the world. The journey from Moscow to Vladivostok takes eight days and covers a distance of 5,777 miles (9,297 km).

◆ LOOK AGAIN ◆

- What kind of fossils have been discovered on the West Siberian Plain?
- On which peninsula is the Klyuchevskaya volcano located?
- Name a form of dance that is popular in Moscow.

ALASKA (U.S.A.)

Chukchi Sea
Bering Strait
East Siberian Sea
CHUKCHI PENINSULA
Harbor seals
Chukchi hunter

OCEAN
NEW SIBERIAN ISLANDS
Laptev Sea
Kittiwake
Arctic fox
Nordvik
Snowy owl
Reindeer sled
Evenki woman and baby
Furs

Polar bears
Walrus
Lynx
Reindeer
Furs
Gold
Wolf
Bering Sea

Yakut woman and children
Verkhoyansk
Natural gas
VERKHOYANSKI MTS.
Lena

KAMCHATKA PENINSULA
Timber
Klyuchevskaya volcano
15,580 ft (4,749 m)
Petropavlovsk-Kamchatskiy

Magadan
Brown bear
Okhotsk
CENTRAL SIBERIAN PLATEAU
Timber
Yakutsk
Osprey
Herring
Salmon
Sea of Okhotsk

Elk (moose)
Diamonds
Lena
Wolf
Gold
Oil
Natural gas
Sakhalin
KURIL ISLANDS

SIA
·gara
Hydroelectricity
Bratsk
Wheat
Coal
Baroque architecture
Irkutsk
YABLANOVYY MTS.
Hydroelectricity
STANOVOY MTS.
Coal
Coal
E Siberian tiger
Amur
Khabarovsk
Udegei dancers
JAPAN

AYAN MTS.
Lake Baikal
Ulan-Ude
Siberian house
Buryat archer
CHINA
Udegei building
Vladivostok
Sea of Japan (East Sea)

MONGOLIA
LOCATION

MATRESHKA DOLLS

These traditional wooden dolls are shaped so that they fit inside one another. Some matreshka sets include more than 12 dolls.

SIBERIAN TIGER

Siberian tigers are the world's biggest tigers. They live in southeastern Siberia and hunt bears, deer and, occasionally, people!

SCALE
MILES
0 100 200 300 400 500
0 200 400 600 800
KILOMETERS

Central Eurasia

EURASIA IS THE LANDMASS that contains Europe and Asia. Central Eurasia extends from the southeastern corner of Europe into the dry heart of Asia. Turkey forms a bridge between the two continents, which are separated by the narrow Bosporus strait. Turkey's interior is hilly and barren, but its fertile coastal regions produce tea, tobacco, and the world's largest crops of hazelnuts and raisins. South of Turkey lies the island of Cyprus, which is home to people of Turkish and Greek descent. Beyond Turkey's eastern border, the countries of Georgia, Armenia and

Azerbaijan are flanked by the massive Caucasus mountains. These countries are rich in minerals: at one time, Baku, the capital of Azerbaijan, supplied half of the world's oil. Across the Caspian Sea, deserts cover most of Turkmenistan, Uzbekistan and Kazakstan. Ancient trade routes between China and Europe passed through these lands, linking cities such as Samarkand and Tashkent. In the north, the desert merges with the Steppe, a vast grassland; in the southeast, the Tien Mountains cover most of Kyrgyzstan and Tajikistan. Many of central Eurasia's rivers are diverted to irrigate crops. This has lowered the levels of some lakes. The Aral Sea, once the world's fourth-largest lake, has shrunk to less than half its former size, stranding fishing villages and boats over 20 miles (30 km) from the shore.

Map labels:

BULGARIA · GREECE · Blue Mosque · Dardanelles · EUROPE · Istanbul · Bosporus · Gate of Majesty, Topkapi Palace · Bursa · Kilim rug · İzmir · Tobacco · Black Sea · Anchovies · Hoopoe · Wheat · Turkish delight (candy) · Olives · RUSSIA · Wild boars · Watermelons · Ruins of Roman theater · ANKARA · Goats · TURKEY · CAUCASUS MOUNTAINS · Atyraū · Antalya · Tea · Folk costume · Flamingo · Turkish coffee pot · Whirling dervish · GEORGIA · Fishing for sturgeon · Sailing · Adana · TBILISI · Wine · Tenghiz oil field · Dogubayazit border fortress · Rock formations, Cappadocia · Copper · ARMENIA · Aqtaū · Tobac · TURKISH FEDERATED STATE OF CYPRUS · Mt. Ararat 16,945 ft (5,165 m) · YEREVAN · Caviar · CYPRUS · NICOSIA · Euphrates · Wheat · Lake Van · Temple of the Fire Worshippers · Shepherd · Olives · SYRIA · Caspian Sea · Manganese · Mediterranean Sea · Tigris · Kara-Bogaz Gol Natural gas · Dashhow · Turquoise · BAKU · Traditional carpet · IRAQ · AZERBAIJAN · Oil · © Sturgeon · Oil · TURKMENISTA · IRAN · Cloth merchant · KOPET-DAG MTS. · ASHKHABA · Cotton · Camel

ARMENIA
POPULATION: 3,330,099 ∗ CAPITAL: YEREVAN

AZERBAIJAN
POPULATION: 7,798,497 ∗ CAPITAL: BAKU

CYPRUS
POPULATION: 767,314 ∗ CAPITAL: NICOSIA

GEORGIA
POPULATION: 4,960,951 ∗ CAPITAL: TBILISI

KAZAKSTAN
POPULATION: 16,741,519 ∗ CAPITAL: ASTANA

KYRGYZSTAN
POPULATION: 4,822,166 ∗ CAPITAL: BISHKEK

TAJIKISTAN
POPULATION: 6,719,567 ∗ CAPITAL: DUSHANBE

TURKEY
POPULATION: 67,308,928 ∗ CAPITAL: ANKARA

TURKMENISTAN
POPULATION: 4,688,963 ∗ CAPITAL: ASHKHABAD

UZBEKISTAN
POPULATION: 25,563,441 ∗ CAPITAL: TASHKENT

BLUE MOSQUE
Built for Sultan Ahmet I in the 17th century, this mosque in Istanbul, Turkey, is named for the more than 21,000 blue tiles that cover its interior.

◆ AMAZING FACT ◆

In Cappadocia in central Turkey, an eerie landscape of strange rock formations has been created by wind and water erosion. Early Christians made homes and churches inside caves cut into the rock. Some of these caves are still in use today.

◆ PROJECT: *Kilim Weaving* ◆

A kilim is a flat, woven rug traditionally made in Turkey. To make a simple kilim, you will first need to make a loom.

❶ Cut notches into the corners of a rectangular piece of cardboard. Tie a length of string to the left-hand notch and then wrap it around the cardboard, moving from left to right and leaving about ½ inch (1 cm) between strings. Tie the string off on the right-hand notch.

❷ Now weave by threading wool under and then over the strings. If you begin the first row weaving under, begin the second row weaving over, and so on. When you add a new piece of wool, tie it to the old piece. As you weave, push the rows tightly together.

❸ When the loom is full, turn it over so that it is face down and cut the two middle strings. Tie them together at the top and bottom edges of the weaving. Repeat with the rest of the strings.

❹ When all the strings have been cut and tied, remove the weaving from the loom. Trim the ends of the tied-off strings to make a fringe for your weaving.

Step 1

Step 2

Step 3

SNOW LEOPARD
Living high in the mountains, the snow leopard needs strong paws for rock climbing and long, thick fur to keep warm.

LOCATION

Map labels

Qostanay
Petropavl
Iron ore
Marmot
Ishim
Irtysh
Aktyubinsk
THE STEPPE
Wheat
Sarsembek herder
ASTANA
Pavlodar
Barley
RUSSIA
Bearded vulture
Stranded fishing boats, Aral Sea
Yurts (nomad tents)
Gold
Textiles
Manganese
Copper
Qaraghandy
Semey
Oskemen
Former coastline 1993
KAZAKSTAN
Coal
Hydroelectricity
Lake Zaysan
Aral Sea
Baykonur Cosmodrome
Baking bread in traditional oven
White-throated kingfisher
Cotton
Lake Balkhash
Tukus
Cotton
Saiga antelope
Spoonbill
Cotton
Kirgiz farmer
Street vendor selling apples
UZBEKISTAN
Chemicals
CHINA
Registan Square
Shymkent
Almaty
Ⓔ Snow leopard
Bukhara
Samarkand
BISHKEK
TASHKENT
KYRGYZSTAN
Turkmenabat
Namangan
Rice
Sheep
Cotton
Osh
Yak
Amu Dar'ya
Syr Dar'ya
DUSHANBE
Cotton
Sheep
Kommunizma 24,590 ft (7,495 m)
Musician playing longhorn
Karakumskiy Canal
TAJIKISTAN
Hissar fortress
AFGHANISTAN
TIEN MTS.

Compass
N
W E
S

SCALE
MILES
0   100   200   300
0   100   200   300   400   500
KILOMETERS

BAYKONUR COSMODROME
Formerly a Soviet Union space center, Baykonur is now leased from Kazakstan by Russia for use as its main space shuttle and rocket launching site.

The Middle East

THE MIDDLE EAST IS A LAND of ancient cities and vast deserts. It is home to some of the world's oldest civilizations and was the birthplace of three of the most widespread religions—Islam, Christianity and Judaism. Though there are narrow strips of fertile land on the densely populated Mediterranean coast, along the Tigris and Euphrates rivers in Iraq, and in the highlands of northern Iran, most of this region is hot, dry and barren. Deserts extend southward from Syria, Jordan and Israel, covering most of the Arabian Peninsula. Parts of this peninsula receive no rain for up to 10 years! Deserts also cover two-thirds of Iran. The enormous Dasht-e Kavīr salt desert in eastern Iran has almost no vegetation. Among its few inhabitants are gazelles that survive on tiny amounts of salty water. Over the centuries, the people of the Middle East have made skillful use of their limited water supplies. For thousands of years, the Tigris and Euphrates rivers have been used to water crops. Today, desalination plants on the shores of the Persian Gulf turn sea water into fresh water. The Gulf region holds half the world's reserves of oil and gas, and this has made some countries very wealthy. On average, people in the United Arab Emirates earn twice as much as people in the United States. In contrast, Yemen, which has little oil, is one of the poorest countries in the world.

BAHRAIN
POPULATION: 656,397 * CAPITAL: MANAMA

IRAN
POPULATION: 66,622,704 * CAPITAL: TEHRAN

IRAQ
POPULATION: 24,001,816 * CAPITAL: BAGHDAD

ISRAEL
POPULATION: 6,029,529 * CAPITAL: JERUSALEM

JORDAN
POPULATION: 5,307,470 * CAPITAL: AMMAN

KUWAIT
POPULATION: 2,111,561 * CAPITAL: KUWAIT

LEBANON
POPULATION: 3,677,780 * CAPITAL: BEIRUT

OMAN
POPULATION: 2,713,462 * CAPITAL: MUSCAT

QATAR
POPULATION: 793,341 * CAPITAL: DOHA

SAUDI ARABIA
POPULATION: 23,513,330 * CAPITAL: RIYADH

SYRIA
POPULATION: 17,155,814 * CAPITAL: DAMASCUS

UNITED ARAB EMIRATES
POPULATION: 2,445,989 * CAPITAL: ABU DHABI

YEMEN
POPULATION: 18,701,257 * CAPITAL: SANAA

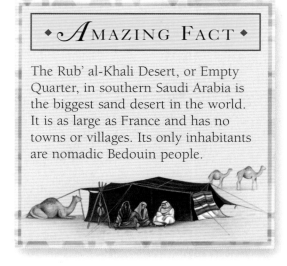

• AMAZING FACT •

The Rub' al-Khali Desert, or Empty Quarter, in southern Saudi Arabia is the biggest sand desert in the world. It is as large as France and has no towns or villages. Its only inhabitants are nomadic Bedouin people.

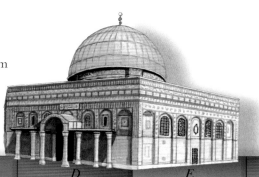

DOME OF THE ROCK
This Muslim temple in Jerusalem backs onto the Western Wall, a site sacred to Jews. Inside the temple is a rock that some say marks the center of the world.

VEILED WOMAN
Traditionally, Muslim women must keep their face and hair hidden from strangers. Many wear a long black cloak and a veil or eye-mask.

ARMENIA   AZERBAIJAN

Tobacco

Araks

• Tabrīz

Barley

• Rasht

Caspian Sea

TURKMENISTAN

Ⓔ Sturgeon

Caviar

• Mashhad

Oil

Mosul

Friday Mosque, Samarra

Cotton

ṬEHRĀN ★

Musician

Winnowing grain

DASHT-E KAVĪR (GREAT SALT DESERT)

Turquoise

ZAGROS MOUNTAINS

Kurdish woman

Royal Mosque

PLATEAU OF IRAN

BAGHDAD ★

Tigris

Q

Bedouin shepherd

• Eṣfahān

Making rugs

IRAN

Ⓔ Leopard

DASHT-E LŪT

AFGHANISTAN

Oil

Stone carvings, Persepolis

• Kermān

Ziggurat (temple), Ur   **Al Basrah**

Ābādān

Oil

• Shīrāz

Wine

Walled city of Bam

Shepherd in traditional felt coat

PAKISTAN

KUWAIT

KUWAIT ★

Oil

Persian Gulf

Oil

Caracal

Eurasian griffon

Goats

Camel race

Oil

BAHRAIN

Ad Dammām •

AL MANAMA ★

QATAR

Oil

Strait of Hormuz

Dubai **OMAN**

Gulf of Oman

Oil tanker

Water tower

AD DAWHAH ★

Natural gas

ABU DHABI

MUSCAT

Date palm

Zubara fort

UNITED ARAB EMIRATES

RIYADH ★

Arabian horse

(UNDEFINED BORDER)

Al Khuwair Mosque

Ṣūr

Bedouin with falcon

SAUDI ARABIA

Solar-powered telephone

Coconuts

Sardines

Arabian Sea

N

W   E

S

Great Mosque

Bedouin tent

RUB' AL-KHALI DESERT (EMPTY QUARTER)

Collecting frankincense

OMAN

Baboon

Sand cat

Woman at well

Ⓔ Arabian oryx

Tiger shark

SCALE

MILES

0   50   100   150   200   250

0   100   200   300   400

KILOMETERS

Wheat   Apricots

SANAA ★

Al Hajrah

YEMEN

Men with narghile

Salālah

Ta'izz •

Coffee

Oil

Aden

Gulf of Aden

Socotra (Yemen)

DJOUTI

ARABIAN ORYX

This antelope may have been the origin of the myth of the unicorn. Viewed from the side, the oryx looks as though it has only one horn.

*L*OCATION

Southern Asia

SOUTHERN ASIA, OR THE Indian Subcontinent as it is also known, is separated from the rest of Asia by a series of massive mountain ranges. In the northeast, the mighty Himalayas, the highest mountains on Earth, tower over northern India and the two small kingdoms of Nepal and Bhutan. In the northwest, the dry, rugged Hindu Kush— the world's second-highest mountain range—spreads across central Afghanistan. South of these mountains, the land drops steeply to a wide, fertile plain that stretches from Pakistan to Bangladesh and covers most of northern India. Southern India consists of a large triangular plateau (the Deccan) fringed by narrow coastal plains. Just off the southeast coast lies the island of Sri Lanka.

Southern Asia has large areas of fertile land, valuable mineral reserves and expanding industries, but these resources barely support the region's huge population, and many people are very poor. One-fifth of the world's people live in southern Asia, and the population is growing rapidly. In India alone, almost 20 million babies are born each year. Four-fifths of southern Asians live in small villages, and most grow their own food. In India, Sri Lanka and Bangladesh, farmers rely on summer rains to water their crops. These rains are brought by winds known as monsoons. If too little rain falls, the crops fail. If too much rain falls, the crops, as well as buildings and people, can be washed away by devastating floods.

AFGHANISTAN
POPULATION: 27,755,775 ♦ CAPITAL: KABUL
BANGLADESH
POPULATION: 133,376,684 ♦ CAPITAL: DHAKA
BHUTAN
POPULATION: 2,094,176 ♦ CAPITAL: THIMPHU
INDIA
POPULATION: 1,045,845,226 ♦ CAPITAL: NEW DELHI
MALDIVES
POPULATION: 320,165 ♦ CAPITAL: MALE
NEPAL
POPULATION: 25,873,917 ♦ CAPITAL: KATHMANDU
PAKISTAN
POPULATION: 147,663,429 ♦ CAPITAL: ISLAMABAD
SRI LANKA
POPULATION: 19,576,783 ♦ CAPITAL: COLOMBO

♦ PROJECT: *Taj Mahal Tile* ♦

The Taj Mahal in India was built by Emperor Shah Jahan in memory of his beloved wife Mumtaz. Construction began in 1631, and it took 20,000 workers about 20 years to complete the building. It is covered in tiles of dazzling white marble. Each tile is carved with floral designs and inlaid with semi-precious stones. You can make your own paper Taj Mahal tile.

❶ Draw floral patterns on a square of white paper.
❷ Color the patterns and then use glitter, sequins, buttons or colored plastic wrap to "fashion" the jewels in the Taj Mahal's intricate designs.

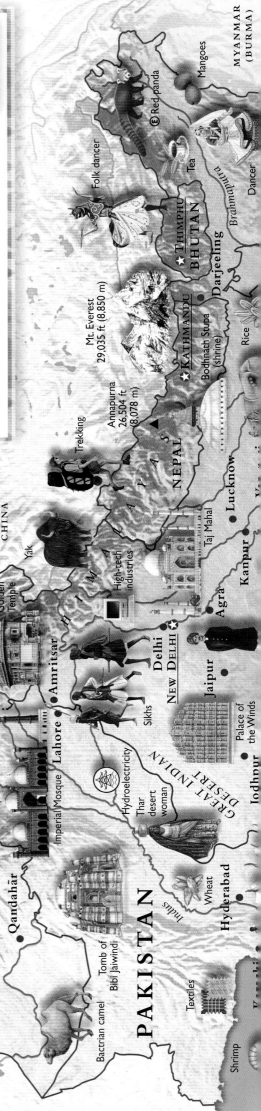

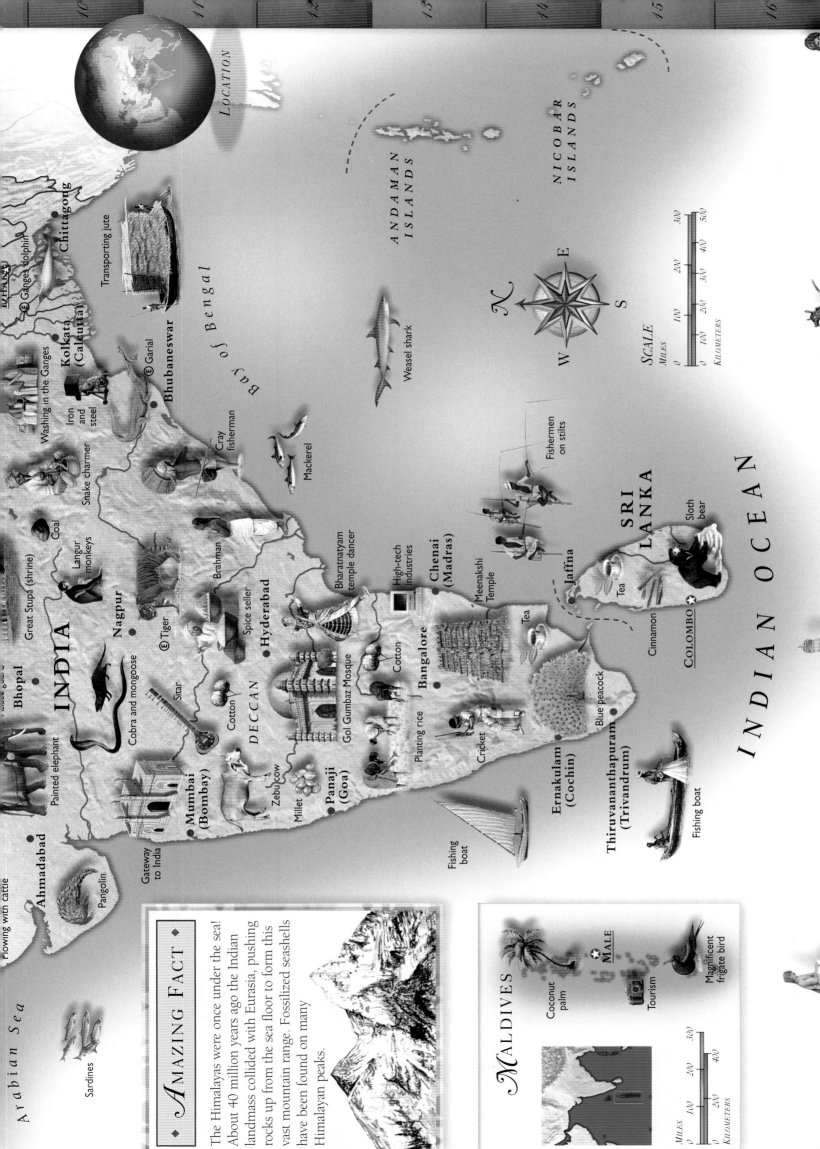

LOCATION

Arabian Sea

Plowing with cattle

Sardines

Ahmadabad

Pangolin

Gateway to India

Bhopal

Painted elephant

Cobra and mongoose

Zebu cow

Millet

Mumbai (Bombay)

Sitar

Panaji (Goa)

Cotton

INDIA

DECCAN

Gol Gumbaz Mosque

Cricket

Planting rice

Bangalore

Cotton

High-tech industries

Bharatnatyam temple dancer

Spice seller

Hyderabad

Brahman

Nagpur

(E) Tiger

Langur monkeys

Great Stupa (shrine)

Coal

Snake charmer

Crab fisherman

Bhubaneswar

(E) Garial

Iron and steel

Kolkata (Calcutta)

Washing in the Ganges

(E) Ganges dolphin

Chittagong

Transporting jute

Bay of Bengal

Mackerel

Weasel shark

ANDAMAN ISLANDS

NICOBAR ISLANDS

N
W   E
S

SCALE

MILES
0   100   200   300

KILOMETERS
0   100   200   300   400   500

Fishermen on stilts

Meenakshi Temple

Chenai (Madras)

Tea

Tea

Jaffna

SRI LANKA

Sloth bear

Cinnamon

COLOMBO

Ernakulam (Cochin)

Blue peacock

Thiruvananthapuram (Trivandrum)

Fishing boat

Fishing boat

INDIAN OCEAN

FOLK DANCER

In Bhutan, dancers taking part in religious festivals wear ornate silk costumes and masks to represent gods and spirits.

BODHNATH STUPA

Begun in the fifth century, this huge shrine in Nepal is decorated with the all-seeing eyes of Buddha, the founder of Buddhism.

PAINTED ELEPHANT

During religious processions in India, elephants are painted and then draped in colorful silks and sparkling jewels.

◆ AMAZING FACT ◆

The Himalayas were once under the sea! About 40 million years ago the Indian landmass collided with Eurasia, pushing rocks up from the sea floor to form this vast mountain range. Fossilized seashells have been found on many Himalayan peaks.

MALDIVES

Coconut palm

MALE

Tourism

Magnificent frigate bird

MILES
0   100   200   300

KILOMETERS
0   100   200   300   400

Southeast Asia

SOUTHEAST ASIA IS MADE UP OF a mainland peninsula and more than 20,000 islands. Throughout this hot, humid region, rugged mountains rise steeply from wide river basins and coastal plains once covered in dense rain forests. Most people live in the river valleys or near the coast, where they fish and grow food. Rice is the most important crop. On the plains, it is planted in wide, flooded fields called rice paddies. On hills and mountains, rice is grown on terraces—narrow strips of land that climb the slopes like giant staircases. In recent years, many Southeast Asians have moved from the countryside to cities in search of work. Bangkok, Ho Chi Minh City, Manila and Jakarta are now among the most crowded and fastest-growing cities in the world. Southeast Asia has many natural resources. Malaysia is the world's leading exporter of tin, Myanmar supplies most of the world's rubies, and oil has made Brunei one of the world's richest countries. Timber is the most widespread resource, and the region's rain forests supply more than three-quarters of the world's tropical hardwoods. But so many trees are being chopped down that several countries could soon run out of forest, and many animal and plant species are now endangered. Some countries restrict logging activities and have turned large areas of forest into magnificent national parks.

BRUNEI
POPULATION: 350,898 • CAPITAL: BANDAR SERI BEGAWAN

CAMBODIA
POPULATION: 12,775,324 • CAPITAL: PHNOM PENH

EAST TIMOR
POPULATION: 952,618 • CAPITAL: DILI

INDONESIA
POPULATION: 231,328,092 • CAPITAL: JAKARTA

LAOS
POPULATION: 5,777,180 • CAPITAL: VIENTIANE

MALAYSIA
POPULATION: 22,662,365 • CAPITAL: KUALA LUMPUR

MYANMAR (BURMA)
POPULATION: 42,238,224 • CAPITAL: YANGON (RANGOON)

PHILIPPINES
POPULATION: 84,525,639 • CAPITAL: MANILA

SINGAPORE
POPULATION: 4,452,732 • CAPITAL: SINGAPORE

THAILAND
POPULATION: 62,354,402 • CAPITAL: BANGKOK

VIETNAM
POPULATION: 81,098,416 • CAPITAL: HANOI

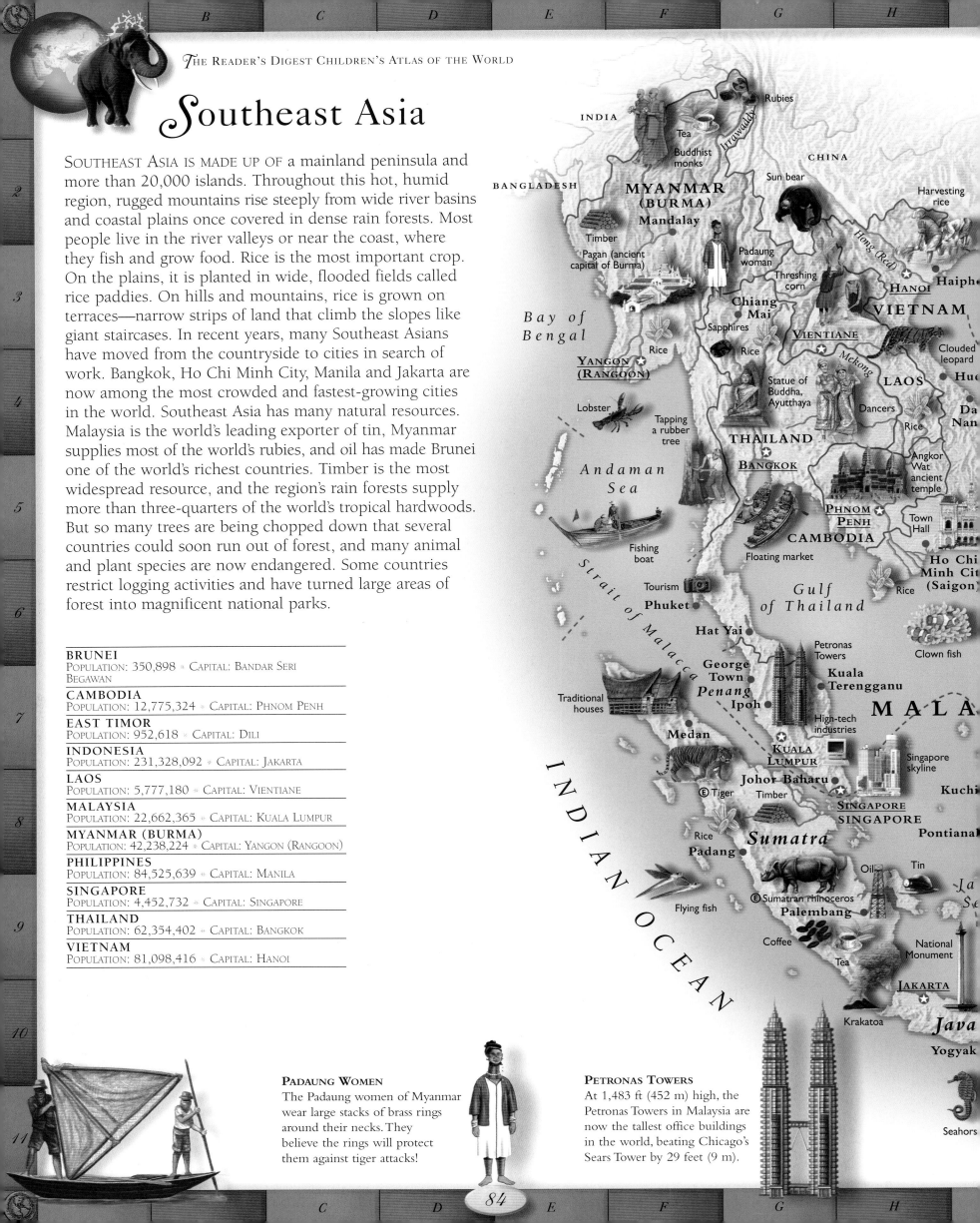

PADAUNG WOMEN
The Padaung women of Myanmar wear large stacks of brass rings around their necks. They believe the rings will protect them against tiger attacks!

PETRONAS TOWERS
At 1,483 ft (452 m) high, the Petronas Towers in Malaysia are now the tallest office buildings in the world, beating Chicago's Sears Tower by 29 feet (9 m).

N   O   P   Q

◆ LOOK AGAIN ◆

- In which country could you shop at a floating market?
- Name a weapon used by hunters in Malaysia.
- What kind of "dragon" lives on an island in Indonesia?

SCALE

MILES

0   100   200   300   400

KILOMETERS

0   150   300   450   600

◆ PROJECT: *Erupting Volcano* ◆

Southeast Asia has more active volcanoes than any other part of the world. The island of Java alone has 50 volcanoes that could erupt at any time. Here's a volcano that will erupt whenever you want it to.

❶ On a tray, use moist soil to model a mountain.

❷ Scoop out a hole from the top of the mountain and put in a container, such as the lid from a spray can.

❸ Pour about ¼ cup warm water into the container. Now stir in 1 tablespoon baking soda, a few drops of red food coloring and a few drops of dishwashing liquid. Pour in ¼ cup vinegar and watch your volcano erupt.

Adding vinegar to the baking soda produces carbon dioxide gas. This causes pressure to build up until the volcano erupts, forcing lava suds out the top. This is similar to the pressure inside Earth's crust that causes a real volcano to erupt.

Dugongs

Jeepney bus

Basket boat

Luzon   ● Baguio

Copper

Ⓔ Philippine eagle

Parrot fish

MANILA ☆

Mindoro   ● Legazpi

Swordfish

PHILIPPINES

Tiger shark

Panay   Pineapples   *Samar*

● Bacolod

Palawan   Fishing with a frame-net   ● Cebu

South China Sea

Negros

Rice

Dayak woman

Sulu Sea

Muslim dancer

Mindanao

● Davao

Oil

Kota Kinabalu   **Sandakan**

BANDAR SERI BEGAWAN

Mt. Kinabalu 13,455 ft (4,101 m)

SABAH

PACIFIC OCEAN

BRUNEI

Celebes Sea

Sea gypsy collecting sea urchins

Diver and giant clam

SARAWAK

Mulu Caves

Hunter with blowpipe

Coconuts   **Manado**

Halmahera

Oil

Greater bird of paradise

Ⓔ Orangutan

Oil

Sail-tailed water lizard

Cloves

Jayapura

Banded pitta

KALIMANTAN

Borneo

● **Balikpapan**

Peppercorns

Asmat tribesman

IRIAN JAYA

ber   Rafflesia flower

Proboscis monkey

Nutmeg   *Ceram*

● **Banjarmasin**

Rice   Tarsier

Buru   ● **Ambon**

Puncak Jaya 16,535 ft (5,040 m)

New Guinea

Ⓔ Leatherback turtle

Ujung Pandang

Sulawesi

Banda Sea

Kai

Aru

PAPUA NEW GUINEA

robudur Temple   ● **Surabaya**

Flores Sea

Komodo dragon

Bumblebee goby

Manta ray

Bananas

Tourism

Bali   *Sumbawa*

Flores

Tanimbar

Arafura Sea

Balinese mask

Lombok   Shadow puppet

Sumba   Corn

☆ **DILI EAST TIMOR**

Hammerhead shark

INDONESIA

Coconuts   ● **Kupang**

Timor Sea

AUSTRALIA

LOCATION

J   K   L   M   N   O   P   Q

Eastern Asia

EASTERN ASIA INCLUDES ONE-QUARTER of the Asian mainland as well as several small islands. It is dominated by China, the third-largest (and most populous) country in the world. China is only slightly larger than the United States, but it has more than four times as many people. Eighty percent live in the eastern third of the country, where the climate is mild and wet, and most of the land is fertile. There are many large cities in eastern China, but most people live in villages where they raise pigs and chickens, and grow rice, wheat and vegetables. Western China is dry, rugged and sparsely populated. The southwestern region—Tibet—is sometimes called the "roof of the world" because it lies on the highest plateau on Earth and contains part of the tallest mountain range, the Himalayas. In the north, the barren Gobi Desert stretches into Mongolia, where many people are nomadic herders. On and around China's coast lie a number of rapidly developing countries and territories. South Korea and Taiwan have many thriving industries, including textile, car and electrical goods manufacturers. Macao, a tiny Portuguese colony on the south coast of China, reverted to Chinese rule in 1999. It is the world's most crowded place, with 57,100 people for every square mile (22,150 per sq. km). Neighboring Hong Kong, a former British territory which was given back to China in 1997, is the world's third-largest financial center. Its modern, high-rise office buildings tower over one of Asia's busiest harbors.

CHINA
POPULATION: 1,284,303,705 • CAPITAL: BEIJING
MONGOLIA
POPULATION: 2,694,432 • CAPITAL: ULAANBAATAR
NORTH KOREA
POPULATION: 22,224,195 • CAPITAL: P'YŎNGYANG
SOUTH KOREA
POPULATION: 48,324,000 • CAPITAL: SEOUL
TAIWAN
POPULATION: 22,548,009 • CAPITAL: TAIPEI

✦ AMAZING FACT ✦

The Great Wall of China stretches for 2,150 miles (3,460 km) across northern China and is so large that astronauts can see it from space. It was built in the third century BC to keep out invaders from the north, and then rebuilt and expanded in the 14th century AD.

SCALE

MILES

0   100   200   300

0 100 200 300 400 500

KILOMETERS

TERRA-COTTA WARRIORS
Chinese emperor Qin Shi Huang had more than 6,000 life-sized clay warriors built to guard his body after his death.

GIANT PANDA
There are only 1,000 giant pandas left in the wild, and they all live in bamboo forests in central China, near Chengdu.

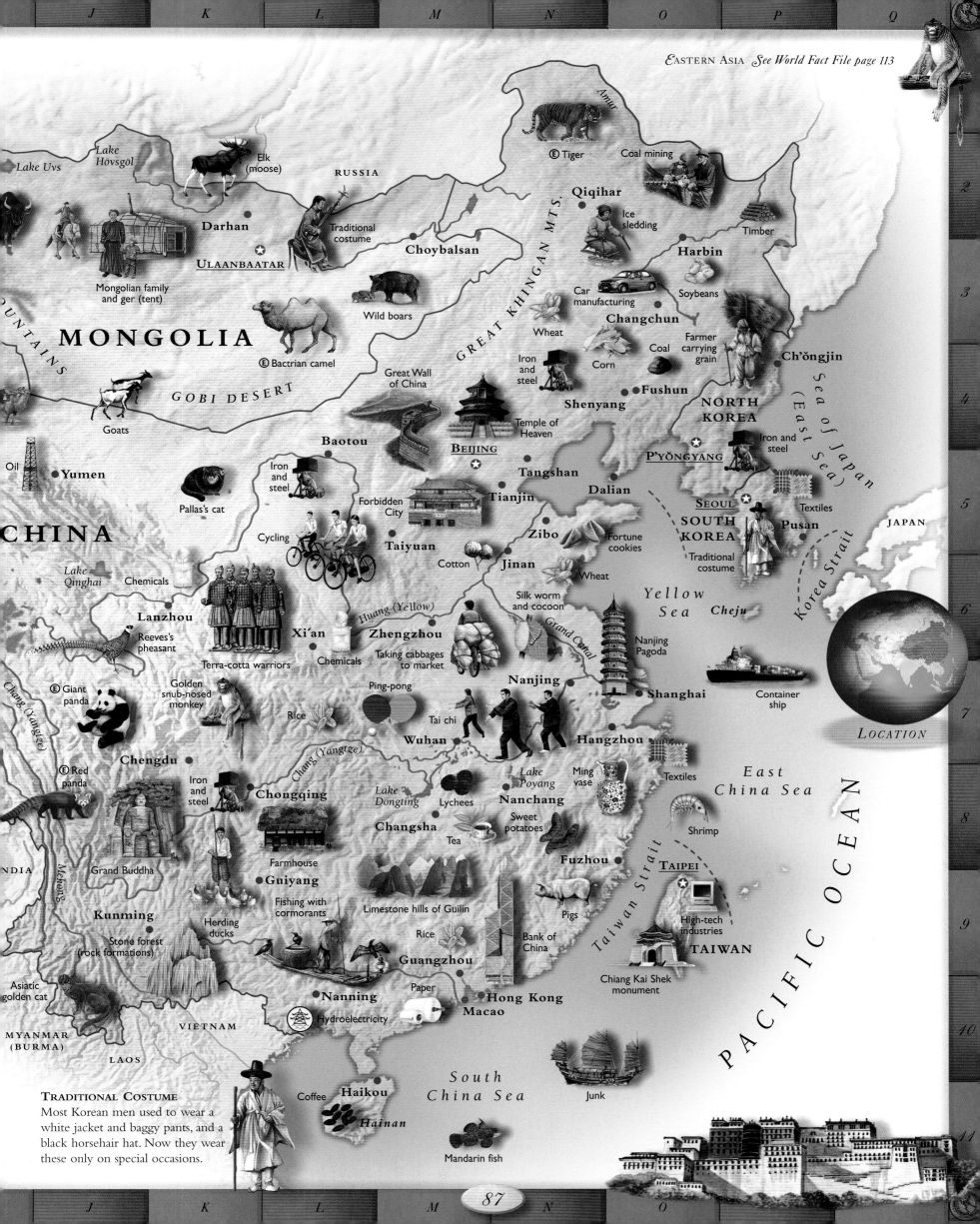

J   K   L   M   N   O   P   Q

Lake Uvs

Lake Hövsgöl

Elk (moose)

RUSSIA

Amur

Tiger

Coal mining

Qiqihar

Ice sledding

Timber

Darhan

Traditional costume

Choybalsan

Harbin

Car manufacturing

Soybeans

Mongolian family and ger (tent)

ULAANBAATAR

Wild boars

Changchun

Wheat

Coal

Farmer carrying grain

MONGOLIA

Corn

Ch'ŏngjin

Bactrian camel

GREAT KHINGAN MTS.

Iron and steel

Fushun

GOBI DESERT

Great Wall of China

Shenyang

NORTH KOREA

Sea of Japan (East Sea)

Goats

Temple of Heaven

P'YŎNGYANG

Iron and steel

Oil

Yumen

BEIJING

Tangshan

Dalian

Textiles

JAPAN

Baotou

Iron and steel

Tianjin

SEOUL

Pusan

Pallas's cat

Forbidden City

Zibo

SOUTH KOREA

CHINA

Cycling

Taiyuan

Cotton

Jinan

Fortune cookies

Traditional costume

Lake Qinghai

Chemicals

Wheat

Lanzhou

Silk worm and cocoon

Yellow Sea

Cheju

Korea Strait

Reeves's pheasant

Xi'an

Huang (Yellow)

Zhengzhou

Grand Canal

Terra-cotta warriors

Chemicals

Taking cabbages to market

Nanjing Pagoda

Giant panda

Golden snub-nosed monkey

Ping-pong

Tai chi

Nanjing

Shanghai

Container ship

LOCATION

Rice

Chang (Yangtze)

Wuhan

Hangzhou

Chengdu

Chang (Yangtze)

Lake Poyang

Ming vase

Textiles

East China Sea

Red panda

Iron and steel

Chongqing

Lake Dongting

Lychees

Nanchang

Sweet potatoes

Grand Buddha

Farmhouse

Changsha

Tea

Fuzhou

Shrimp

Guiyang

TAIPEI

Kunming

Herding ducks

Fishing with cormorants

Limestone hills of Guilin

Rice

Pigs

High-tech industries

Stone forest (rock formations)

Bank of China

TAIWAN

Asiatic golden cat

Guangzhou

Taiwan Strait

Chiang Kai Shek monument

Paper

PACIFIC OCEAN

Nanning

Hong Kong

Macao

MYANMAR (BURMA)

VIETNAM

Hydroelectricity

South China Sea

LAOS

Coffee

Haikou

Junk

TRADITIONAL COSTUME
Most Korean men used to wear a white jacket and baggy pants, and a black horsehair hat. Now they wear these only on special occasions.

Hainan

Mandarin fish

J   K   L   M   N   O

Japan

JAPAN CONSISTS OF a long chain of 4 main islands and more than 4,000 smaller islands that lies off the east coast of the Asian mainland. The northern half of Japan has a cold temperate climate with snowy winters and mild summers. In the south the weather is more tropical, with mild winters and a summer wet season. Most of the land is mountainous, and almost two-thirds is covered in forests. Earthquakes are common, and there are many active volcanoes. Japan occupies an area smaller than the U.S. state of Montana but has 150 times as many people. Three-quarters live in cities, the largest of which are located on the large island of Honshū. Japan's capital, Tokyo, sprawls across more than 80 neighboring towns, forming the biggest urban area in the world, and is home to almost 27 million people. So many workers commute to the city center each day that railroad stations employ guards known as "pushers" to cram passengers into trains. Despite having little farmland, Japan manages to produce most of its food, including large quantities of rice. Fish is the country's most important resource, and the Japanese fishing fleet is the largest in the world. Although it has few other natural resources, Japan has become a major industrial power by importing raw materials and manufacturing high-quality goods. It is the world's top car manufacturer, has the world's foremost shipbuilding industry, and is a leading exporter of electronic goods.

RUSSIA

Sea of Okhotsk

Hokkaidō

Salmon

Dairy cattle

Ainu man

Brown bear

Kushiro

Coal

Great white shark

Pollock

Mackerel

Timber

Sapporo snow festival

Asahikawa

Rice

Sapporo

Otaru

Halibut

Serows

Hakodate

Japanese crane

Tsugaru Strait

Macaques

Apples

Japanese spider crab

Aomori

Morioka

Sushi

Akita

Carp streamers

Making chopsticks

Rice

Kokechi doll

Shiogama festival

Sendai

Sardines

Dancer in traditional costume

Fukushima

Niigata

Shinano

JAPAN

Mako shark

Sado

Ninja

Sea of Japan (East Sea)

Rebun

Rishiri

Wakkanai

Skiing

RUSSIA

JAPAN
POPULATION: 126,974,628 • CAPITAL: TOKYO

◆ LOOK AGAIN ◆

- What kind of festival takes place in Sapporo?
- Name two kinds of shark found off the west coast of Honshū.
- Which famous mountain lies southwest of Japan's capital?

RYUKYU ISLANDS

East China Sea

Rice

AMAMI ISLANDS

Long-tailed carpet shark

Karate

OKINAWA ISLANDS

Tourism

Pineapples

Naha

MILES
0   25   50   75
KILOMETERS
0   50   100   150

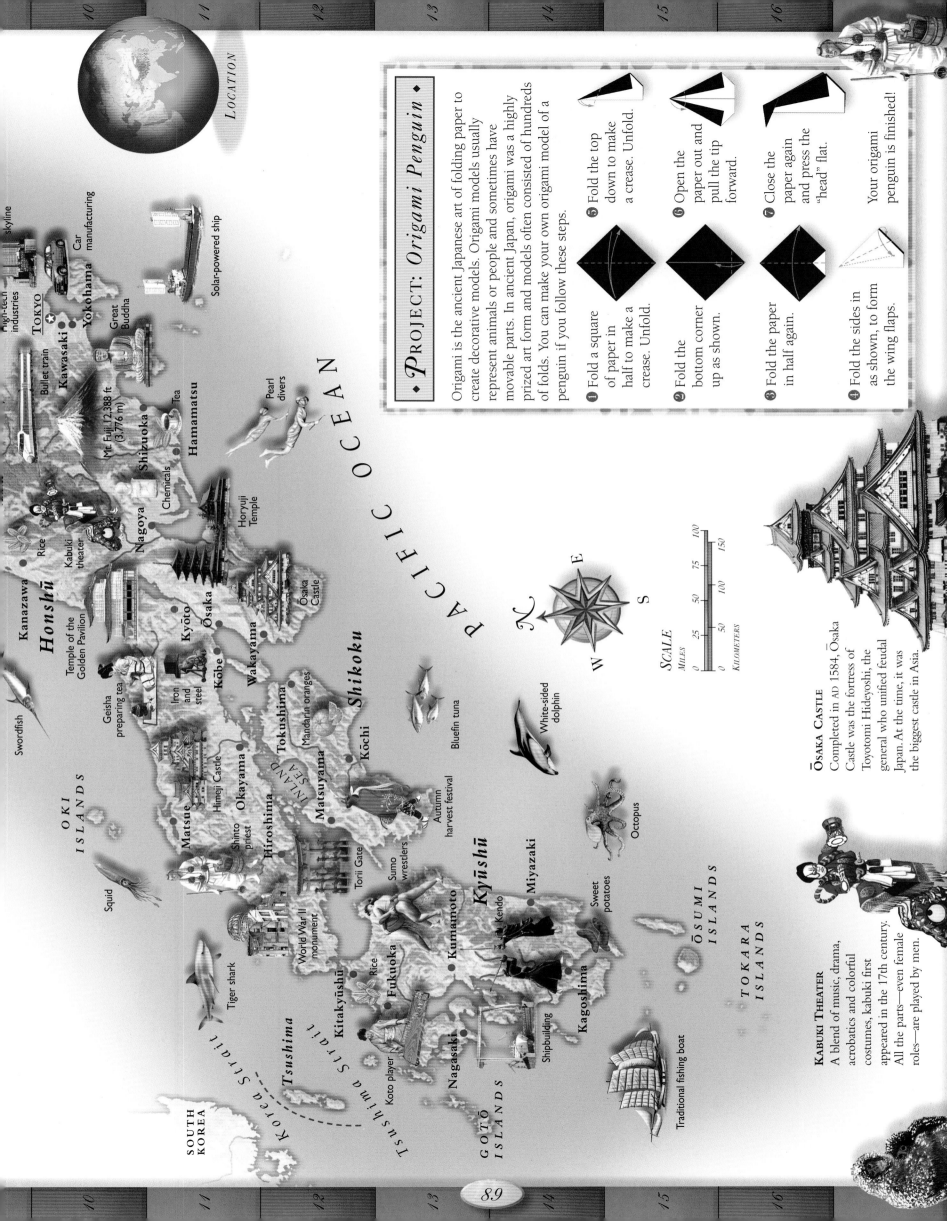

LOCATION

◆ PROJECT: *Origami Penguin* ◆

Origami is the ancient Japanese art of folding paper to create decorative models. Origami models usually represent animals or people and sometimes have movable parts. In ancient Japan, origami was a highly prized art form and models often consisted of hundreds of folds. You can make your own origami model of a penguin if you follow these steps.

① Fold a square of paper in half to make a crease. Unfold.

② Fold the bottom corner up as shown.

③ Fold the paper in half again.

④ Fold the sides in as shown, to form the wing flaps.

⑤ Fold the top down to make a crease. Unfold.

⑥ Open the paper out and pull the tip forward.

⑦ Close the paper again and press the "head" flat.

Your origami penguin is finished!

PACIFIC OCEAN

Honshū

Kanazawa

Tokyo ★

Yokohama
Kawasaki

High-tech industries
skyline
Car manufacturing
Solar-powered ship
Bullet train
Great Buddha
Mt. Fuji 12,388 ft (3,776 m)
Tea
Shizuoka
Hamamatsu
Pearl divers
Chemicals
Nagoya
Rice
Kabuki theater
Temple of the Golden Pavilion
Horyuji Temple
Kyōto
Ōsaka
Ōsaka Castle
Kōbe
Wakayama
Geisha preparing tea
Iron and steel
Himeji Castle
Mandarin oranges
Okayama
Matsue
Shinto priest
Hiroshima
World War II monument
Torii Gate
Sumo wrestlers
Tokushima
Matsuyama
Kōchi
Shikoku
INLAND SEA
Autumn harvest festival
Bluefin tuna
White-sided dolphin
Octopus
Squid
Swordfish
OKI ISLANDS
Tiger shark
Tsushima
Koto player
Korea Strait
Tsushima Strait
SOUTH KOREA
Kitakyūshū
Fukuoka
Rice
Nagasaki
GOTŌ ISLANDS
Shipbuilding
Kumamoto
Kendo
Kyūshū
Miyazaki
Sweet potatoes
Kagoshima
ŌSUMI ISLANDS
TOKARA ISLANDS
Traditional fishing boat

N E S W

SCALE
MILES 0 25 50 75 100
KILOMETERS 0 50 100 150

ŌSAKA CASTLE
Completed in AD 1584, Ōsaka Castle was the fortress of Toyotomi Hideyoshi, the general who unified feudal Japan. At the time, it was the biggest castle in Asia.

KABUKI THEATER
A blend of music, drama, acrobatics and colorful costumes, kabuki first appeared in the 17th century. All the parts—even female roles—are played by men.

Africa

THE WORLD'S SECOND-LARGEST CONTINENT, Africa is an enormous plateau surrounded by narrow coastal plains. A thick band of tropical rain forest covers much of the center of the continent. To the north and south of this forest lie grasslands, known as savannas, and deserts. The Sahara Desert, the biggest desert in the world, spans the entire width of northern Africa, from the Atlantic Ocean to the Red Sea, and covers an area almost as large as the United States. The Kalahari and Namib deserts extend across much of the southwest. In the east, the Great Rift Valley, a series of valleys formed by cracks in Earth's crust, stretches from Syria, in Asia, to Mozambique. Africa includes 53 countries ranging from vast, mainly arid Sudan to the tiny tropical islands of the Seychelles. Arab peoples form the majority of the population in the north. The south's mainly black population is made up of hundreds of native tribes.

Continent Facts

Regional land area: 11,716,972 sq. miles (30,354,852 sq. km)
Regional population: 840,449,396
Independent countries: Algeria, Angola, Benin, Botswana, Burkina Faso, Burundi, Cameroon, Cape Verde Islands, Central African Republic, Chad, Comoros, Congo, Côte d'Ivoire (Ivory Coast), Democratic Republic of the Congo (Zaire), Djibouti, Egypt, Equatorial Guinea, Eritrea, Ethiopia, Gabon, Gambia, Ghana, Guinea, Guinea-Bissau, Kenya, Lesotho, Liberia, Libya, Madagascar, Malawi, Mali, Mauritania, Mauritius, Morocco, Mozambique, Namibia, Niger, Nigeria, Rwanda, São Tomé and Príncipe, Senegal, Seychelles, Sierra Leone, Somalia, South Africa, Sudan, Swaziland, Tanzania, Togo, Tunisia, Uganda, Zambia, Zimbabwe

Major Mountains and Rivers

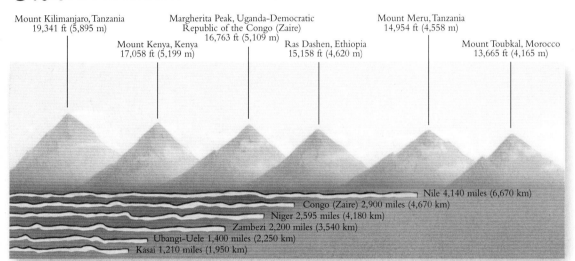

Mount Kilimanjaro, Tanzania 19,341 ft (5,895 m)
Mount Kenya, Kenya 17,058 ft (5,199 m)
Margherita Peak, Uganda-Democratic Republic of the Congo (Zaire) 16,763 ft (5,109 m)
Ras Dashen, Ethiopia 15,158 ft (4,620 m)
Mount Meru, Tanzania 14,954 ft (4,558 m)
Mount Toubkal, Morocco 13,665 ft (4,165 m)

Nile 4,140 miles (6,670 km)
Congo (Zaire) 2,900 miles (4,670 km)
Niger 2,595 miles (4,180 km)
Zambezi 2,200 miles (3,540 km)
Ubangi-Uele 1,400 miles (2,250 km)
Kasai 1,210 miles (1,950 km)

World Records

WORLD'S LARGEST DESERT
SAHARA DESERT, NORTHERN AFRICA, 3,579,000 SQ. MILES (9,269,000 SQ. KM)

WORLD'S LONGEST RIVER
NILE RIVER, NORTHERN AFRICA, 4,140 MILES (6,670 KM)

WORLD'S LARGEST ARTIFICIAL LAKE
LAKE VOLTA, GHANA, 3,275 SQ. MILES (8,482 SQ. KM)

WORLD'S HIGHEST TEMPERATURE
AL-'AZĪZĪYA, LIBYA, SHADE TEMPERATURE OF 136°F (58°C) RECORDED ON SEPTEMBER 13, 1922

Continent Records

HIGHEST MOUNTAIN
KILIMANJARO, TANZANIA, 19,341 FT (5,895 M)

LOWEST POINT
LAKE ASSAL, DJIBOUTI, 500 FT (152 M) BELOW SEA LEVEL

LARGEST LAKE
LAKE VICTORIA, EAST AFRICA, 26,828 SQ. MILES (69,485 SQ. KM)

LARGEST COUNTRY BY AREA
SUDAN, 967,500 SQ. MILES (2,505,825 SQ. KM)

LARGEST COUNTRY BY POPULATION
NIGERIA, POPULATION 129,934,911

LARGEST CITY BY POPULATION
CAIRO, EGYPT, POPULATION 12,399,000

Political Map

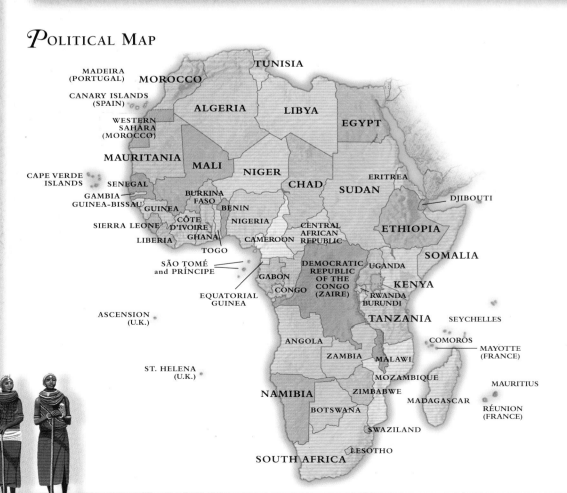

MADEIRA (PORTUGAL)
MOROCCO
TUNISIA
CANARY ISLANDS (SPAIN)
WESTERN SAHARA (MOROCCO)
ALGERIA
LIBYA
EGYPT
MAURITANIA
MALI
NIGER
CHAD
SUDAN
ERITREA
DJIBOUTI
CAPE VERDE ISLANDS
SENEGAL
GAMBIA
GUINEA-BISSAU
GUINEA
BURKINA FASO
BENIN
CÔTE D'IVOIRE
NIGERIA
SIERRA LEONE
GHANA
TOGO
CAMEROON
CENTRAL AFRICAN REPUBLIC
ETHIOPIA
SOMALIA
LIBERIA
SÃO TOMÉ and PRÍNCIPE
GABON
CONGO
DEMOCRATIC REPUBLIC OF THE CONGO (ZAIRE)
UGANDA
RWANDA
BURUNDI
KENYA
EQUATORIAL GUINEA
ASCENSION (U.K.)
TANZANIA
SEYCHELLES
ANGOLA
COMOROS
MAYOTTE (FRANCE)
ST. HELENA (U.K.)
ZAMBIA
MALAWI
MOZAMBIQUE
MAURITIUS
NAMIBIA
ZIMBABWE
MADAGASCAR
RÉUNION (FRANCE)
BOTSWANA
SWAZILAND
LESOTHO
SOUTH AFRICA

• Amazing Fact •

The huge volume of water that pours over Victoria Falls, on the border between Zambia and Zimbabwe, creates a deafening roar and a cloud of spray that can be seen from more than 20 miles (32 km) away. Because of this, locals refer to the falls as "the smoke that thunders."

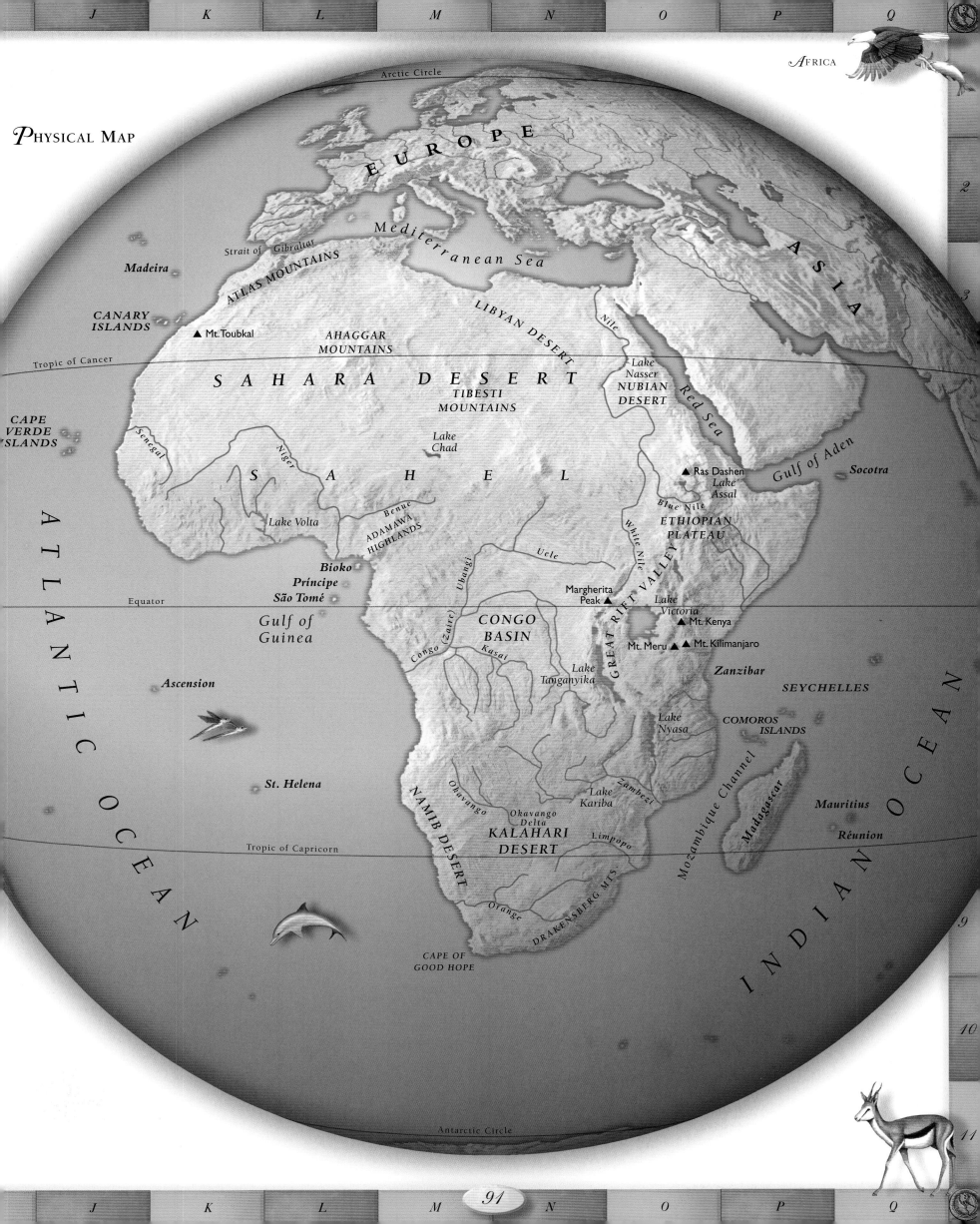

AFRICA

PHYSICAL MAP

EUROPE

ASIA

Arctic Circle

Mediterranean Sea

Madeira

Strait of Gibraltar

ATLAS MOUNTAINS

Nile

CANARY
ISLANDS

▲ Mt. Toubkal

AHAGGAR
MOUNTAINS

LIBYAN DESERT

Tropic of Cancer

SAHARA DESERT

Lake
Nasser

NUBIAN
DESERT

Red Sea

CAPE
VERDE
ISLANDS

TIBESTI
MOUNTAINS

S A H E L

Senegal

Niger

Lake
Chad

Ras Dashen ▲
Lake
Assal

Gulf of Aden

Socotra

Blue Nile

Lake Volta

Benue

ADAMAWA
HIGHLANDS

Uele

White Nile

ETHIOPIAN
PLATEAU

ATLANTIC OCEAN

Bioko
Príncipe
São Tomé

Ubangi

Margherita
Peak ▲

Equator

Gulf of
Guinea

Congo (Zaire)

Kasai

CONGO
BASIN

GREAT RIFT VALLEY

Lake
Victoria

▲ Mt. Kenya

Mt. Meru ▲ ▲ Mt. Kilimanjaro

Ascension

Lake
Tanganyika

Zanzibar

SEYCHELLES

Lake
Nyasa

COMOROS
ISLANDS

St. Helena

Okavango

Okavango
Delta

NAMIB DESERT

KALAHARI
DESERT

Lake
Kariba

Zambezi

Limpopo

Mozambique Channel

Madagascar

Mauritius

Réunion

Tropic of Capricorn

Orange

DRAKENSBERG MTS.

INDIAN OCEAN

CAPE OF
GOOD HOPE

Antarctic Circle

Northern Africa

THE SAHARA DESERT, the largest desert in the world, covers more than half of northern Africa. On its barren, rocky plains and rolling sand dunes, the heat is fierce, water is scarce and there is little land that can be farmed. Most of the people of the Sahara are nomads, who move their camels, sheep and goats around the desert in search of water and pasture. The only usable fertile land north or east of the Sahara lies in the valleys of the Atlas Mountains and along the banks of the Nile River in Egypt. People have farmed the Nile valley for thousands of years, and it is now one of the most densely populated places on Earth. There is little farmland in Algeria and Libya, but both countries possess large oil and gas reserves which have helped them overcome serious poverty. South of the Sahara lies a wide belt of dry grasslands known as the Sahel. These grasslands suffer frequent droughts, and overfarming is turning some areas into desert. Farther south, the Sahel gives way to the tropical rain forests of central Africa. Around the Gulf of Guinea, much of the forest has been cleared to make way for farms and large plantations where cocoa beans, coffee and cotton are grown. Oil and other minerals have been discovered in a number of Gulf countries, and this has created some wealth and industries. However, only a minority of the region's huge population benefit and most people are still very poor.

ALGERIA
POPULATION: 32,277,942 * CAPITAL: ALGIERS

BENIN
POPULATION: 6,787,625 * CAPITALS: COTONOU, PORTO-NOVO

BURKINA FASO
POPULATION: 12,603,185 * CAPITAL: OUAGADOUGOU

CAMEROON
POPULATION: 16,184,748 * CAPITAL: YAOUNDÉ

CAPE VERDE ISLANDS
POPULATION: 408,760 * CAPITAL: PRAIA

CENTRAL AFRICAN REPUBLIC
POPULATION: 3,642,739 * CAPITAL: BANGUI

CHAD
POPULATION: 8,997,237 * CAPITAL: N'DJAMENA

CÔTE D'IVOIRE (IVORY COAST)
POPULATION: 16,804,784 * CAPITALS: ABIDJAN, YAMOUSSOUKRO

DJIBOUTI
POPULATION: 472,810 * CAPITAL: DJIBOUTI

EGYPT
POPULATION: 70,712,345 * CAPITAL: CAIRO

EQUATORIAL GUINEA
POPULATION: 498,144 * CAPITAL: MALABO

ERITREA
POPULATION: 4,465,651 * CAPITAL: ASMARA

ETHIOPIA
POPULATION: 67,673,031 * CAPITAL: ADDIS ABABA

GAMBIA
POPULATION: 1,455,842 * CAPITAL: BANJUL

GHANA
POPULATION: 20,244,154 * CAPITAL: ACCRA

GUINEA
POPULATION: 7,775,065 * CAPITAL: CONAKRY

GUINEA-BISSAU
POPULATION: 1,345,479 * CAPITAL: BISSAU

LIBERIA
POPULATION: 3,288,198 * CAPITAL: MONROVIA

LIBYA
POPULATION: 5,368,585 * CAPITAL: TRIPOLI

MALI
POPULATION: 11,340,480 * CAPITAL: BAMAKO

MAURITANIA
POPULATION: 2,828,858 * CAPITAL: NOUAKCHOTT

MOROCCO
POPULATION: 31,167,783 * CAPITAL: RABAT

NIGER
POPULATION: 10,639,744 * CAPITAL: NIAMEY

NIGERIA
POPULATION: 129,934,911 * CAPITAL: ABUJA

SENEGAL
POPULATION: 10,589,571 * CAPITAL: DAKAR

SIERRA LEONE
POPULATION: 5,614,743 * CAPITAL: FREETOWN

SOMALIA
POPULATION: 7,753,310 * CAPITAL: MOGADISHU

SUDAN
POPULATION: 37,090,298 * CAPITAL: KHARTOUM

TOGO
POPULATION: 5,285,501 * CAPITAL: LOMÉ

TUNISIA
POPULATION: 9,815,644 * CAPITAL: TUNIS

SPAIN

Sardines · Tangier · Ceuta (SPAIN) · **ALGIERS**
RABAT · Fès · Melilla · Oran
MADEIRA (PORTUGAL) · Casablanca · (SPAIN) · Roman arch
MOROCCO · Wheat
Kouttoubia Mosque minaret · Marrakech
CANARY ISLANDS (SPAIN) · Mt. Toubkal 13,665 ft (4,165 m) · ATLAS MTS. · Dyeing wool for carpets
Sheep
El Aaiún · Tindouf · **ALGERIA**
WESTERN SAHARA (MOROCCO) · Nomads carrying water · Scorpion
Dolphin · Nomad with camel
Imraguen fisherman · Chinguetti man making tea · Tamanrasset
Pounding millet · MAURITANIA · Woman carrying goods to market · SAH · AHAGGA MTS.
Nouakchott · Secretary bird · Hippopotamus · **MALI**
Senegal · **Tombouctou (Timbuktu)** · Ostrich
Dakar · Fishing traps · Niger · SAHEL
SENEGAL · Bororro man
Banjul · Ségou · **BURKINA FASO** · **Niamey** · Marad
GAMBIA · **Bamako** · **Ouagadougou** · Fishing hut
GUINEA-BISSAU · Bissau · GUINEA · Ivorian carrying palm wine · Cotton
Bauxite (aluminum) · **BENIN** · Yams
Conakry · Diana monkey · Cocoa · Niger · **ABU**
Freetown · Diamonds · CÔTE D'IVOIRE (IVORY COAST) · Lake Volta · TOGO · **GHANA** · Bananas · **NI**
SIERRA LEONE · Cassava · **Yamoussoukro** · **Cotonou** · Ibadan
Monrovia · Coffee · **Lomé** · Lagos
LIBERIA · Bananas · **Abidjan** · **Accra** · **Porto-Novo** · Oil · Pea
Gulf of Guinea · Bioko

OSTRICH
The largest bird in the world, the ostrich, is unable to fly but can run at up to 40 miles per hour (65 kph).

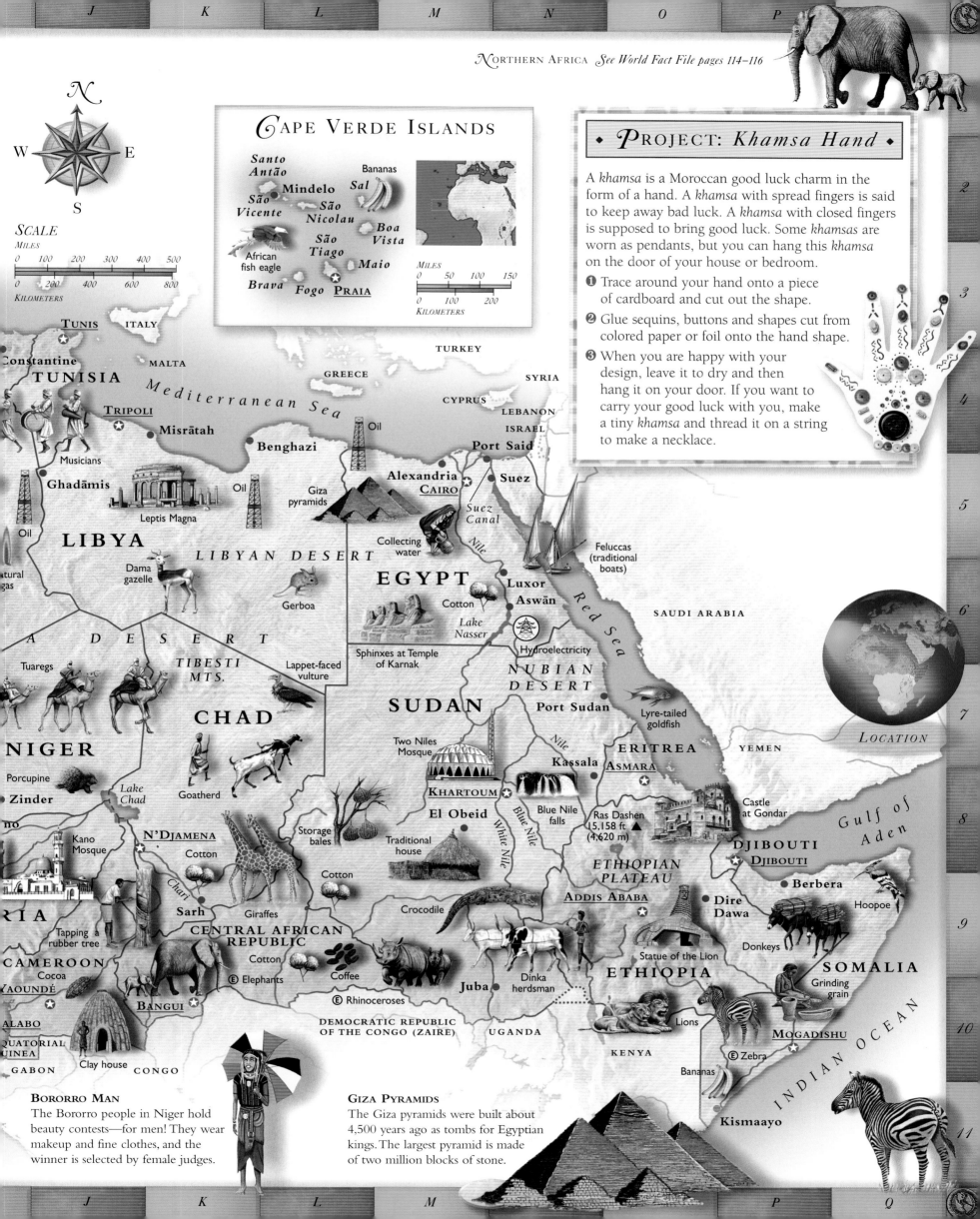

Grid labels (top): J K L M N O P

Compass: N W E S

SCALE
MILES
0 100 200 300 400 500
KILOMETERS
0 200 400 600 800

CAPE VERDE ISLANDS

Santo Antão
Mindelo
São Vicente
São Nicolau
Sal
Bananas
Boa Vista
São Tiago
Maio
African fish eagle
Brava
Fogo
Praia

MILES
0 50 100 150
KILOMETERS
0 100 200

PROJECT: *Khamsa Hand*

A *khamsa* is a Moroccan good luck charm in the form of a hand. A *khamsa* with spread fingers is said to keep away bad luck. A *khamsa* with closed fingers is supposed to bring good luck. Some *khamsas* are worn as pendants, but you can hang this *khamsa* on the door of your house or bedroom.

❶ Trace around your hand onto a piece of cardboard and cut out the shape.

❷ Glue sequins, buttons and shapes cut from colored paper or foil onto the hand shape.

❸ When you are happy with your design, leave it to dry and then hang it on your door. If you want to carry your good luck with you, make a tiny *khamsa* and thread it on a string to make a necklace.

Map labels:

TUNIS
ITALY
TUNISIA
Musicians
TRIPOLI
Misrātah
MALTA
GREECE
TURKEY
CYPRUS
SYRIA
LEBANON
ISRAEL
Port Said
Benghazi
Oil
Alexandria
CAIRO
Suez
Constantine
Ghadāmis
Leptis Magna
Oil
Oil
LIBYA
LIBYAN DESERT
Giza pyramids
Suez Canal
Mediterranean Sea
Natural gas
Oil
Dama gazelle
Gerboa
EGYPT
Collecting water
Luxor
Aswān
Nile
Feluccas (traditional boats)
Red Sea
SAUDI ARABIA
Cotton
Lake Nasser
Sphinxes at Temple of Karnak
Hydroelectricity
NUBIAN DESERT
YEMEN
LOCATION
Tuaregs
TIBESTI MTS.
Lappet-faced vulture
CHAD
SUDAN
Port Sudan
Lyre-tailed goldfish
NIGER
Porcupine
Lake Chad
Goatherd
Two Niles Mosque
KHARTOUM
Nile
ERITREA
Asmara
Kassala
Castle at Gondar
Gulf of Aden
Zinder
El Obeid
Blue Nile falls
Ras Dashen 15,158 ft (4,620 m) ▲
Kano Mosque
N'DJAMENA
Cotton
Storage bales
Traditional house
Blue Nile
White Nile
ETHIOPIAN PLATEAU
DJIBOUTI
DJIBOUTI
Berbera
Hoopoe
Tapping a rubber tree
Sarh
Giraffes
Cotton
Crocodile
ADDIS ABABA
Dire Dawa
Donkeys
CENTRAL AFRICAN REPUBLIC
Cotton
Coffee
Statue of the Lion
SOMALIA
CAMEROON
Cocoa
YAOUNDÉ
Ⓔ Elephants
Ⓔ Rhinoceroses
Juba
Dinka herdsman
ETHIOPIA
Lions
Grinding grain
BANGUI
Chari
DEMOCRATIC REPUBLIC OF THE CONGO (ZAIRE)
UGANDA
KENYA
MOGADISHU
MALABO
EQUATORIAL GUINEA
Clay house
CONGO
GABON
Bananas
Ⓔ Zebra
Kismaayo
INDIAN OCEAN

BORORRO MAN
The Bororro people in Niger hold beauty contests—for men! They wear makeup and fine clothes, and the winner is selected by female judges.

GIZA PYRAMIDS
The Giza pyramids were built about 4,500 years ago as tombs for Egyptian kings. The largest pyramid is made of two million blocks of stone.

Grid labels (bottom): J K L M N O P Q

Southern Africa

IN THE NORTHWESTERN PART of this region, the Congo River and its many tributaries flow through immense tropical rain forests. Crocodiles swim the waterways, and the jungles are home to chimpanzees, gorillas and tropical birds. Most of the local people live in villages near the rivers and grow their own food on small plots of cleared land. The rain forests stretch eastward across the continent toward the Great Rift Valley, a chain of dramatic, steep-sided valleys that runs down the eastern side of Africa. Within these valleys lie many deep lakes as well as a number of volcanoes, including Mount Kilimanjaro, Africa's highest mountain. On the valley floors and across the surrounding grassland plateaus, enormous herds of zebras, wildebeests and antelopes are hunted by lions, cheetahs and other predators. To protect the region's wildlife, many countries have created nature preserves, which attract tourists from all over the world. From the southern end of the Rift Valley, in Mozambique, high grasslands known as the Veld spread westward toward the Kalahari and Namib deserts. In South Africa the Veld is an important farming region that is also rich in mineral resources including copper, gold and diamonds. Off the coast of Mozambique lies Madagascar, the world's fourth-largest island. Madagascar is famous for its unique wildlife, which includes many species of lemurs, unusual relatives of monkeys.

ANGOLA
POPULATION: 10,593,171 • CAPITAL: LUANDA

BOTSWANA
POPULATION: 1,591,232 • CAPITAL: GABORONE

BURUNDI
POPULATION: 6,373,002 • CAPITAL: BUJUMBURA

COMOROS
POPULATION: 614,382 • CAPITAL: MORONI

CONGO
POPULATION: 2,958,448 • CAPITAL: BRAZZAVILLE

DEMOCRATIC REPUBLIC OF THE CONGO (ZAIRE)
POPULATION: 55,225,478 • CAPITAL: KINSHASA

GABON
POPULATION: 1,233,353 • CAPITAL: LIBREVILLE

KENYA
POPULATION: 31,138,735 • CAPITAL: NAIROBI

LESOTHO
POPULATION: 2,207,954 • CAPITAL: MASERU

MADAGASCAR
POPULATION: 16,473,477 • CAPITAL: ANTANANARIVO

MALAWI
POPULATION: 10,701,824 • CAPITAL: LILONGWE

MAURITIUS
POPULATION: 1,200,206 • CAPITAL: PORT LOUIS

MOZAMBIQUE
POPULATION: 19,607,519 • CAPITAL: MAPUTO

NAMIBIA
POPULATION: 1,820,916 • CAPITAL: WINDHOEK

RWANDA
POPULATION: 7,398,074 • CAPITAL: KIGALI

SÃO TOMÉ AND PRÍNCIPE
POPULATION: 170,372 • CAPITAL: SÃO TOMÉ

SEYCHELLES
POPULATION: 80,098 • CAPITAL: VICTORIA

SOUTH AFRICA
POPULATION: 43,647,658 • CAPITALS: BLOEMFONTEIN, CAPE TOWN, PRETORIA

SWAZILAND
POPULATION: 1,123,605 • CAPITAL: MBABANE

TANZANIA
POPULATION: 37,187,939 • CAPITALS: DAR ES SALAAM, DODOMA

UGANDA
POPULATION: 24,699,073 • CAPITAL: KAMPALA

ZAMBIA
POPULATION: 9,959,037 • CAPITAL: LUSAKA

ZIMBABWE
POPULATION: 11,376,676 • CAPITAL: HARARE

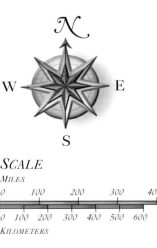

SCALE

MILES

0   100   200   300   400

0   100   200   300   400   500   600

KILOMETERS

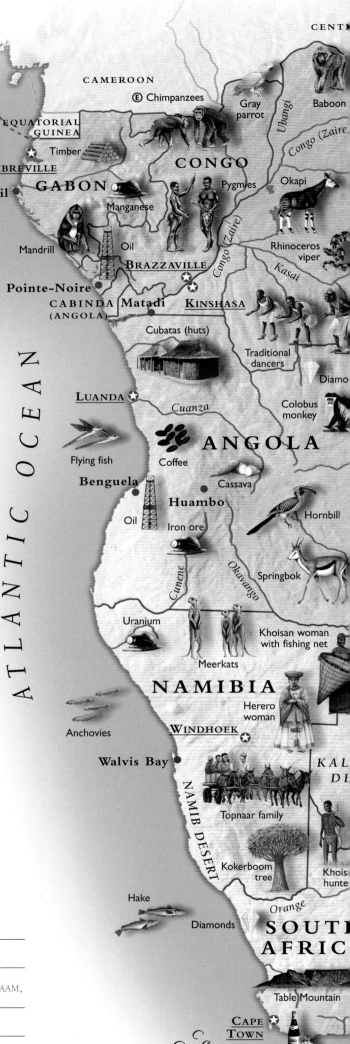

ATLANTIC OCEAN

CAMEROON

SÃO TOMÉ AND PRÍNCIPE
Príncipe
São Tomé
SÃO TOMÉ

EQUATORIAL GUINEA

CENT

Chimpanzees

Gray parrot

Baboon

Ubangi

Congo (Zaire)

CONGO

GABON
Timber
LIBREVILLE

Port-Gentil

Manganese

Pygmies

Okapi

Mandrill

Oil

Rhinoceros viper

BRAZZAVILLE

Kasai

Pointe-Noire

CABINDA (ANGOLA)   Matadi   KINSHASA

Cubatas (huts)

Traditional dancers

Diamo

LUANDA

Cuanza

Colobus monkey

Flying fish

ANGOLA

Coffee

Benguela

Cassava

Huambo

Hornbill

Oil   Iron ore

Cunene   Okavango

Springbok

Uranium

Khoisan woman with fishing net

Meerkats

NAMIBIA

Herero woman

Anchovies

WINDHOEK

Walvis Bay

KAL DE

NAMIB DESERT

Topnaar family

Kokerboom tree

Khois hunte

Hake

Orange

Diamonds

SOUTI AFRIC

Table Mountain

CAPE TOWN

Wine

Cape of Good Hope

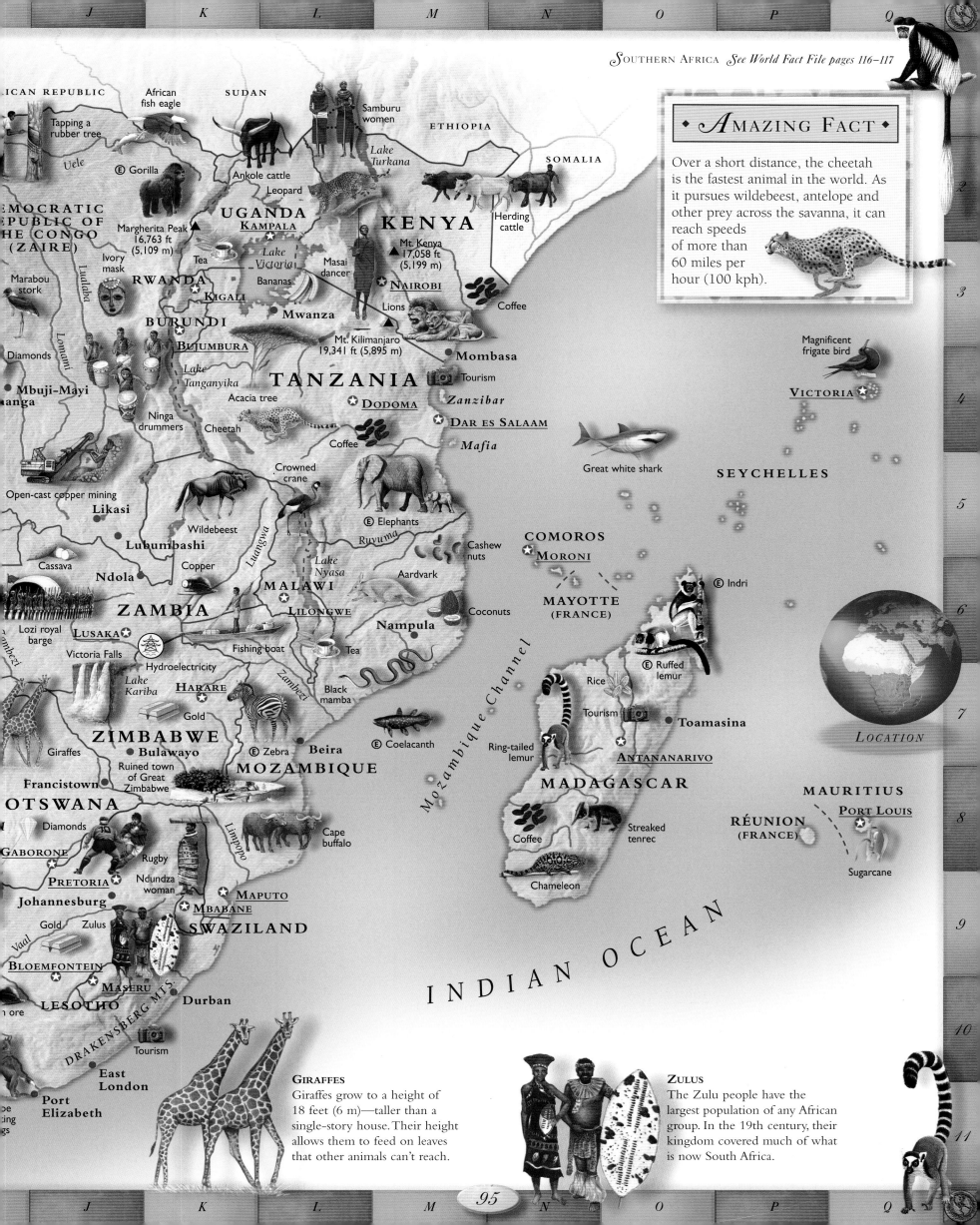

JICAN REPUBLIC

SUDAN

ETHIOPIA

SOMALIA

African fish eagle

Tapping a rubber tree

Uele

Samburu women

Lake Turkana

Herding cattle

Ⓔ Gorilla

Ankole cattle

Leopard

UGANDA

KAMPALA

KENYA

Mt. Kenya 17,058 ft (5,199 m) ▲

DEMOCRATIC REPUBLIC OF THE CONGO (ZAIRE)

Margherita Peak 16,763 ft (5,109 m) ▲

Ivory mask

Tea

Lake Victoria

Masai dancer

RWANDA

Bananas

★ **NAIROBI**

Marabou stork

★ **KIGALI**

Mwanza

Lions

Lualaba

Lomami

BURUNDI

★ **BUJUMBURA**

Mt. Kilimanjaro 19,341 ft (5,895 m)

☐ Tourism

Coffee

Mombasa

Diamonds

Lake Tanganyika

TANZANIA

Ninga drummers

Acacia tree

☉ **DODOMA**

Zanzibar

Mbuji-Mayi

anga

Cheetah

★ **DAR ES SALAAM**

Coffee

Mafia

AMAZING FACT

Over a short distance, the cheetah is the fastest animal in the world. As it pursues wildebeest, antelope and other prey across the savanna, it can reach speeds of more than 60 miles per hour (100 kph).

Magnificent frigate bird

VICTORIA ★

Great white shark

SEYCHELLES

Open-cast copper mining

Crowned crane

Ⓔ Elephants

Likasi

Wildebeest

Luangwa

Ruvuma

Cashew nuts

COMOROS

Ⓔ Indri

Lubumbashi

Copper

Lake Nyasa

Aardvark

☆ **MORONI**

Cassava

MALAWI

Coconuts

MAYOTTE (FRANCE)

Ⓔ Ruffed lemur

Ndola

★ **LILONGWE**

Nampula

Lozi royal barge

ZAMBIA

Fishing boat

Tea

Rice

Tourism ☐

Toamasina

★ **LUSAKA**

Victoria Falls

Hydroelectricity

Black mamba

Ⓔ Coelacanth

Ring-tailed lemur

Zambezi

Lake Kariba

★ **HARARE**

Zambezi

★ **ANTANANARIVO**

Giraffes

Gold

ZIMBABWE

Ⓔ Zebra

Beira

MADAGASCAR

MAURITIUS

Francistown

● **Bulawayo**

Ruined town of Great Zimbabwe

MOZAMBIQUE

Mozambique Channel

Coffee

Streaked tenrec

RÉUNION (FRANCE)

★ **PORT LOUIS**

OTSWANA

Diamonds

Rugby

Limpopo

Cape buffalo

Sugarcane

★ **GABORONE**

Ndundza woman

★ **PRETORIA**

Johannesburg

Chameleon

★ **MAPUTO**

★ **MBABANE**

Gold

Zulus

SWAZILAND

BLOEMFONTEIN

★ **MASERU**

n ore

LESOTHO

DRAKENSBERG MTS.

Durban

Tourism ☐

INDIAN OCEAN

East London

Port Elizabeth

LOCATION

GIRAFFES
Giraffes grow to a height of 18 feet (6 m)—taller than a single-story house. Their height allows them to feed on leaves that other animals can't reach.

ZULUS
The Zulu people have the largest population of any African group. In the 19th century, their kingdom covered much of what is now South Africa.

Australia and Oceania

STRETCHING FROM THE INDIAN OCEAN to the center of the Pacific Ocean, Australia and Oceania cover a vast area of the globe. But because most of this region is ocean, it has a relatively small population. Australia is by far the largest landmass. This island is so big that it is considered a continent. Oceania consists of thousands of much smaller islands that are scattered across the Pacific Ocean to the east of Australia. They are divided into three groups: Micronesia, Melanesia, and Polynesia, which includes the large islands of New Zealand. There are two main types of Pacific island: high, rugged islands that are the peaks of undersea volcanoes and submerged mountain ranges; and coral atolls—low, sandy islands formed by coral reefs growing on the tops of undersea mountains. Many of the Pacific islands are so small that they do not appear on regular maps.

Continent Facts

Regional land area: 3,283,993 sq. miles (8,507,753 sq. km)
Regional population: 30,885,204
Independent countries: Australia, Federated States of Micronesia, Fiji, Kiribati, Marshall Islands, Nauru, New Zealand, Palau, Papua New Guinea, Samoa, Solomon Islands, Tonga, Tuvalu, Vanuatu

World Records

WORLD'S LONGEST CORAL REEF
THE GREAT BARRIER REEF, AUSTRALIA, 1,260 MILES (2,025 KM)

WORLD'S LARGEST ROCK
ULURU (AYERS ROCK), AUSTRALIA, 1,143 FT (348 M) HIGH; 1.5 MILES (2.5 KM) LONG; 1 MILE (1.6 KM) WIDE

WORLD'S LARGEST SAND ISLAND
FRASER ISLAND, AUSTRALIA, 75 MILES (120 KM) LONG

Continent Records

HIGHEST MOUNTAIN
MOUNT WILHELM, PAPUA NEW GUINEA, 14,762 FEET (4,500 M)

LOWEST POINT
LAKE EYRE, AUSTRALIA, 52 FT (16 M) BELOW SEA LEVEL

LARGEST LAKE
LAKE EYRE, AUSTRALIA, 3,600 SQ. MILES (9,324 SQ. KM)

LONGEST RIVER
MURRAY-DARLING, AUSTRALIA, 2,330 MILES (3,750 KM)

LARGEST COUNTRY BY AREA
AUSTRALIA, 2,967,909 SQ. MILES (7,686,884 SQ. KM)

LARGEST COUNTRY BY POPULATION
AUSTRALIA, POPULATION 19,546,792

LARGEST CITY BY POPULATION
SYDNEY, AUSTRALIA, POPULATION 4,175,000

Major Mountains and Rivers

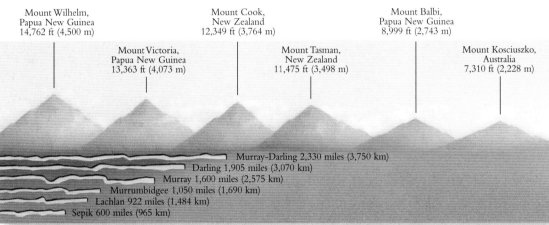

Mount Wilhelm, Papua New Guinea 14,762 ft (4,500 m)
Mount Victoria, Papua New Guinea 13,363 ft (4,073 m)
Mount Cook, New Zealand 12,349 ft (3,764 m)
Mount Tasman, New Zealand 11,475 ft (3,498 m)
Mount Balbi, Papua New Guinea 8,999 ft (2,743 m)
Mount Kosciuszko, Australia 7,310 ft (2,228 m)

Murray-Darling 2,330 miles (3,750 km)
Darling 1,905 miles (3,070 km)
Murray 1,600 miles (2,575 km)
Murrumbidgee 1,050 miles (1,690 km)
Lachlan 922 miles (1,484 km)
Sepik 600 miles (965 km)

Political Map

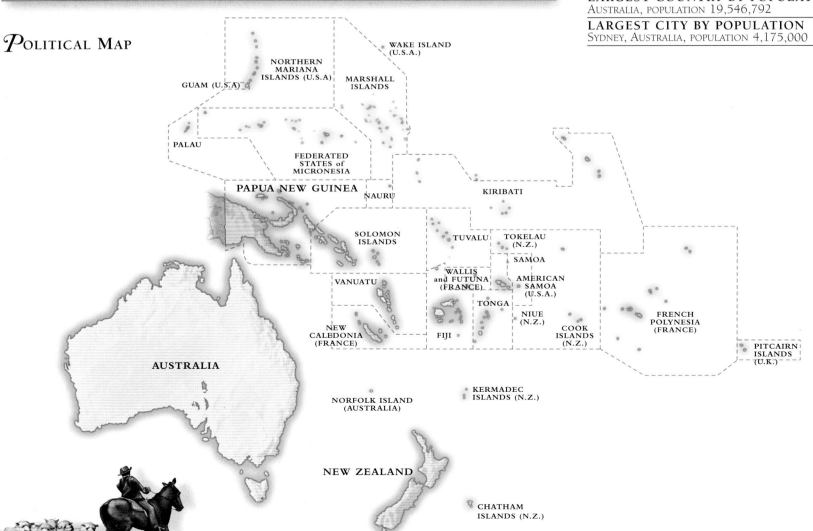

WAKE ISLAND (U.S.A.)
NORTHERN MARIANA ISLANDS (U.S.A)
GUAM (U.S.A)
MARSHALL ISLANDS
PALAU
FEDERATED STATES of MICRONESIA
PAPUA NEW GUINEA
NAURU
KIRIBATI
SOLOMON ISLANDS
TUVALU
TOKELAU (N.Z.)
SAMOA
WALLIS and FUTUNA (FRANCE)
AMERICAN SAMOA (U.S.A.)
VANUATU
TONGA
NIUE (N.Z.)
COOK ISLANDS (N.Z.)
FRENCH POLYNESIA (FRANCE)
NEW CALEDONIA (FRANCE)
FIJI
PITCAIRN ISLANDS (U.K.)
AUSTRALIA
KERMADEC ISLANDS (N.Z.)
NORFOLK ISLAND (AUSTRALIA)
NEW ZEALAND
CHATHAM ISLANDS (N.Z.)

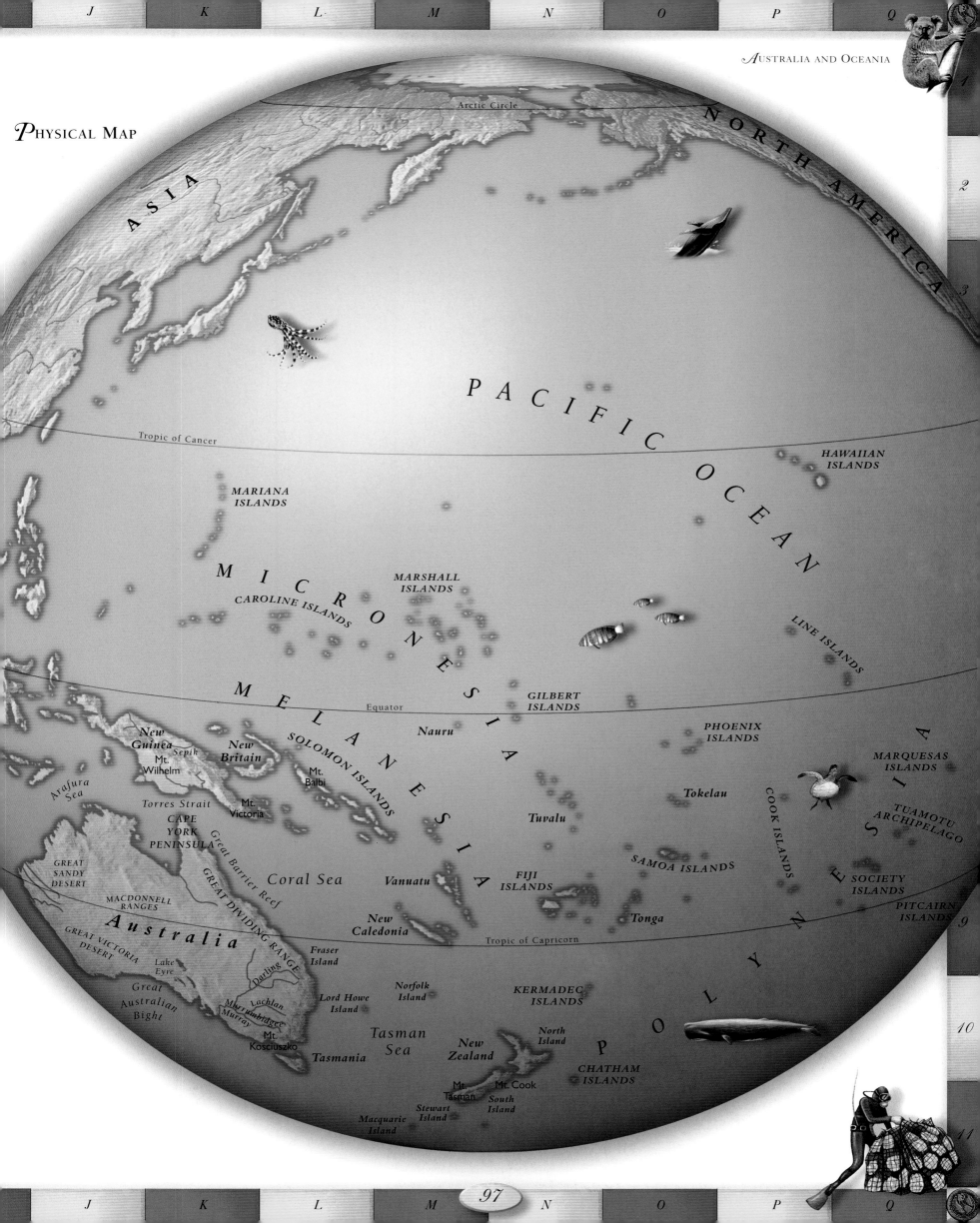

Australia and Papua New Guinea

AUSTRALIA IS AS BIG AS the United States mainland but has a smaller population than Texas. The vast, dry interior, known as the outback, consists mainly of deserts and grasslands. It contains mineral reserves and is used for grazing huge numbers of sheep and cattle, but few people live there. Most Australians live in or near cities along the east, southeast and southwest coasts, where the climate is temperate and the land fertile. The far northeast is tropical, with areas of dense rain forest. The southeast is cooler, and mountain snowfalls are common. Most of Australia's native peoples, the Aborigines, live in towns and cities, but some still follow old traditions in the outback. Aborigines originally came to Australia more than 40,000 years ago, having crossed over from the island of New Guinea when it was still attached to Australia. Papua New Guinea, an Australian territory until 1975, is made up of several island chains and half the island of New Guinea. This main island is covered in jungle and surrounded by swampy plains. Most people live in small villages, where they grow food in gardens and raise animals. Many communities have little contact with the outside world and have retained their own traditions and languages. Papua New Guinea has over 700 languages—more than any other country in the world.

AUSTRALIA
Population: 19,546,792 · Capital: Canberra

PAPUA NEW GUINEA
Population: 5,172,033 · Capital: Port Moresby

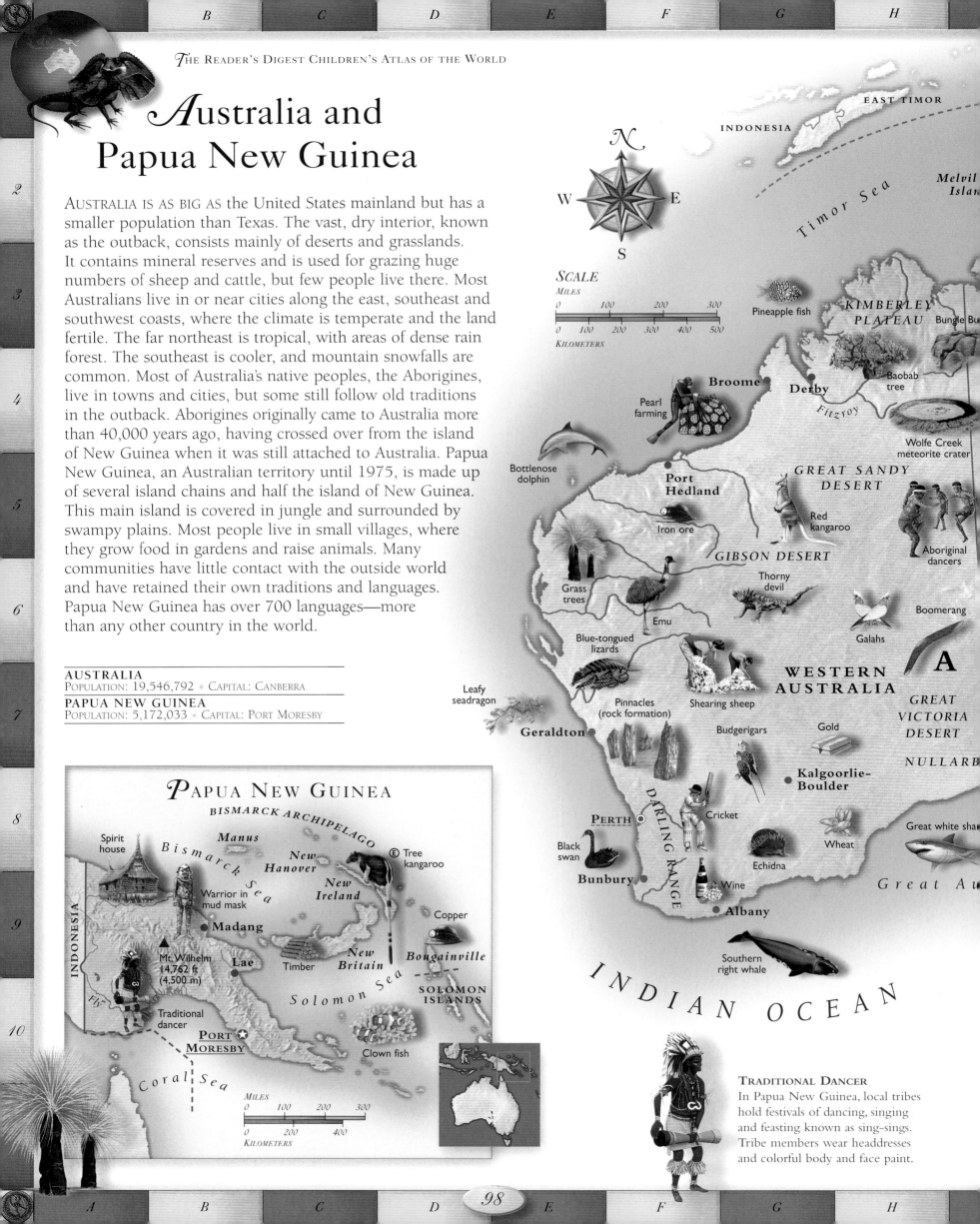

SCALE
MILES
0   100   200   300
0   100   200   300   400   500
KILOMETERS

EAST TIMOR
INDONESIA
Timor Sea
Melvil Islan
Pineapple fish
KIMBERLEY PLATEAU
Bungle Bu
Broome
Derby
Baobab tree
Pearl farming
Fitzroy
Wolfe Creek meteorite crater
Bottlenose dolphin
GREAT SANDY DESERT
Port Hedland
Iron ore
Red kangaroo
Aboriginal dancers
GIBSON DESERT
Thorny devil
Grass trees
Emu
Galahs
Boomerang
Blue-tongued lizards
WESTERN AUSTRALIA
A
Leafy seadragon
Pinnacles (rock formation)
Shearing sheep
GREAT VICTORIA DESERT
Geraldton
Budgerigars
Gold
NULLARB
Kalgoorlie-Boulder
Cricket
DARLING RANGE
PERTH
Great white shar
Black swan
Wheat
Bunbury
Echidna
Wine
Great Au
Albany
Southern right whale
INDIAN OCEAN

PAPUA NEW GUINEA

BISMARCK ARCHIPELAGO

Spirit house
Manus
New Hanover
Tree kangaroo
Bismarck Sea
Warrior in mud mask
New Ireland
Madang
Copper
Mt. Wilhelm 14,762 ft (4,500 m)
Lae
Timber
New Britain
Bougainville
INDONESIA
Fly
Solomon Sea
SOLOMON ISLANDS
Traditional dancer
PORT MORESBY
Clown fish
Coral Sea
MILES
0   100   200   300
0   200   400
KILOMETERS

TRADITIONAL DANCER
In Papua New Guinea, local tribes hold festivals of dancing, singing and feasting known as sing-sings. Tribe members wear headdresses and colorful body and face paint.

INDONESIA PAPUA NEW GUINEA

Arafura Sea

Torres Strait

Dugongs

Bauxite (aluminum)

Harlequin fish

DARWIN   ARNHEM LAND

Groote Island

Saltwater crocodile

CAPE YORK PENINSULA

Playing the didgeridoo

Gulf of Carpentaria

Scuba diving

Coral reef

Cassowary

Tourism

NORTHERN TERRITORY

Giant termite mound

Road train

Carpet snake

Cairns

Dingo

Copper

Mount Isa

Wallaby

Pineapples

Townsville

Devil's Marbles (rock formation)

Sugarcane

Mackay

rilled zard

School of the Air (school by radio)

Royal Flying Doctor Service

Coal

ACDONNELL RANGES

Hot-air ballooning

Alice Springs

QUEENSLAND

Sulfur-crested cockatoo

Rockhampton

Blue-ringed octopus

Uluru (Ayers Rock)

Gum tree

Homestead

Rugby league

Fraser Island

Maryborough

SIMPSON DESERT

Brumbies (wild horses)

Magpie

TRALIA

Herding sheep

Camel

Opals

Lake Eyre

Gray kangaroo

BRISBANE

Gold Coast

Toowoomba

SOUTH AUSTRALIA

Windmill

Koala

Kookaburra

Platypus

Coal

Tourism

AIN

Lake Gairdner

Lake Torrens

Merino sheep

Steelworker

Surf-lifesavers

Iron and steel

Port Augusta

Darling

Broken Hill

NEW SOUTH WALES

Newcastle

lian Bight

Whyalla

Zinc

Wine

Australian Rules football

Wollongong

Wombat

SYDNEY

Opera House and Harbour Bridge

ADELAIDE

Wheat

Murray

CANBERRA

AUSTRALIAN CAPITAL TERRITORY

Kangaroo Island

Surfing

VICTORIA

Mt. Kosciuszko 7,310 ft (2,228 m)

Sailing

MELBOURNE

Ballarat

Geelong

Tram

Bass Strait

Twelve Apostles (rock formation)

King Island

Flinders Island

Tasmanian devil

Launceston

TASMANIA

Apples

Port Arthur historic site

HOBART

GREAT BARRIER Reef

GREAT DIVIDING RANGE

PACIFIC OCEAN

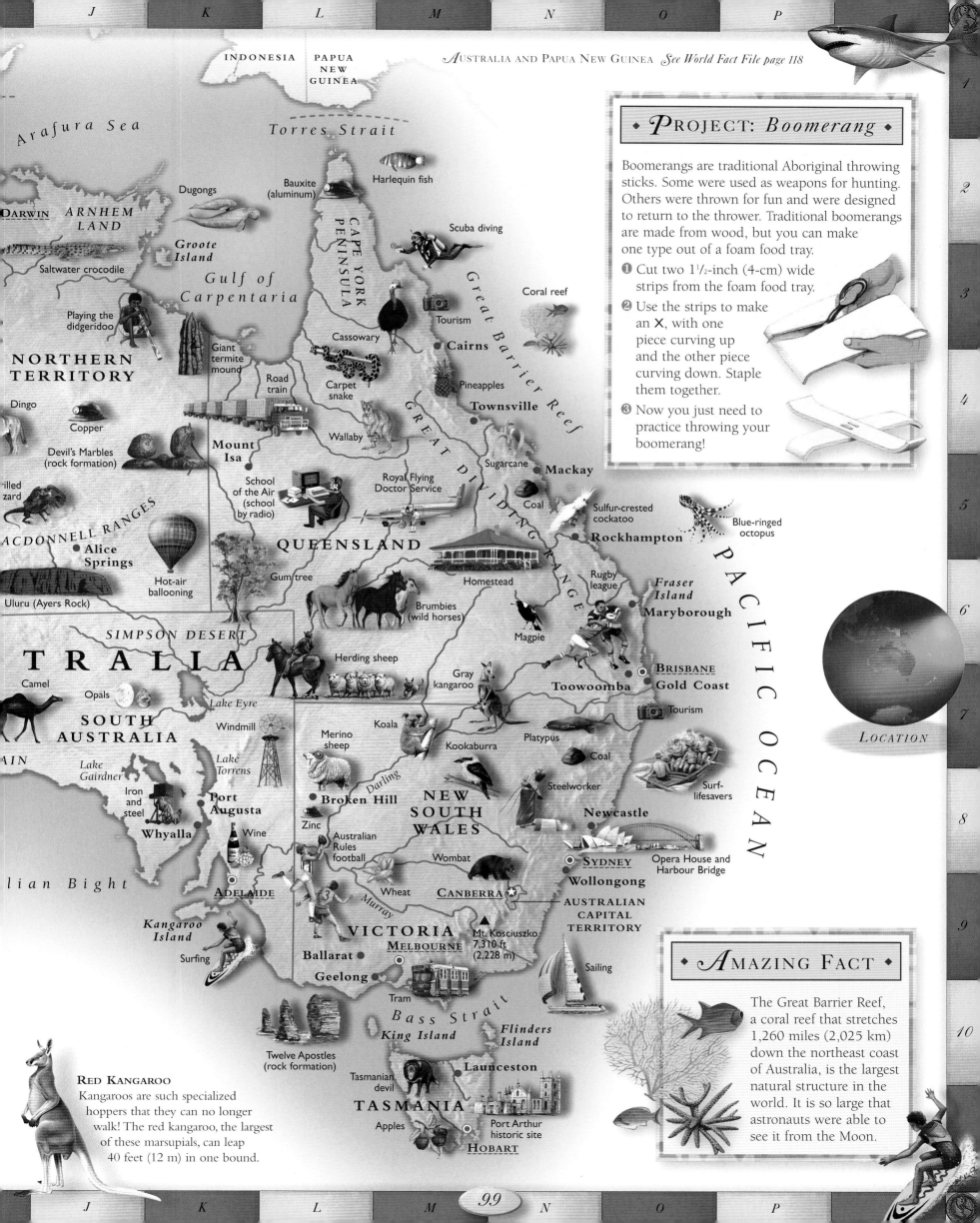

◆ PROJECT: *Boomerang* ◆

Boomerangs are traditional Aboriginal throwing sticks. Some were used as weapons for hunting. Others were thrown for fun and were designed to return to the thrower. Traditional boomerangs are made from wood, but you can make one type out of a foam food tray.

❶ Cut two 1½-inch (4-cm) wide strips from the foam food tray.

❷ Use the strips to make an **X**, with one piece curving up and the other piece curving down. Staple them together.

❸ Now you just need to practice throwing your boomerang!

◆ AMAZING FACT ◆

The Great Barrier Reef, a coral reef that stretches 1,260 miles (2,025 km) down the northeast coast of Australia, is the largest natural structure in the world. It is so large that astronauts were able to see it from the Moon.

RED KANGAROO
Kangaroos are such specialized hoppers that they can no longer walk! The red kangaroo, the largest of these marsupials, can leap 40 feet (12 m) in one bound.

New Zealand and the Southwestern Pacific

SCATTERED ACROSS A VAST EXPANSE of ocean and separated from each other by great distances, the islands of the southwestern Pacific are among the most isolated places on Earth. The largest and most southerly group is New Zealand, consisting of two large islands—the North Island and the South Island—and several smaller islands. New Zealand is a modern, industrialized country. About 70 percent of the population live on the North Island, which has several active volcanoes. Lake Taupo, New Zealand's largest lake, lies in a crater that formed when a volcano exploded. The nearby volcanoes, Ruapehu and Ngauruhoe, have erupted several times in recent years. The Southern Alps form the "backbone" of the South Island. On their western side, temperate rain forests have grown up around a line of mighty glaciers that run down to the coast. More than half of New Zealand is used for growing crops and grazing animals—there are 20 sheep for every New Zealander! The country's original inhabitants, the Maori people, make up one-sixth of the population. Most other New Zealanders are descendants of British immigrants. Thousands of tropical islands lie to the north and east of New Zealand. Tourism is a growing industry in countries such as Fiji and Vanuatu. Some islands have developing towns with new businesses, but most islanders live in small villages. They fish for crabs, lobsters, turtles and tuna, and grow sweet potatoes and bananas. One of the most important export products is copra (dried coconut meat), which is used in making soap and candles.

FIJI
POPULATION: 856,346 * CAPITAL: SUVA

NEW ZEALAND
POPULATION: 3,908,037 * CAPITAL: WELLINGTON

SAMOA
POPULATION: 256,177 * CAPITAL: APIA

SOLOMON ISLANDS
POPULATION: 494,786 * CAPITAL: HONIARA

TONGA
POPULATION: 106,137 * CAPITAL: NUKU'ALOFA

VANUATU
POPULATION: 196,178 * CAPITAL: PORT VILA

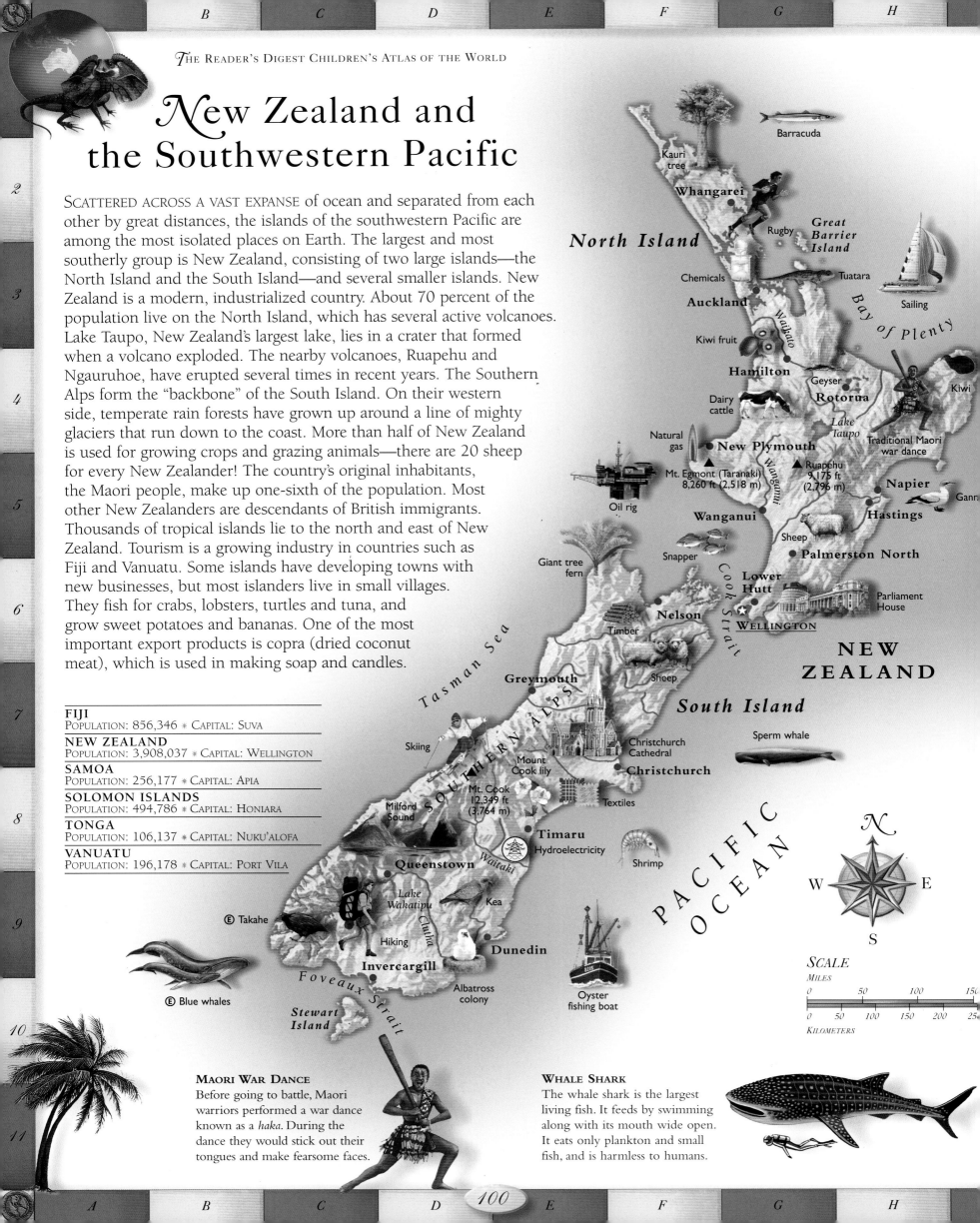

Barracuda

Kauri tree

Whangarei

North Island

Rugby

Great Barrier Island

Chemicals

Tuatara

Sailing

Auckland

Waikato

Bay of Plenty

Kiwi fruit

Hamilton

Geyser

Rotorua

Kiwi

Dairy cattle

Lake Taupo

Traditional Maori war dance

Natural gas

New Plymouth

Wanganui

Ruapehu 9,175 ft (2,796 m)

Napier

Oil rig

Mt. Egmont (Taranaki) 8,260 ft (2,518 m)

Ganne

Hastings

Wanganui

Snapper

Sheep

Palmerston North

Giant tree fern

Lower Hutt

Cook Strait

Parliament House

Nelson

Timber

WELLINGTON

Tasman Sea

Greymouth

South Island

NEW ZEALAND

Sheep

Sperm whale

Christchurch Cathedral

Skiing

Christchurch

SOUTHERN ALPS

Mount Cook lily

Textiles

Milford Sound

Mt. Cook 12,349 ft (3,764 m)

Timaru

Hydroelectricity

Shrimp

PACIFIC OCEAN

Queenstown

Waitaki

Lake Wakatipu

Kea

Chutha

(E) Takahe

Hiking

Dunedin

Invercargill

(E) Blue whales

Foveaux Strait

Albatross colony

Oyster fishing boat

Stewart Island

N / W / E / S

SCALE

MILES
0 — 50 — 100 — 150

KILOMETERS
0 — 50 — 100 — 150 — 200 — 250

MAORI WAR DANCE
Before going to battle, Maori warriors performed a war dance known as a *haka*. During the dance they would stick out their tongues and make fearsome faces.

WHALE SHARK
The whale shark is the largest living fish. It feeds by swimming along with its mouth wide open. It eats only plankton and small fish, and is harmless to humans.

SOLOMON ISLANDS

House on stilts

Choiseul

Santa Isabel

Spotted cuscus

MILES
0   100   200

0   100   200   300
KILOMETERS

NEW GEORGIA ISLANDS

HONIARA ★

Malaita

Guadalcanal

Timber

Bananas

San Cristóbal

Harlequin tuskfish

Rennell

SANTA CRUZ ISLANDS

Coral Sea

SAMOA ISLANDS

SAMOA

Coconuts

Sala'ilua

Savai'i

Making tapa cloth

Bottlenose dolphin

APIA ★

Upolu

AMERICAN SAMOA (U.S.A.)

Pago-Pago

Preparing copra

Tau

Tutuila

MANUA ISLANDS

MILES
0   25   50

0   25   50   75
KILOMETERS

Manta ray

Bluefin tuna

VANUATU AND NEW CALEDONIA

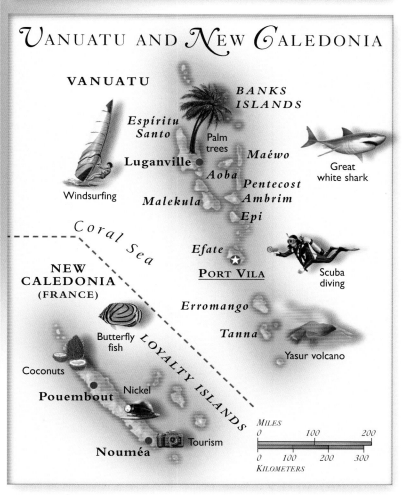

VANUATU

BANKS ISLANDS

Espíritu Santo

Palm trees

Maéwo

Great white shark

Luganville

Aoba

Pentecost

Windsurfing

Malekula

Ambrim

Epi

Coral Sea

Efate

PORT VILA ★

Scuba diving

NEW CALEDONIA (FRANCE)

Butterfly fish

Erromango

Tanna

Yasur volcano

LOYALTY ISLANDS

Coconuts

Pouembout

Nickel

Tourism

Nouméa

MILES
0   100   200

0   100   200   300
KILOMETERS

SOLOMON ISLANDS

FIJI

SAMOA ISLANDS

VANUATU AND NEW CALEDONIA

TONGA

SOCIETY ISLANDS

NEW ZEALAND

FIJI

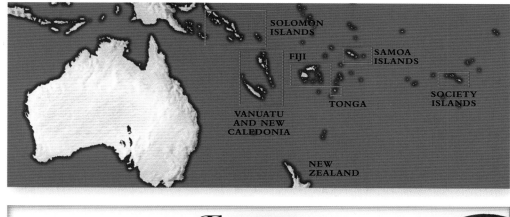

Sugarcane

Vanua Levu

Taveuni

Koro

Tourism

Cocoa

Viti Levu

Walking on hot coals

Koro Sea

LAU GROUP

SUVA ★

Gau

Lakeba

Magnificent frigate bird

Moala

Coconuts

Kandavu

Angelfish

MILES
0   25   50   75

0   50   100   150
KILOMETERS

LOCATION

TONGA

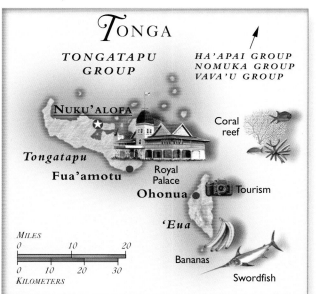

TONGATAPU GROUP

HA'APAI GROUP
NOMUKA GROUP
VAVA'U GROUP

NUKU'ALOFA ★

Coral reef

Tongatapu

Fua'amotu

Royal Palace

Ohonua

Tourism

'Eua

MILES
0   10   20

0   10   20   30
KILOMETERS

Bananas

Swordfish

SOCIETY ISLANDS

Tupai Atoll

Bora-Bora

Lobster

FRENCH POLYNESIA (FRANCE)

Maupiti

Tahaa

HUAHINE ISLANDS

Green turtle

Tourism

Outrigger boat

Raiatea

Pearls

Tetiaroa Atoll

LEEWARD ISLANDS

Surfer in traditional dress

WINDWARD ISLANDS

Paopao

Papeete

Moorea

Whale shark

Palm trees

Maiao

Tahiti

Bananas

MILES
0   25   50

0   25   50   75
KILOMETERS

Taravao

The Polar Regions

THE REGIONS THAT SURROUND the North and South poles are the coldest and windiest parts of our planet. Both are permanently covered in snow and ice, and during winter months there is little or no daylight. Antarctica is a frozen continent surrounded by ocean. The Arctic is an area of frozen ocean surrounded by continents. In winter, the Arctic ice spreads southward, reaching North America, Europe and Asia. The northern fringes of these continents are home to native peoples who have adapted to Arctic life. They include the Saami (Lapps) of Scandinavia and the Inuit of Canada, Alaska, Greenland and Russia. A Danish territory, Greenland is the world's largest island. Most of it lies under a thick sheet of ice. Antarctica is the only continent with no permanent population. Scientists spend part of the year at research stations, but many leave Antarctica before the cold, dark winter sets in. The continent is covered by a vast ice sheet which is two miles (3 km) thick in some places. Along the coast, the ice sheet forms huge ice shelves over the ocean. Giant blocks of ice break off and float away as icebergs. Some icebergs are as large as small countries and take years to melt. There is little life in the Antarctic interior, but whales, seals and fish swim just offshore, and during the summer enormous colonies of seabirds nest along the coast and on nearby islands.

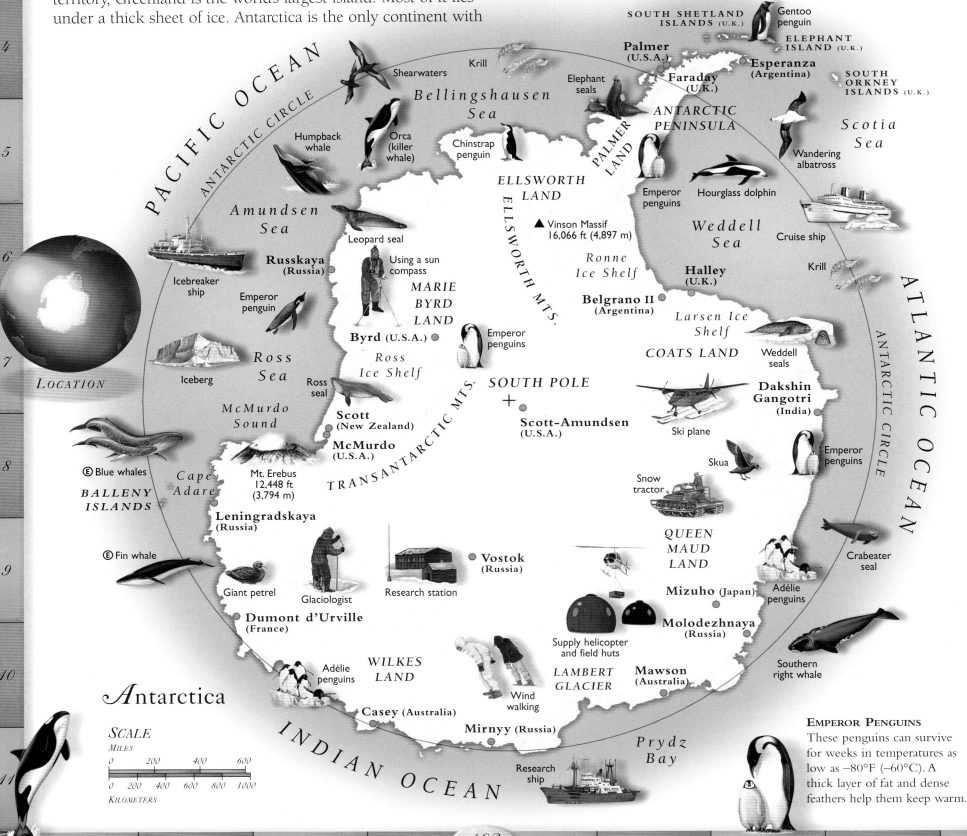

LOCATION

Antarctica

SCALE
MILES
0   200   400   600

0   200   400   600   800   1000
KILOMETERS

EMPEROR PENGUINS
These penguins can survive for weeks in temperatures as low as −80°F (−60°C). A thick layer of fat and dense feathers help them keep warm.

The Arctic

SCALE

MILES

0   200   400   600

0   200   400   600   800   1000

KILOMETERS

· **LOOK AGAIN** ·

● Name four kinds of penguins that live in Antarctica.

● Which minerals are mined on Banks Island in Canada?

● What kind of whale lives in the Barents Sea?

Icebreaker ship

Reindeer

Chukchi hunter

ALASKA (U.S.A.)

Arctic hare

Oil

Chukchi Sea

Pevek

Ambarchik

Wrangel Island

ARCTIC CIRCLE

CANADA

Barrow

Prudhoe Bay

East Siberian Sea

Narwhal

Walrus

NEW SIBERIAN ISLANDS

Gray whale

Snow goose

Beaufort Sea

Arctic tern

Banks Island

Skua

Lena

Ptarmigan

Yakut woman and children

Musk-ox

Zinc and lead

Polar bears

Laptev Sea

RUSSIA

Victoria Island

Snowy owl

ARCTIC OCEAN

Nordvik

Kittiwake

Wolf

Snowmobile

Walrus

SEVERNAYA ZEMLYA

Arctic fox

QUEEN ELIZABETH ISLANDS

NORTH POLE
+

Ⓔ Beluga whale

Dudinka

Resolute

Kara Sea

Hudson Bay

Ellesmere Island

FRANZ JOSEF LAND

Natural gas

ARCTIC CIRCLE

Baffin Island

Walrus tusk carvings

Harp seals

NOVAYA ZEMLYA

Inuit fishing through ice

Thule

Hooded seal

Svalbard reindeer

Haddock

Nenet woman

Jakobshavn houses

Baffin Bay

SVALBARD (NORWAY)

CANADA

Upernavik

Longyearbyen

Barents Sea

Tourism

LOCATION

GREENLAND (DENMARK)

Spitsbergen

Nar'yan-Mar

Davis Strait

Musk-ox

Inuit hunter

Bowhead whale

Harbor seals

Nuuk

Snowmobile

Cod

Orca (killer whale)

NORTH CAPE

Murmansk

Iceberg

Mt. Gunnbjørn 12,139 ft (3,700 m)

Hammerfest

Tourism

Julianehåb

Jan Mayen Island (NORWAY)

Sami (Lapp) man

FINLAND

Denmark Strait

Puffins

Norwegian Sea

CAPE FAREWELL

ICELAND

NORWAY

SWEDEN

CHUKCHI HUNTER

Traditionally, Chukchi people hunted seals, walruses and whales from kayaks, using ivory-tipped harpoons. Now most hunters use rifles and travel in motorboats.

REINDEER

Huge herds of reindeer roam over the tundra in search of food. Their large hooves prevent them from sinking into the snow and help them dig through to reach plants and lichens.

World Fact File

NORTH AMERICA

CANADA

PRONUNCIATION: KA-nuh-duh
AREA: 3,851,809 sq. miles (9,976,185 sq. km)
POPULATION: 31,902,268
CAPITAL: Ottawa
CURRENCY: 100 cents = 1 Canadian dollar (Can$)
OFFICIAL LANGUAGES: English, French
MAIN RELIGION: Christianity 82%
EXPORTS: Newsprint, wood pulp, timber, crude petroleum, machinery, natural gas, aluminum, motor vehicles and parts, telecommunications equipment, electricity

UNITED STATES OF AMERICA

PRONUNCIATION: yoo-NEYE-tuhd STAYTS of uh-MEHR-uh-kuh
AREA: 3,717,800 sq. miles (9,629,091 sq. km)
POPULATION: 280,562,489
CAPITAL: Washington, D.C.
CURRENCY: 100 cents = 1 United States dollar (US$)
OFFICIAL LANGUAGE: English
OTHER LANGUAGE: Spanish
MAIN RELIGIONS: Christianity 84%, Judaism 2%
EXPORTS: Motor vehicles, raw materials, consumer goods, agricultural products, industrial supplies

MEXICO

PRONUNCIATION: MEK-si-koh
AREA: 761,600 sq. miles (1,972,544 sq. km)
POPULATION: 103,400,165
CAPITAL: Mexico City
CURRENCY: 100 centavos = 1 Mexican peso (Mex$)
OFFICIAL LANGUAGE: Spanish
OTHER LANGUAGES: Regional languages
MAIN RELIGION: Christianity 95%
EXPORTS: Crude oil, oil products, coffee, silver, engines, motor vehicles, cotton, electronic goods

GUATEMALA

PRONUNCIATION: gwah-tuh-MAH-luh
AREA: 42,042 sq. miles (108,889 sq. km)
POPULATION: 13,314,079
CAPITAL: Guatemala
CURRENCY: 100 centavos = 1 Guatemalan quetzal (Q)
OFFICIAL LANGUAGE: Spanish
OTHER LANGUAGES: Quiche, Cakchiquel, Kekchi, and other regional languages
MAIN RELIGIONS: Christianity 99%, traditional Mayan religions
EXPORTS: Coffee, bananas, cotton, sugar, minerals, textiles, petroleum

BELIZE

PRONUNCIATION: buh-LEEZ
AREA: 8,867 sq. miles (22,966 sq. km)
POPULATION: 262,999
CAPITAL: Belmopan
CURRENCY: 100 cents = 1 Belizean dollar (Bz$)
OFFICIAL LANGUAGE: English
OTHER LANGUAGES: Spanish, Maya, Garifuna, Creole
MAIN RELIGION: Christianity 92%
EXPORTS: Sugar, molasses, citrus fruit, bananas, clothing, fish products, timber

HONDURAS

PRONUNCIATION: hahn-DER-uhs
AREA: 43,277 sq. miles (112,087 sq. km)
POPULATION: 6,560,608
CAPITAL: Tegucigalpa
CURRENCY: 100 centavos = 1 lempira (L)
OFFICIAL LANGUAGE: Spanish
OTHER LANGUAGES: Regional languages
MAIN RELIGION: Christianity 97%
EXPORTS: Sugar, coffee, textiles, clothing, timber and timber products

EL SALVADOR

PRONUNCIATION: el SAL-vuh-dor
AREA: 8,260 sq. miles (21,393 sq. km)
POPULATION: 6,353,681
CAPITAL: San Salvador
CURRENCY: 100 centavos = 1 Salvadoran colón (C)
OFFICIAL LANGUAGE: Spanish
OTHER LANGUAGE: Nahua
MAIN RELIGION: Christianity 92%
EXPORTS: Coffee, sugarcane, shrimp, raw materials

NICARAGUA

PRONUNCIATION: ni-kuh-RAH-gwuh
AREA: 49,998 sq. miles (129,494 sq. km)
POPULATION: 5,023,818
CAPITAL: Managua
CURRENCY: 100 centavos = 1 gold cordoba (C$)
OFFICIAL LANGUAGE: Spanish
OTHER LANGUAGES: English, regional languages
MAIN RELIGION: Christianity 100%
EXPORTS: Coffee, cotton, sugar, bananas, seafood, gold, beef, tobacco

COSTA RICA

PRONUNCIATION: kaws-tuh REE-kuh
AREA: 19,652 sq. miles (50,899 sq. km)
POPULATION: 3,834,934
CAPITAL: San José
CURRENCY: 100 centimos = 1 Costa Rican colón (C)
OFFICIAL LANGUAGE: Spanish
OTHER LANGUAGE: English
MAIN RELIGION: Christianity 92%
EXPORTS: Coffee, bananas, sugar, textiles, pineapples

PANAMA

PRONUNCIATION: PA-nuh-mah
AREA: 33,659 sq. miles (87,177 sq. km)
POPULATION: 2,882,329
CAPITAL: Panama
CURRENCY: 100 centesimos = 1 balboa (B)

PRONUNCIATION KEY

"a" sounds		"i" sounds		"u" sounds		zh *as in* mea<u>s</u>ure
a	*as in* p<u>a</u>t	i	*as in* p<u>i</u>t	uh	*as in* b<u>u</u>t	s *as in* <u>s</u>et
ah	*as in* f<u>a</u>ther	eye	*as in* b<u>i</u>te		*and* comm<u>a</u>	ch *as in* <u>ch</u>ase
ar	*as in* d<u>ar</u>k	ihr	*as in* h<u>ear</u>	u	*as in* p<u>u</u>t	j *as in* <u>j</u>ug
ay	*as in* b<u>ay</u>				*and* b<u>oo</u>k	g *as in* <u>g</u>ame
air	*as in* p<u>air</u>	"o" sounds		oo	*as in* b<u>oo</u>t	ng *as in* si<u>ng</u>
		o	*as in* p<u>o</u>t	yoo	*as in* m<u>u</u>sic	
"e" sounds		oh	*as in* b<u>oa</u>t			Emphasize the part
e	*as in* p<u>e</u>t	aw	*as in* p<u>aw</u>	other sounds		of the word that
ee	*as in* f<u>ee</u>t	or	*as in* p<u>oor</u>	th	*as in* <u>th</u>in	is written in
er	*as in* p<u>er</u>t	ow	*as in* h<u>ow</u>		*and* <u>th</u>en	**BOLD CAPITAL**
ehr	*as in* S<u>ie</u>rra	oy	*as in* b<u>oy</u>	sh	*as in* <u>sh</u>ow	**LETTERS**

OFFICIAL LANGUAGE: Spanish
OTHER LANGUAGES: English, regional languages
MAIN RELIGION: Christianity 100%
EXPORTS: Bananas, shrimp, sugar, coffee, clothing

THE BAHAMAS

PRONUNCIATION: the buh-HAH-muhz
AREA: 5,386 sq. miles
(13,950 sq. km)
POPULATION: 300,529
CAPITAL: Nassau
CURRENCY: 100 cents = 1 Bahamian dollar (B$)
OFFICIAL LANGUAGE: English
OTHER LANGUAGE: Bahamian creole
MAIN RELIGION: Christianity 95%
EXPORTS: Pharmaceuticals, cement, rum, crayfish, refined petroleum products

CUBA

PRONUNCIATION: KYOO-buh
AREA: 42,804 sq. miles
(110,862 sq. km)
POPULATION: 11,224,321
CAPITAL: Havana
CURRENCY: 100 centavos = 1 Cuban peso (Cu$)
OFFICIAL LANGUAGE: Spanish
MAIN RELIGION: Christianity 85%
EXPORTS: Sugar, fish and shellfish, citrus fruit, coffee, tobacco, nickel, medical products

JAMAICA

PRONUNCIATION: juh-MAY-kuh
AREA: 4,243 sq. miles
(10,990 sq. km)
POPULATION: 2,680,029
CAPITAL: Kingston
CURRENCY: 100 cents = 1 Jamaican dollar (J$)
OFFICIAL LANGUAGE: English
OTHER LANGUAGE: Jamaican creole
MAIN RELIGION: Christianity 65%
EXPORTS: Bauxite, sugar, bananas, rum, alumina

HAITI

PRONUNCIATION: HAY-tee
AREA: 10,714 sq. miles
(27,749 sq. km)
POPULATION: 7,063,722
CAPITAL: Port-au-Prince
CURRENCY: 100 centimes = 1 gourde (G)
OFFICIAL LANGUAGES: French, Haitian creole
MAIN RELIGION: Christianity 96%
EXPORTS: Clothing, coffee, sugar, manufactured goods, oils, mangoes

DOMINICAN REPUBLIC

PRONUNCIATION: duh-MI-ni-kuhn ri-PUH-blik
AREA: 18,657 sq. miles (48,322 sq. km)
POPULATION: 8,721,594
CAPITAL: Santo Domingo
CURRENCY: 100 centavos = 1 Dominican peso (RD$)
OFFICIAL LANGUAGE: Spanish
MAIN RELIGION: Christianity 95%
EXPORTS: Minerals, coffee, cocoa, gold, tobacco

ANTIGUA AND BARBUDA

PRONUNCIATION: an-TEE-guh and bar-BOO-duh
AREA: 171 sq. miles (443 sq. km)
POPULATION: 67,448
CAPITAL: St. John's
CURRENCY: 100 cents = 1 East Caribbean dollar (EC$)
OFFICIAL LANGUAGE: English
OTHER LANGUAGES: Regional languages
MAIN RELIGIONS: Christianity 97%, indigenous religions 3%
EXPORTS: Petroleum products, manufactured goods, machinery and transportation equipment, food and livestock

ST. KITTS–NEVIS

PRONUNCIATION: saynt KITS NEE-vuhs
AREA: 104 sq. miles (269 sq. km)
POPULATION: 38,736
CAPITAL: Basseterre
CURRENCY: 100 cents = 1 East Caribbean dollar (EC$)
OFFICIAL LANGUAGE: English
MAIN RELIGION: Christianity 86%
EXPORTS: Machinery, food, beverages, electronics, tobacco

DOMINICA

PRONUNCIATION: dah-muh-NEE-kuh
AREA: 289 sq. miles (749 sq. km)
POPULATION: 70,158
CAPITAL: Roseau
CURRENCY: 100 cents = 1 East Caribbean dollar (EC$)
OFFICIAL LANGUAGE: English
OTHER LANGUAGE: French patois
MAIN RELIGION: Christianity 92%
EXPORTS: Bananas, grapefruit, oranges, vegetables, soap, bay oil

ST. LUCIA

PRONUNCIATION: saynt LOO-shuh
AREA: 238 sq. miles (616 sq. km)
POPULATION: 160,145
CAPITAL: Castries
CURRENCY: 100 cents = 1 East Caribbean dollar (EC$)
OFFICIAL LANGUAGE: English
OTHER LANGUAGE: French patois
MAIN RELIGION: Christianity 100%
EXPORTS: Bananas, clothing, cocoa, coconut oil, fruit and vegetables

BARBADOS

PRONUNCIATION: bar-BAY-dohs
AREA: 166 sq. miles (430 sq. km)
POPULATION: 276,607
CAPITAL: Bridgetown
CURRENCY: 100 cents = 1 Barbadian dollar (Bds$)
OFFICIAL LANGUAGE: English
OTHER LANGUAGE: Barbadian creole
MAIN RELIGION: Christianity 71%
EXPORTS: Sugar and molasses, rum, chemicals, foods and beverages, electrical components, clothing

ST. VINCENT AND THE GRENADINES

PRONUNCIATION: saynt VIN-suhnt and the gren-uh-DEENZ
AREA: 150 sq. miles (389 sq. km)
POPULATION: 116,394
CAPITAL: Kingstown
CURRENCY: 100 cents = 1 East Caribbean dollar (EC$)
OFFICIAL LANGUAGE: English
OTHER LANGUAGE: French patois
MAIN RELIGION: Christianity 75%
EXPORTS: Bananas, taro, tennis rackets, arrowroot

GRENADA

PRONUNCIATION: gruh-NAY-duh
AREA: 133 sq. miles (344 sq. km)
POPULATION: 89,211
CAPITAL: St. George's
CURRENCY: 100 cents = 1 East Caribbean dollar (EC$)
OFFICIAL LANGUAGE: English
OTHER LANGUAGE: French patois
MAIN RELIGION: Christianity 100%
EXPORTS: Bananas, fruit and vegetables, cocoa, nutmeg, clothing, mace

TRINIDAD AND TOBAGO

PRONUNCIATION: TRI-nuh-dad and tuh-BAY-goh
AREA: 1,980 sq. miles (5,128 sq. km)
POPULATION: 1,163,724
CAPITAL: Port-of-Spain
CURRENCY: 100 cents = 1 Trinidad and Tobago dollar (TT$)
OFFICIAL LANGUAGE: English
OTHER LANGUAGES: Hindi, French, Spanish, Chinese
MAIN RELIGIONS: Christianity 44%, Hinduism 24%, Islam 6%
EXPORTS: Petroleum and petroleum products, chemicals, steel products, fertilizer, sugar, cocoa, coffee, citrus fruit, flowers

SOUTH AMERICA

COLOMBIA
PRONUNCIATION: kuh-LUHM-bee-uh
AREA: 439,735 sq. miles
(1,138,914 sq. km)
POPULATION: 41,008,227
CAPITAL: Bogota
CURRENCY: 100 centavos = 1 Colombian
peso (Col$)
OFFICIAL LANGUAGE: Spanish
MAIN RELIGION: Christianity 90%
EXPORTS: Petroleum, coffee, coal, bananas, flowers

VENEZUELA
PRONUNCIATION: ve-nuh-ZWAY-luh
AREA: 352,143 sq. miles
(912,050 sq. km)
POPULATION: 24,287,670
CAPITAL: Caracas
CURRENCY: 100 centimos = 1 bolivar (Bs)
OFFICIAL LANGUAGE: Spanish
OTHER LANGUAGES: Regional languages
MAIN RELIGION: Christianity 98%
EXPORTS: Petroleum, bauxite and aluminum,
steel, chemicals, agricultural products, basic
manufactured goods

GUYANA
PRONUNCIATION: geye-AH-nuh
AREA: 83,000 sq. miles
(214,970 sq. km)
POPULATION: 698,209
CAPITAL: Georgetown
CURRENCY: 100 cents = 1 Guyanese dollar (G$)
OFFICIAL LANGUAGE: English
OTHER LANGUAGES: Local languages, Hindi, Urdu
MAIN RELIGIONS: Christianity 50%,
Hinduism 33%, Islam 9%
EXPORTS: Sugar, molasses, bauxite, rice, shrimp

SURINAME
PRONUNCIATION: SUR-uh-nah-muh
AREA: 63,039 sq. miles
(163,270 sq. km)
POPULATION: 436,494
CAPITAL: Paramaribo
CURRENCY: 100 cents = 1 Surinamese guilder or
florin (Sf)
OFFICIAL LANGUAGE: Dutch
OTHER LANGUAGES: English, Sranang Tongo,
Hindustani, Javanese
MAIN RELIGIONS: Christianity 48%,
Hinduism 27%, Islam 20%, regional religions 5%
EXPORTS: Aluminum, fish,
shrimp, timber, rice,
bananas, crude oil

ECUADOR
PRONUNCIATION: E-kwuh-dor
AREA: 109,483 sq. miles
(283,561 sq. km)
POPULATION: 13,447,494
CAPITAL: Quito
CURRENCY: 100 cents = 1 United States dollar (US$)
OFFICIAL LANGUAGE: Spanish
OTHER LANGUAGES: Quechua, other regional
languages
MAIN RELIGION: Christianity 95%
EXPORTS: Petroleum, bananas, shrimp, cocoa,
coffee, flowers, fish

PERU
PRONUNCIATION: puh-ROO
AREA: 496,222 sq. miles
(1,285,215 sq. km)
POPULATION: 27,949,639
CAPITAL: Lima
CURRENCY: 100 centimos = 1 nuevo sol (S/.)
OFFICIAL LANGUAGES: Spanish, Quechua
OTHER LANGUAGE: Aymara
MAIN RELIGION: Christianity 90%
EXPORTS: Copper, zinc, petroleum products, lead,
coffee, cotton, fish and fish products, sugar

BRAZIL
PRONUNCIATION: bruh-ZIL
AREA: 3,286,470 sq. miles
(8,511,965 sq. km)
POPULATION: 176,029,560
CAPITAL: Brasília
CURRENCY: 100 centavos = 1 real (R$)
OFFICIAL LANGUAGE: Portuguese
OTHER LANGUAGES: Spanish, English, French
MAIN RELIGION: Christianity 80%
EXPORTS: Iron ore, soybean bran, coffee, sugar,
footwear, manufactured goods

BOLIVIA
PRONUNCIATION: buh-LI-vee-uh
AREA: 424,162 sq. miles
(1,098,579 sq. km)
POPULATION: 8,445,134
CAPITALS: La Paz (seat of government),
Sucre (legal and judicial)
CURRENCY: 100 centavos = 1 boliviano ($B)
OFFICIAL LANGUAGES: Spanish, Quechua, Aymara
MAIN RELIGION: Christianity 100%
EXPORTS: Natural gas, soybeans, zinc, gold
jewelry, timber

CHILE
PRONUNCIATION: CHI-lee
AREA: 292,257 sq. miles
(756,946 sq. km)
POPULATION: 15,498,930
CAPITAL: Santiago
CURRENCY: 100 centavos = 1 Chilean peso (Ch$)
OFFICIAL LANGUAGE: Spanish
OTHER LANGUAGES: Regional languages
MAIN RELIGION: Christianity 99%
EXPORTS: Copper, metals and minerals, timber
products, fish, fruit, chemicals

PARAGUAY
PRONUNCIATION: PAR-uh-gweye
AREA: 157,043 sq. miles
(406,741 sq. km)
POPULATION: 5,884,491
CAPITAL: Asunción
CURRENCY: 100 centimos = 1 guarani (G)
OFFICIAL LANGUAGES: Spanish, Guarani
MAIN RELIGION: Christianity 97%
EXPORTS: Cotton, soybeans, timber, vegetable
oils, meat products, coffee, electricity, feed
for livestock

ARGENTINA
PRONUNCIATION: ar-juhn-TEE-nuh
AREA: 1,068,296 sq. miles
(2,766,884 sq. km)
POPULATION: 37,812,817
CAPITAL: Buenos Aires
CURRENCY: 100 centavos = 1 Argentine peso (ARS)
OFFICIAL LANGUAGE: Spanish
OTHER LANGUAGES: English, Italian,
German, French
MAIN RELIGIONS: Christianity 92%, Judaism 2%
EXPORTS: Manufactured goods, meat, wheat, corn,
vegetable oil, fuel and energy

URUGUAY
PRONUNCIATION: OOR-uh-gweye
AREA: 68,039 sq. miles
(176,221 sq. km)
POPULATION: 3,386,575
CAPITAL: Montevideo
CURRENCY: 100 centesimos = 1 Uruguayan peso
($Ur)
OFFICIAL LANGUAGE: Spanish
OTHER LANGUAGE: Brazilero
MAIN RELIGIONS: Christianity 68%, Judaism 1%
EXPORTS: Wool, textiles, beef and other animal
products, leather, rice

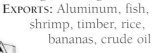

EUROPE

UNITED KINGDOM

PRONUNCIATION: yoo-NEYE-tuhd KING-duhm
AREA: 94,525 sq. miles (244,820 sq. km)
POPULATION: 58,836,700
CAPITAL: London
CURRENCY: 100 pence = 1 British pound (£)
OFFICIAL LANGUAGE: English
OTHER LANGUAGES: Welsh, Scottish Gaelic, Irish Gaelic
MAIN RELIGIONS: Christianity 90%, Islam 3%, Sikh 1%, Hinduism 1%, Judaism 1%
EXPORTS: Manufactured goods, machinery, fuels, chemicals, food and beverages, tobacco

IRELAND

PRONUNCIATION: EYER-luhnd
AREA: 26,600 sq. miles (68,894 sq. km)
POPULATION: 3,883,159
CAPITAL: Dublin
CURRENCY: 100 cents = 1 euro (€)
OFFICIAL LANGUAGES: English, Irish (Gaelic)
MAIN RELIGION: Christianity 94%
EXPORTS: Chemicals, data processing equipment, industrial machinery, livestock, animal products, pharmacueticals

PORTUGAL

PRONUNCIATION: POR-chi-guhl
AREA: 35,383 sq. miles (91,642 sq. km)
POPULATION: 10,084,245
CAPITAL: Lisbon
CURRENCY: 100 cents = 1 euro (€)
OFFICIAL LANGUAGE: Portuguese
MAIN RELIGION: Christianity 98%
EXPORTS: Clothing, footwear, machinery, cork, paper products, animal hides, chemicals

SPAIN

PRONUNCIATION: spayn
AREA: 194,881 sq. miles (504,742 sq. km)
POPULATION: 40,077,100
CAPITAL: Madrid
CURRENCY: 100 cents = 1 euro (€)
OFFICIAL LANGUAGE: Castilian Spanish
OTHER LANGUAGES: Catalan, Galician, Basque
MAIN RELIGION: Christianity 99%
EXPORTS: Motor vehicles, manufactured goods, food, machinery, consumer goods

ANDORRA

PRONUNCIATION: an-DOR-uh
AREA: 180 sq. miles (482 sq. km)
POPULATION: 68,403
CAPITAL: Andorra la Vella
CURRENCIES: 100 cents = 1 euro (€)
OFFICIAL LANGUAGE: Catalan
OTHER LANGUAGES: French, Castilian Spanish
MAIN RELIGION: Christianity 95%
EXPORTS: Electricity, tobacco products, timber, furniture

FRANCE

PRONUNCIATION: frans
AREA: 211,209 sq. miles (547,030 sq. km)
POPULATION: 59,765,983
CAPITAL: Paris
CURRENCY: 100 cents = 1 euro (€)
OFFICIAL LANGUAGE: French
OTHER LANGUAGES: Occitan, Breton, Catalan, Basque, Arabic, Corsican, Flemish, Alsatian
MAIN RELIGIONS: Christianity 92%, Judaism 1%, Islam 3%
EXPORTS: Machinery and transportation equipment, chemicals, food, agricultural products, iron and steel, textiles, clothing, pharmacueticals

MONACO

PRONUNCIATION: MAH-nuh-koh
AREA: 0.58 sq. miles (1.5 sq. km)
POPULATION: 31,987
CAPITAL: Monaco
CURRENCY: 100 cents = 1 euro (€)
OFFICIAL LANGUAGE: French
OTHER LANGUAGES: English, Italian, Monégasque
MAIN RELIGION: Christianity 95%
EXPORTS: Pharmaceuticals, perfumes, clothing

THE NETHERLANDS

PRONUNCIATION: the NE-ther-luhndz
AREA: 16,033 sq. miles (41,525 sq. km)
POPULATION: 16,067,754
CAPITALS: Amsterdam; The Hague (judicial)
CURRENCY: 100 cents = 1 euro (€)
OFFICIAL LANGUAGE: Dutch
MAIN RELIGIONS: Christianity 52%, Islam 4%
EXPORTS: Metal products, chemicals, processed food, tobacco, agricultural products, machinery and equipment

BELGIUM

PRONUNCIATION: bel-juhm
AREA: 11,781 sq. miles (30,513 sq. km)
POPULATION: 10,274,595
CAPITAL: Brussels
CURRENCY: 100 cents = 1 euro (€)
OFFICIAL LANGUAGES: Dutch (Flemish), French
OTHER LANGUAGE: German
MAIN RELIGION: Christianity 100%
EXPORTS: Iron and steel, machinery and equipment, chemicals, diamonds, petroleum products

LUXEMBOURG

PRONUNCIATION: LUK-suhm-berg
AREA: 999 sq. miles (2,587 sq. km)
POPULATION: 429,100
CAPITAL: Luxembourg
CURRENCY: 100 cents = 1 euro (€)
OFFICIAL LANGUAGES: Luxembourgish (Letzeburgesh), German, French
OTHER LANGUAGE: English
MAIN RELIGIONS: Christianity 99%, Judaism 1%
EXPORTS: Steel products, chemicals, rubber products, glass, aluminum, machinery and equipment

GERMANY

PRONUNCIATION: JER-muh-nee
AREA: 137,735 sq. miles (356,734 sq. km)
POPULATION: 83,251,851
CAPITAL: Berlin
CURRENCY: 100 cents = 1 euro (€)
OFFICIAL LANGUAGE: German
MAIN RELIGIONS: Christianity 72%, Islam 2%
EXPORTS: Machines and machine tools, chemicals, motor vehicles, iron and steel products, textiles, agricultural products, raw materials

SWITZERLAND

PRONUNCIATION: SWIT-suhr-luhnd
AREA: 15,941 sq. miles (41,287 sq. km)
POPULATION: 7,301,994
CAPITAL: Bern
CURRENCY: 100 centimes = 1 Swiss franc (CHF)
OFFICIAL LANGUAGES: German, French, Italian
OTHER LANGUAGE: Romansch
MAIN RELIGION: Christianity 86%
EXPORTS: Machinery, precision instruments, metal products, food, textiles, chemicals

LIECHTENSTEIN

PRONUNCIATION: LIK-tuhn-shteyen
AREA: 62 sq. miles (161 sq. km)
POPULATION: 32,842
CAPITAL: Vaduz
CURRENCY: 100 centimes = 1 Swiss franc (CHF)
OFFICIAL LANGUAGE: German
MAIN RELIGION: Christianity 87%
EXPORTS: Machinery, dental products, stamps, hardware, pottery

AUSTRIA

PRONUNCIATION: AWS-tree-uh
AREA: 32,375 sq. miles
(83,851 sq. km)
POPULATION: 8,169,929
CAPITAL: Vienna
CURRENCY: 100 cents = 1 euro (€)
OFFICIAL LANGUAGE: German
MAIN RELIGION: Christianity 82%
EXPORTS: Machinery, electrical equipment, iron and steel, lumber, textiles, paper and paper products, chemicals, foodstuffs, metal goods

ITALY

PRONUNCIATION: IT-uh-lee
AREA: 116,313 sq. miles
(301,251 sq. km)
POPULATION: 57,715,625
CAPITAL: Rome
CURRENCY: 100 cents = 1 euro (€)
OFFICIAL LANGUAGE: Italian
OTHER LANGUAGES: German, French, Slovene
MAIN RELIGION: Christianity 98%
EXPORTS: Textiles, clothing, machinery, motor vehicles, transportation equipment, chemicals, food products, minerals

SAN MARINO

PRONUNCIATION: san muh-REE-noh
AREA: 24 sq. miles (62 sq. km)
POPULATION: 27,730
CAPITAL: San Marino
CURRENCY: 100 cents = 1 euro (€)
OFFICIAL LANGUAGE: Italian
MAIN RELIGION: Christianity 95%
EXPORTS: Building stone, lime, timber, chestnuts, wheat, wine, baked goods, animal skins, ceramics

VATICAN CITY

PRONUNCIATION: VA-ti-kuhn city
AREA: 0.17 sq. miles (0.44 sq. km)
POPULATION: 900
CAPITAL: Vatican City
CURRENCY: 100 cents = 1 euro (€)
OFFICIAL LANGUAGES: Italian, Latin, French
MAIN RELIGION: Christianity 100%
EXPORTS: None

MALTA

PRONUNCIATION: MAWL-tuh
AREA: 122 sq. miles (316 sq. km)
POPULATION: 397,499
CAPITAL: Valletta
CURRENCY: 100 cents = 1 Maltese lira (LM)
OFFICIAL LANGUAGES: Maltese, English
MAIN RELIGION: Christianity 98%
EXPORTS: Machinery and transportation equipment, clothing, footwear

SLOVENIA

PRONUNCIATION: sloh-VEE-nee-uh
AREA: 7,819 sq. miles (20,251 sq. km)
POPULATION: 1,932,917
CAPITAL: Ljubljana
CURRENCY: 100 stotins = 1 tolar (SIT)
OFFICIAL LANGUAGE: Slovenian
OTHER LANGUAGE: Serbo-Croatian
MAIN RELIGIONS: Christianity 72%, Islam 1%
EXPORTS: Motor vehicles, furniture, machinery, manufactured goods, chemicals, textiles, food, raw materials

CROATIA

PRONUNCIATION: kroh-AY-shuh
AREA: 21,829 sq. miles
(56,537 sq. km)
POPULATION: 4,390,751
CAPITAL: Zagreb
CURRENCY: 100 lipas = 1 Croatian kuna (HRK)
OFFICIAL LANGUAGE: Serbo-Croatian
MAIN RELIGIONS: Christianity 88%, Islam 1%
EXPORTS: Machinery and transportation equipment, other manufactured goods, chemicals, food, livestock, raw materials, fuels, textiles

BOSNIA AND HERZEGOVINA

PRONUNCIATION: BAHZ-nee-uh and hert-suh-goh-VEE-nuh
AREA: 19,740 sq. miles (51,129 sq. km)
POPULATION: 3,964,388
CAPITAL: Sarajevo
CURRENCY: 100 pfenniga = 1 marka (BAM)
OFFICIAL LANGUAGES: Serbo-Croatian, Bosnian
MAIN RELIGIONS: Christianity 50%, Islam 40%
EXPORTS: Timber, furniture

YUGOSLAVIA

PRONUNCIATION: yoo-goh-SLAH-vee-uh
AREA: 39,449 sq. miles (102,173 sq. km)
POPULATION: 10,656,929
CAPITAL: Belgrade
CURRENCY: 100 paras = 1 Yugoslav new dinar (YD)
OFFICIAL LANGUAGE: Serbo-Croatian
OTHER LANGUAGE: Albanian
MAIN RELIGIONS: Christianity 70%, Islam 19%
EXPORTS: Manufactured goods, raw materials, food

ROMANIA

PRONUNCIATION: roh-MAY-nee-uh
AREA: 91,699 sq. miles (237,500 sq. km)
POPULATION: 22,317,730
CAPITAL: Bucharest
CURRENCY: 100 bani = 1 leu (L)
OFFICIAL LANGUAGE: Romanian
OTHER LANGUAGES: Hungarian, German
MAIN RELIGION: Christianity 82%
EXPORTS: Metals and metal products, minerals and fuels, textiles and footwear, electrical goods, machinery and equipment

BULGARIA

PRONUNCIATION: buhl-GAIR-ee-uh
AREA: 42,823 sq. miles
(110,912 sq. km)
POPULATION: 7,621,337
CAPITAL: Sofia
CURRENCY: 100 stotinki = 1 lev (Lv)
OFFICIAL LANGUAGE: Bulgarian
MAIN RELIGIONS: Christianity 86%, Islam 13%, Judaism 1%
EXPORTS: Machinery and equipment, fuels, minerals and raw materials, metals, clothing, footwear

ALBANIA

PRONUNCIATION: al-BAY-nee-uh
AREA: 11,100 sq. miles
(28,749 sq. km)
POPULATION: 3,544,841
CAPITAL: Tiranë
CURRENCY: 100 qintars = 1 lek (L)
OFFICIAL LANGUAGE: Albanian (Tosk dialect)
OTHER LANGUAGE: Greek
MAIN RELIGIONS: Islam 70%, Christianity 30%
EXPORTS: Asphalt, metals and metallic ores, electricity, crude oil, fruit and vegetables, tobacco

MACEDONIA

PRONUNCIATION: ma-suh-DOH-nee-uh
AREA: 9,928 sq. miles (25,714 sq. km)
POPULATION: 2,054,800
CAPITAL: Skopje
CURRENCY: 100 deni = 1 Macedonian denar (MKD)
OFFICIAL LANGUAGE: Macedonian
OTHER LANGUAGES: Albanian, Turkish, Serbo-Croatian
MAIN RELIGIONS: Christianity 67%, Islam 30%
EXPORTS: Manufactured goods, machinery and transportation equipment, food, beverages, tobacco, iron and steel

GREECE

PRONUNCIATION: grees
AREA: 50,944 sq. miles
(131,945 sq. km)
POPULATION: 10,645,343
CAPITAL: Athens
CURRENCY: 100 cents = 1 euro (€)
OFFICIAL LANGUAGE: Greek
OTHER LANGUAGES: English, French
MAIN RELIGIONS: Christianity 98%, Islam 1%
EXPORTS: Manufactured goods, food, petroleum

ESTONIA

PRONUNCIATION: e-STOH-nee-uh
AREA: 17,413 sq. miles
(45,100 sq. km)
POPULATION: 1,415,681
CAPITAL: Tallinn
CURRENCY: 100 cents = 1 Estonian kroon (EEK)
OFFICIAL LANGUAGE: Estonian
OTHER LANGUAGES: Russian, Ukrainian, English
MAIN RELIGION: Christianity 99%
EXPORTS: Textiles, food, machinery, timber

LATVIA

PRONUNCIATION: lat-vee-uh

AREA: 24,938 sq. miles (64,589 sq. km)

POPULATION: 2,366,515

CAPITAL: Riga

CURRENCY: 100 santims = 1 Latvian lat (LVL)

OFFICIAL LANGUAGE: Latvian (Lettish)

OTHER LANGUAGES: Lithuanian, Russian

MAIN RELIGION: Christianity 100%

EXPORTS: Timber, metals, dairy products, furniture, textiles, machinery and equipment

LITHUANIA

PRONUNCIATION: li-thuh-WAY-nee-uh

AREA: 25,174 sq. miles (65,201 sq. km)

POPULATION: 3,601,138

CAPITAL: Vilnius

CURRENCY: 100 centas = 1 Lithuan litas (Lt)

OFFICIAL LANGUAGE: Lithuanian

OTHER LANGUAGES: Polish, Russian

MAIN RELIGION: Christianity 98%

EXPORTS: Machinery, minerals, chemicals, textiles and clothing, food

BELARUS

PRONUNCIATION: be-luh-ROOS

AREA: 80,154 sq. miles (207,599 sq. km)

POPULATION: 10,335,382

CAPITAL: Minsk

CURRENCY: Belarussian rubel (BR)

OFFICIAL LANGUAGE: Belarussian

OTHER LANGUAGE: Russian

MAIN RELIGION: Christianity 80%

EXPORTS: Machinery and equipment, chemicals, food, metals, textiles

POLAND

PRONUNCIATION: POH-luhnd

AREA: 120,756 sq. miles (312,758 sq. km)

POPULATION: 38,625,478

CAPITAL: Warsaw

CURRENCY: 100 groszy = 1 zloty (Zl)

OFFICIAL LANGUAGE: Polish

MAIN RELIGION: Christianity 95%

EXPORTS: Machinery and transportation equipment, manufactured goods, food and livestock, fuels

CZECH REPUBLIC

PRONUNCIATION: chek ri-PUH-blik

AREA: 30,450 sq. miles (78,866 sq. km)

POPULATION: 10,256,760

CAPITAL: Prague

CURRENCY: 100 haleru = 1 Czech koruna (CZK)

OFFICIAL LANGUAGE: Czech

MAIN RELIGION: Christianity 47%

EXPORTS: Manufactured goods, raw materials and fuels, machinery and transportation equipment, chemicals, agricultural products

SLOVAKIA

PRONUNCIATION: sloh-VAH-kee-uh

AREA: 18,923 sq. miles (49,011 sq. km)

POPULATION: 5,422,366

CAPITAL: Bratislava

CURRENCY: 100 halierov = 1 Slovak koruna (Sk)

OFFICIAL LANGUAGE: Slovak

OTHER LANGUAGE: Hungarian

MAIN RELIGION: Christianity 73%

EXPORTS: Machinery and transportation equipment, chemicals, minerals and metals, manufactured goods, agricultural products

UKRAINE

PRONUNCIATION: yoo-KRAYN

AREA: 233,089 sq. miles (603,701 sq. km)

POPULATION: 48,396,470

CAPITAL: Kiev

CURRENCY: 100 kopiykas = 1 hryvnia

OFFICIAL LANGUAGE: Ukrainian

OTHER LANGUAGES: Russian, Romanian, Polish, Hungarian

MAIN RELIGIONS: Christianity 90%, Judaism 2%

EXPORTS: Metals, chemicals, machinery and transportation equipment, grain, meat, fuel and petroleum products

HUNGARY

PRONUNCIATION: HUHNG-uh-ree

AREA: 35,919 sq. miles (93,030 sq. km)

POPULATION: 10,075,034

CAPITAL: Budapest

CURRENCY: 100 filler = 1 forint (Ft)

OFFICIAL LANGUAGE: Hungarian

MAIN RELIGION: Christianity 93%

EXPORTS: Raw materials, machinery and transportation equipment, manufactured goods, food products, agriculture, fuels, energy

MOLDOVA

PRONUNCIATION: mawl-DOH-vuh

AREA: 13,012 sq. miles (33,701 sq. km)

POPULATION: 4,434,547

CAPITAL: Chişinău

CURRENCY: Moldovan Leu (L)

OFFICIAL LANGUAGE: Moldovan

OTHER LANGUAGES: Russian, Gagauz

MAIN RELIGIONS: Christianity 98%, Judaism 2%

EXPORTS: Food, wine, tobacco, textiles, footwear, machinery, chemicals

ICELAND

PRONUNCIATION: EYES-luhnd

AREA: 39,702 sq. miles (102,828 sq. km)

POPULATION: 279,384

CAPITAL: Reykjavik

CURRENCY: 100 aurar = 1 Icelandic krona (IKr)

OFFICIAL LANGUAGE: Icelandic

MAIN RELIGION: Christianity 99%

EXPORTS: Fish and fish products, animal products, minerals

NORWAY

PRONUNCIATION: nor-way

AREA: 125,181 sq. miles (324,220 sq. km)

POPULATION: 4,525,116

CAPITAL: Oslo

CURRENCY: 100 oere = 1 Norwegian krone (NKr)

OFFICIAL LANGUAGE: Norwegian

OTHER LANGUAGES: Finnish, Sami

MAIN RELIGION: Christianity 89%

EXPORTS: Petroleum and petroleum products, metals, fish and fish products, chemicals, ships, machinery and equipment, natural gas

SWEDEN

PRONUNCIATION: swee-duhn

AREA: 173,665 sq. miles (449,792 sq. km)

POPULATION: 8,912,000

CAPITAL: Stockholm

CURRENCY: 100 oere = 1 Swedish krona (SKr)

OFFICIAL LANGUAGE: Swedish

OTHER LANGUAGES: Finnish, Sami

MAIN RELIGION: Christianity 96%

EXPORTS: Machinery, motor vehicles, paper products, pulp and wood, iron and steel products, chemicals, petroleum products

FINLAND

PRONUNCIATION: FIN-luhnd

AREA: 130,128 sq. miles (337,032 sq. km)

POPULATION: 5,183,545

CAPITAL: Helsinki

CURRENCY: 100 cents = 1 euro (€)

OFFICIAL LANGUAGES: Finnish, Swedish

OTHER LANGUAGES: Sami, Russian

MAIN RELIGION: Christianity 90%

EXPORTS: Paper and pulp, machinery and equipment, chemicals, metals, timber

DENMARK

PRONUNCIATION: den-mark

AREA: 16,629 sq. miles (43,069 sq. km)

POPULATION: 5,368,854

CAPITAL: Copenhagen

CURRENCY: 100 ore = 1 Danish krone (DKr)

OFFICIAL LANGUAGE: Danish

OTHER LANGUAGES: Faroese, Greenlandic, German

MAIN RELIGION: Christianity 98%

EXPORTS: Meat and meat products, dairy products, ships, fish, chemicals, machinery and instruments, furniture, windmills

ASIA

RUSSIA

PRONUNCIATION: RUH-shuh
AREA: 6,592,812 sq. miles
(17,075,383 sq. km)
POPULATION: 144,978,573
CAPITAL: Moscow
CURRENCY: 100 kopecks = 1 Russian ruble (R)
OFFICIAL LANGUAGE: Russian
MAIN RELIGIONS: Christianity 75%, Islam,
Buddhism
EXPORTS: Petroleum and petroleum products,
natural gas, timber and timber products, metals,
chemicals, manufactured goods

TURKEY

PRONUNCIATION: TER-kee
AREA: 301,380 sq. miles
(780,574 sq. km)
POPULATION: 67,308,928
CAPITAL: Ankara
CURRENCY: Turkish lira (TL)
OFFICIAL LANGUAGE: Turkish
OTHER LANGUAGES: Kurdish, Arabic, Armenian
MAIN RELIGION: Islam 99%
EXPORTS: Manufactured goods, food, textiles
and clothing, transport equipment

CYPRUS

PRONUNCIATION: SEYE-pruhs
AREA: 3,572 sq. miles (9,251 sq. km)
POPULATION: 767,314
CAPITAL: Nicosia
CURRENCY: 100 cents = 1 Cypriot pound (£C);
100 kurus = 1 Turkish lira (TL)
OFFICIAL LANGUAGES: Greek, Turkish
OTHER LANGUAGE: English
MAIN RELIGIONS: Christianity 78%, Islam 18%
EXPORTS: Citrus fruit, potatoes, grapes, wine,
cement, textiles and clothing, shoes

GEORGIA

PRONUNCIATION: JOR-juh
AREA: 26,911 sq. miles
(69,699 sq. km)
POPULATION: 4,960,951
CAPITAL: T'bilisi
CURRENCY: Lari (GEL)
OFFICIAL LANGUAGE: Georgian
OTHER LANGUAGES: Russian, Armenian, Azeri
MAIN RELIGIONS: Christianity 83%, Islam 11%
EXPORTS: Citrus fruit, tea, wine, machinery,
metals, textiles, chemicals, fuel re-exports

ARMENIA

PRONUNCIATION: ar-MEE-nee-uh
AREA: 11,506 sq. miles
(29,800 sq. km)
POPULATION: 3,330,099
CAPITAL: Yerevan
CURRENCY: 100 luma = 1 dram (AMD)
OFFICIAL LANGUAGE: Armenian
OTHER LANGUAGES: Russian, Azeri
MAIN RELIGION: Christianity 94%
EXPORTS: Diamonds, scrap metal, machinery
and equipment, brandy, copper ore

AZERBAIJAN

PRONUNCIATION: a-zuhr-beye-ZHAHN
AREA: 33,436 sq. miles
(86,599 sq. km)
POPULATION: 7,798,497
CAPITAL: Baku
CURRENCY: 100 gopiks = 1 Azerbaijani manat (AzM)
OFFICIAL LANGUAGE: Azerbaijani
OTHER LANGUAGES: Russian, Armenian
MAIN RELIGIONS: Islam 94%, Christianity 5%
EXPORTS: Oil, gas, chemicals, oil field equipment,
textiles, cotton, foodstuffs

KAZAKSTAN

PRONUNCIATION: kuh-zahk-STAHN
AREA: 1,049,150 sq. miles
(2,717,300 sq. km)
POPULATION: 16,741,519
CAPITAL: Astana
CURRENCY: 100 tiyn = 1 tenge (KZT)
OFFICIAL LANGUAGES: Kazak, Russian
MAIN RELIGIONS: Islam 47%, Christianity 46%
EXPORTS: Oil, metals, chemicals, grain, wool,
cotton, machinery, ferrous and non-ferrous metals,
meat and livestock, coal

UZBEKISTAN

PRONUNCIATION: uz-be-ki-STAN
AREA: 172,741 sq. miles
(447,400 sq. km)
POPULATION: 25,563,441
CAPITAL: Tashkent
CURRENCY: Uzbekistani Sum (UKS)
OFFICIAL LANGUAGE: Uzbek
OTHER LANGUAGES: Russian, Tajik
MAIN RELIGIONS: Islam 88%, Christianity 9%
EXPORTS: Cotton, gold, natural gas, mineral
fertilizer, metals, textiles, food, automobiles

TURKMENISTAN

PRONUNCIATION: terk-me-nuh-STAN
AREA: 188,455 sq. miles
(488,098 sq. km)
POPULATION: 4,688,963
CAPITAL: Ashkhabad
CURRENCY: 100 tenesi = 1 Turkmen manat (TMM)
OFFICIAL LANGUAGE: Turkmen
OTHER LANGUAGES: Russian, Uzbek
MAIN RELIGIONS: Islam 89%, Christianity 9%
EXPORTS: Natural gas, cotton, petroleum products,
textiles, carpets

KYRGYZSTAN

PRONUNCIATION: kihr-gi-STAN
AREA: 76,641 sq. miles
(198,500 sq. km)
POPULATION: 4,822,166
CAPITAL: Bishkek
CURRENCY: 100 tyiyn = 1 Kyrgyzstani som (KGS)
OFFICIAL LANGUAGES: Kyrgyz (Kirghiz), Russian
MAIN RELIGIONS: Islam 75%, Christianity 20%
EXPORTS: Wool, chemicals, cotton, metals, shoes,
machinery, tobacco, potatoes, vegetables, fruits,
sheep, goats, cattle

TAJIKISTAN

PRONUNCIATION: tah-ji-ki-STAN
AREA: 55,251 sq. miles
(143,100 sq. km)
POPULATION: 6,719,567
CAPITAL: Dushanbe
CURRENCY: 100 diram = 1 somoni (SM)
OFFICIAL LANGUAGE: Tajik
OTHER LANGUAGE: Russian
MAIN RELIGION: Islam 85%
EXPORTS: Cotton, aluminum, fruits, vegetable oil,
textiles, electricity

SYRIA

PRONUNCIATION: SIHR-ee-uh
AREA: 71,498 sq. miles
(185,180 sq. km)
POPULATION: 17,155,814
CAPITAL: Damascus
CURRENCY: 100 piastres = 1 Syrian pound (£S)
OFFICIAL LANGUAGE: Arabic
OTHER LANGUAGES: Kurdish, Armenian, Aramaic,
Circassian, French, English
MAIN RELIGIONS: Islam 90%, Christianity 10%
EXPORTS: Petroleum, textiles, raw cotton, fruit
and vegetables, live sheep, phosphates

IRAQ

PRONUNCIATION: i-RAHK
AREA: 168,927 sq. miles (437,521 sq. km)
POPULATION: 24,001,816
CAPITAL: Baghdad
CURRENCY: 1,000 fils = 1 Iraqi dinar (ID)
OFFICIAL LANGUAGES: Arabic, Kurdish (in Kurdish regions)
OTHER LANGUAGES: Assyrian, Armenian
MAIN RELIGIONS: Islam 97%, Christianity 3%
EXPORTS: Crude oil and refined products, fertilizer, sulfur

IRAN

PRONUNCIATION: i-RAHN
AREA: 635,932 sq. miles (1,647,064 sq. km)
POPULATION: 66,622,704
CAPITAL: Tehran
CURRENCY: 100 dinars = 1 Iranian rial (R)
OFFICIAL LANGUAGE: Farsi (Persian)
OTHER LANGUAGES: Turkic, Kurdish, Luri
MAIN RELIGION: Islam 99%
EXPORTS: Petroleum, carpets, fruit, nuts, iron and steel, chemicals

LEBANON

PRONUNCIATION: LE-buh-nuhn
AREA: 3,949 sq. miles (10,228 sq. km)
POPULATION: 3,677,780
CAPITAL: Beirut
CURRENCY: 100 piastres = 1 Lebanese pound (£L)
OFFICIAL LANGUAGE: Arabic
OTHER LANGUAGES: Armenian, English, French
MAIN RELIGIONS: Islam 70%, Christianity 30%
EXPORTS: Agricultural products, chemicals, paper, textiles, metals, jewelry, electrical products

ISRAEL

PRONUNCIATION: IZ-ray-uhl
AREA: 7,992 sq. miles (20,699 sq. km)
POPULATION: 6,029,529
CAPITAL: Jerusalem
CURRENCY: 100 new agorot = 1 new Israeli shekel (ILS)
OFFICIAL LANGUAGES: Hebrew, Arabic
OTHER LANGUAGE: English
MAIN RELIGIONS: Judaism 80%, Islam 15%, Christianity 2%
EXPORTS: Machinery, cut diamonds, chemicals, textiles, agricultural products, metals, software

JORDAN

PRONUNCIATION: JOR-duhn
AREA: 35,637 sq. miles (92,300 sq. km)
POPULATION: 5,307,470
CAPITAL: Amman
CURRENCY: 1,000 fils = 1 Jordanian dinar (JD)
OFFICIAL LANGUAGE: Arabic
OTHER LANGUAGE: English
MAIN RELIGIONS: Islam 92%, Christianity 6%
EXPORTS: Phosphates, fertilizer, potash, agricultural products, manufactured goods

SAUDI ARABIA

PRONUNCIATION: SOW-dee uh-RAY-bee-uh
AREA: 756,981 sq. miles (1,960,582 sq. km)
POPULATION: 23,513,330
CAPITAL: Riyadh
CURRENCY: 100 halalas = 1 Saudi riyal (SR)
OFFICIAL LANGUAGE: Arabic
MAIN RELIGION: Islam 100%
EXPORTS: Petroleum and petroleum products

KUWAIT

PRONUNCIATION: koo-WAYT
AREA: 6,880 sq. miles (17,819 sq. km)
POPULATION: 2,111,561
CAPITAL: Kuwait
CURRENCY: 1,000 fils = 1 Kuwaiti dinar (KD)
OFFICIAL LANGUAGE: Arabic
OTHER LANGUAGE: English
MAIN RELIGIONS: Islam 85%, Christianity 8%, Hinduism and Parsi 2%
EXPORTS: Oil and refined products, fertilizers

BAHRAIN

PRONUNCIATION: bah-RAYN
AREA: 255 sq. miles (661 sq. km)
POPULATION: 656,397
CAPITAL: Manama
CURRENCY: 1,000 fils = 1 Bahraini dinar (BD)
OFFICIAL LANGUAGE: Arabic
OTHER LANGUAGES: English, Farsi, Urdu
MAIN RELIGION: Islam 100%
EXPORTS: Petroleum and petroleum products, aluminum

QATAR

PRONUNCIATION: KAH-tuhr
AREA: 4,400 sq. miles (11,395 sq. km)
POPULATION: 793,341
CAPITAL: Doha
CURRENCY: 100 dirhams = 1 Qatari rial (QR)
OFFICIAL LANGUAGE: Arabic
OTHER LANGUAGE: English
MAIN RELIGION: Islam 95%
EXPORTS: Petroleum products, steel, fertilizer

UNITED ARAB EMIRATES

PRONUNCIATION: yoo-NEYE-tuhd A-ruhb EM-uh-ruhts
AREA: 32,000 sq. miles (82,880 sq. km)
POPULATION: 2,445,989
CAPITAL: Abu Dhabi
CURRENCY: 100 fils = 1 Emirati dirham (Dh)
OFFICIAL LANGUAGE: Arabic
OTHER LANGUAGES: Persian, English, Hindi, Urdu
MAIN RELIGION: Islam 96%
EXPORTS: Crude oil, natural gas, dried fish, dates

OMAN

PRONUNCIATION: oh-MAHN
AREA: 82,000 sq. miles (212,380 sq. km)
POPULATION: 2,713,462
CAPITAL: Muscat
CURRENCY: 1,000 baiza = 1 Omani rial (RO)
OFFICIAL LANGUAGE: Arabic
OTHER LANGUAGES: English, Baluchi, Urdu, Indian languages
MAIN RELIGIONS: Islam 86%, Hinduism 13%
EXPORTS: Petroleum, fish, metals, textiles

YEMEN

PRONUNCIATION: YE-muhn
AREA: 203,849 sq. miles (527,969 sq. km)
POPULATION: 18,701,257
CAPITAL: Sanaa
CURRENCY: Yemeni rial (YRI)
OFFICIAL LANGUAGE: Arabic
MAIN RELIGION: Islam 99%
EXPORTS: Crude oil, cotton, coffee, animal skins, vegetables, dried and salted fish

AFGHANISTAN

PRONUNCIATION: af-GA-nuh-stan
AREA: 250,775 sq. miles
(649,507 sq. km)
POPULATION: 27,755,775
CAPITAL: Kabul
CURRENCY: 100 puls = 1 afghani (AF)
OFFICIAL LANGUAGES: Afghan, Persian (Dari), Pashtu
OTHER LANGUAGES: Uzbek, Turkmen, Balochi
MAIN RELIGIONS: Islam 99%, Hinduism and Judaism 1%
EXPORTS: Opium, fruit, nuts, handwoven carpets, wool, cotton, animal skins, precious and semiprecious gemstones

PAKISTAN

PRONUNCIATION: pa-ki-STAN
AREA: 310,403 sq. miles
(803,944 sq. km)
POPULATION: 147,663,429
CAPITAL: Islamabad
CURRENCY: 100 paisa = 1 Pakistani rupee (PRe)
OFFICIAL LANGUAGES: Urdu, English
OTHER LANGUAGES: Punjabi, Sindhi, Siraiki Pashtu, Balochi, Hindko
MAIN RELIGION: Islam 97%
EXPORTS: Cotton, textiles, clothing, rice, yarn leather, carpets, agricultural products

INDIA

PRONUNCIATION: IN-dee-uh
AREA: 1,269,338 sq. miles
(3,287,590 sq. km)
POPULATION: 1,045,845,226
CAPITAL: New Delhi
CURRENCY: 100 paise = 1 Indian rupee (Re)
OFFICIAL LANGUAGES: Hindi, English, Bengali, Telugu, Marathi, Tamil, Urdu, Gujarati, Malayalam, Kannada, Oriya, Punjabi, Assamese, Kashmiri, Sindhi, Sanskrit
OTHER LANGUAGES: Hindustani, Rajasthani
MAIN RELIGIONS: Hinduism 81%, Islam 12%, Christianity 2%, Sikh 2%
EXPORTS: Clothing and textiles, gemstones and jewelry, engineering equipment, chemicals, leather goods, cotton yarn, fabric

NEPAL

PRONUNCIATION: nuh-PAHL
AREA: 54,362 sq. miles
(140,798 sq. km)
POPULATION: 25,873,917
CAPITAL: Kathmandu
CURRENCY: 100 paisa = 1 Nepalese rupee (NR)
OFFICIAL LANGUAGE: Nepali
MAIN RELIGIONS: Hinduism 86%, Buddhism 8%, Islam 4%
EXPORTS: Carpets, clothing, leather goods, jute goods, grain

BHUTAN

PRONUNCIATION: boo-TAHN
AREA: 18,147 sq. miles
(47,000 sq. km)
POPULATION: 2,094,176
CAPITAL: Thimphu
CURRENCY: 100 chetrums = 1 ngultrum (Nu); Indian currency is also legal tender
OFFICIAL LANGUAGE: Dzongkha
OTHER LANGUAGES: Tibetan and Nepali
MAIN RELIGIONS: Buddhism 75%, Hinduism 25%
EXPORTS: Timber, handicrafts, cement, fruit, electricity, gemstones, spices, gypsum

BANGLADESH

PRONUNCIATION: bahng-gluh-DESH
AREA: 55,598 sq. miles
(144,000 sq. km)
POPULATION: 133,376,684
CAPITAL: Dhaka
CURRENCY: 100 paisa = 1 taka (Tk)
OFFICIAL LANGUAGE: Bengali (Bangla)
OTHER LANGUAGE: English
MAIN RELIGIONS: Islam 83%, Hinduism 16%,
EXPORTS: Clothing and textiles, jute and jute goods, leather, frozen fish and seafood, agricultural products

MALDIVES

PRONUNCIATION: MAWL-deevz
AREA: 115 sq. miles (298 sq. km)
POPULATION: 320,165
CAPITAL: Male
CURRENCY: 100 laari = 1 rufiyaa (Rf)
OFFICIAL LANGUAGE: Maldivian Dhivehi
OTHER LANGUAGE: English
MAIN RELIGION: Islam 100%
EXPORTS: Fish, clothing

SRI LANKA

PRONUNCIATION: sree LAHNG-kuh
AREA: 25,332 sq. miles
(65,610 sq. km)
POPULATION: 19,576,783
CAPITAL: Colombo
CURRENCY: 100 cents = 1 Sri Lankan rupee (SLRe)
OFFICIAL LANGUAGES: Sinhala, Tamil
OTHER LANGUAGE: English

MAIN RELIGIONS: Buddhism 70%, Hinduism 15%, Christianity 8%, Islam 7%
EXPORTS: Textiles, tea, diamonds and other precious gemstones, petroleum products, rubber products, agricultural products, marine products

MYANMAR (BURMA)

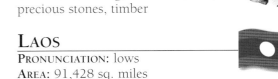

PRONUNCIATION: MYAHN-mar (BER-muh)
AREA: 261,789 sq. miles
(678,034 sq. km)
POPULATION: 42,238,224
CAPITAL: Yangon (Rangoon)
CURRENCY: 100 pyas = 1 kyat (K)
OFFICIAL LANGUAGE: Burmese
OTHER LANGUAGE: ethnic languages
MAIN RELIGIONS: Buddhism 89%, Christianity 4%, Islam 4%, animist 1%
EXPORTS: Clothing, foodstuffs, rice, precious stones, timber

LAOS

PRONUNCIATION: lows
AREA: 91,428 sq. miles
(236,799 sq. km)
POPULATION: 5,777,180
CAPITAL: Vientiane
CURRENCY: 100 at = 1 kip (LAK)
OFFICIAL LANGUAGE: Lao
OTHER LANGUAGES: French, English, local dialects
MAIN RELIGIONS: Buddhism 60%, animism 34%, Christianity 2%
EXPORTS: Electricity, timber products, coffee, tin, textiles and clothing

VIETNAM

PRONUNCIATION: vee-et-NAHM
AREA: 127,243 sq. miles
(329,560 sq. km)
POPULATION: 81,098,416
CAPITAL: Hanoi
CURRENCY: 100 xu = 1 new dong (D)
OFFICIAL LANGUAGE: Vietnamese
OTHER LANGUAGES: French, Chinese languages, English, Khmer, tribal languages
MAIN RELIGIONS: Buddhism 55%, Christianity 7%, Taoism, indigenous religions, Islam
EXPORTS: Crude oil, rice, clothing and footwear, rubber, tea, marine products, coffee

THAILAND

PRONUNCIATION: TEYE-land
AREA: 198,455 sq. miles
(513,998 sq. km)
POPULATION: 62,354,402
CAPITAL: Bangkok
CURRENCY: 100 satang = 1 baht (B)
OFFICIAL LANGUAGE: Thai
OTHER LANGUAGES: English, Chinese languages, Malay, regional languages
MAIN RELIGIONS: Buddhism 95%, Islam 4%
EXPORTS: Computers and parts, textiles, integrated circuits, rice

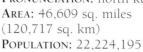

CAMBODIA

PRONUNCIATION: kam-BOH-dee-uh
AREA: 69,898 sq. miles (181,036 sq. km)
POPULATION: 12,775,324
CAPITAL: Phnom Penh
CURRENCY: 100 sen = 1 new riel (CR)
OFFICIAL LANGUAGE: Khmer
OTHER LANGUAGES: French, English
MAIN RELIGIONS: Buddhism 95%, Islam 2%
EXPORTS: Timber, rubber, clothing, rice, fish

MALAYSIA

PRONUNCIATION: muh-LAY-zhuh
AREA: 127,316 sq. miles (329,750 sq. km)
POPULATION: 22,662,365
CAPITAL: Kuala Lumpur
CURRENCY: 100 sen = 1 ringgit (MYR)
OFFICIAL LANGUAGE: Malay (Bahasa Melayu)
OTHER LANGUAGES: English, Chinese languages, Tamil, Telugu, regional languages
MAIN RELIGIONS: Islam 53%, Buddhism 17%, Confucianism 12%, Christianity 9%, Hinduism 7%
EXPORTS: Electronic equipment, petroleum, liquified natural gas, palm oil, timber and timber products, rubber, textiles

PHILIPPINES

PRONUNCIATION: FI-luh-peenz
AREA: 115,651 sq. miles (299,536 sq. km)
POPULATION: 84,525,639
CAPITAL: Manila
CURRENCY: 100 centavos = 1 Philippine peso (P)
OFFICIAL LANGUAGES: Filipino, English
OTHER LANGUAGES: Regional languages
MAIN RELIGIONS: Christianity 92%, Islam 5%, Buddhism 3%
EXPORTS: Electronics, machinery and transport equipment, textiles, coconut products, copper, fish

SINGAPORE

PRONUNCIATION: SING-uh-por
AREA: 200 sq. miles (648 sq. km)
POPULATION: 4,452,732
CAPITAL: Singapore
CURRENCY: 100 cents = 1 Singapore dollar (S$)
OFFICIAL LANGUAGES: Chinese, Malay, Tamil, English
MAIN RELIGIONS: Buddhism 28%, Islam 15%, Christianity 13%, Taoism 13%, Hinduism 5%
EXPORTS: Computer equipment, chemicals, mineral fuels, telecommunications equipment

BRUNEI

PRONUNCIATION: broo-NEYE
AREA: 2,226 sq. miles (5,765 sq. km)
POPULATION: 350,898
CAPITAL: Bandar Seri Begawan
CURRENCY: 100 cents = 1 Bruneian dollar (B$)
OFFICIAL LANGUAGE: Malay
OTHER LANGUAGES: English, Chinese
MAIN RELIGIONS: Islam 67%, Buddhist 13%, Christianity 10%, indigenous religions
EXPORTS: Crude oil, liquefied natural gas, petroleum products

INDONESIA

PRONUNCIATION: in-duh-NEE-zhuh
AREA: 741,096 sq. miles (1,919,440 sq. km)
POPULATION: 216,109,000
CAPITAL: Jakarta
CURRENCY: 100 sen = 1 Indonesian rupiah (IDR)
OFFICIAL LANGUAGE: Bahasa Indonesia
OTHER LANGUAGES: English, Dutch, Javanese, regional languages
MAIN RELIGIONS: Islam 88%, Christianity 8%, Hinduism 2%, Buddhism 1%
EXPORTS: Manufactured goods, oil and gas, textiles, rubber, plywood

EAST TIMOR

PRONUNCIATION: EEST TEE-mor
AREA: 7,000 sq. miles (19,000 sq.km)
POPULATION: 952,618
CAPITAL: Dili
CURRENCY: 100 cents = 1 United States dollar (US$)
OFFICIAL LANGUAGE: Tetum, Portuguese
OTHER LANGUAGES: Bahasa Indonesia, English
MAIN RELIGION: Christianity 93%, Islam 4%
EXPORTS: Coffee, sandalwood, marble

CHINA

PRONUNCIATION: CHEYE-nuh
AREA: 3,705,386 sq. miles (9,596,960 sq. km)
POPULATION: 1,284,303,705
CAPITAL: Beijing
CURRENCY: 10 jiao = 1 yuan (Y)
OFFICIAL LANGUAGE: Mandarin
OTHER LANGUAGES: Cantonese, Shanghaiese, Fuzhou, Hokkien-Taiwanese, regional languages
MAIN RELIGIONS: Daoism (Taoism) 20%, Buddhism 6%, Islam 3%, Christianity 1%
EXPORTS: Textiles and clothing, shoes, toys, machinery and equipment, mineral fuels

MONGOLIA

PRONUNCIATION: mahn-GOHL-yuh
AREA: 604,247 sq. miles (1,565,000 sq. km)
POPULATION: 2,694,432
CAPITAL: Ulaanbaatar
CURRENCY: 100 mongos = 1 togrog/tugrik (Tug)
OFFICIAL LANGUAGE: Khalkha Mongol
OTHER LANGUAGES: Turkic, Russian, Chinese

MAIN RELIGIONS: Buddhism 95%, Islam 4%
EXPORTS: Copper, livestock, animal products, cashmere, wool, animal skins, non-ferrous metals

NORTH KOREA

PRONUNCIATION: north kuh-REE-uh
AREA: 46,609 sq. miles (120,717 sq. km)
POPULATION: 22,224,195
CAPITAL: P'yŏngyang
CURRENCY: 100 chon = 1 North Korean won (Wn)
OFFICIAL LANGUAGE: Korean
MAIN RELIGIONS: Chondogyo 14%, Buddhism 2%, Christianity 1%
EXPORTS: Minerals, metal products, agricultural and fishery products, manufactured goods

SOUTH KOREA

PRONUNCIATION: sowth kuh-REE-uh
AREA: 38,022 sq. miles (98,477 sq. km)
POPULATION: 48,324,000
CAPITAL: Seoul
CURRENCY: 100 chon = 1 South Korean won (W)
OFFICIAL LANGUAGE: Korean
OTHER LANGUAGE: English
MAIN RELIGIONS: Christianity 49%, Buddhism 47%, Confucianism 3%
EXPORTS: Electronic and electrical equipment, machinery, steel, motor vehicles, ships, textiles, clothing, shoes, fish

TAIWAN

PRONUNCIATION: TEYE-WAHN
AREA: 13,887 sq. miles (35,967 sq. km)
POPULATION: 22,548,009
CAPITAL: Taipei
CURRENCY: 100 cents = 1 New Taiwan dollar (NT$)
OFFICIAL LANGUAGE: Mandarin
OTHER LANGUAGES: Taiwanese, Hakka dialects
MAIN RELIGIONS: Buddhism 43%, Daoism (Taoism) 21%, Christianity 5%, Confucianism
EXPORTS: Electrical machinery, electronic goods, textiles, metals, plastics, chemicals

JAPAN

PRONUNCIATION: juh-PAN
AREA: 145,882 sq. miles (377,835 sq. km)
POPULATION: 126,974,628
CAPITAL: Tokyo
CURRENCY: 100 sen = 1 yen (¥)
OFFICIAL LANGUAGE: Japanese
MAIN RELIGIONS: Shinto and Buddhism 84%, Christianity 1%
EXPORTS: Machinery, motor vehicles, consumer electronics, chemicals, semiconductors

AFRICA

MOROCCO

PRONUNCIATION: muh-RAH-koh
AREA: 172,413 sq. miles
(446,550 sq. km)
POPULATION: 31,167,783
CAPITAL: Rabat
CURRENCY: 100 centimes = 1 Moroccan
dirham (DH)
OFFICIAL LANGUAGE: Arabic
OTHER LANGUAGES: French, Berber dialects
MAIN RELIGIONS: Islam 99%, Christianity 1%
EXPORTS: Food, beverages, consumer goods,
phosphates and fertilizers, minerals

ALGERIA

PRONUNCIATION: al-JIHR-ee-uh
AREA: 919,590 sq. miles
(2,381,740 sq. km)
POPULATION: 32,277,942
CAPITAL: Algiers
CURRENCY: 100 centimes = 1 Algerian dinar (DA)
OFFICIAL LANGUAGE: Arabic
OTHER LANGUAGES: French, Berber dialects
MAIN RELIGIONS: Islam 99%, Christianity
and Judaism 1%
EXPORTS: Petroleum products, natural gas

TUNISIA

PRONUNCIATION: too-NEE-zhuh
AREA: 63,378 sq. miles
(164,149 sq. km)
POPULATION: 9,815,644
CAPITAL: Tunis
CURRENCY: 1,000 millimes = 1 Tunisian dinar (TD)
OFFICIAL LANGUAGE: Arabic
OTHER LANGUAGE: French
MAIN RELIGIONS: Islam 98%, Christianity 1%,
Judaism 1%
EXPORTS: Agricultural products, chemicals,
textiles, mechanical goods, phosphates

LIBYA

PRONUNCIATION: LI-bee-uh
AREA: 679,360 sq. miles
(1,759,540 sq. km)
POPULATION: 5,368,585
CAPITAL: Tripoli

CURRENCY: 1,000 dirhams =
1 Libyan dinar (LD)
OFFICIAL LANGUAGE: Arabic
OTHER LANGUAGES: Italian,
English
MAIN RELIGION: Islam 97%
EXPORTS: Crude oil, refined
petroleum products

CAPE VERDE ISLANDS

PRONUNCIATION: kayp VAIRD islands
AREA: 1,557 sq. miles (4,033 sq. km)
POPULATION: 408,760
CAPITAL: Praia
CURRENCY: 100 centavos = 1 Cape Verdean
escudo (CVE)
OFFICIAL LANGUAGE: Portuguese
OTHER LANGUAGE: Cape Verde creole (Crioulo)
MAIN RELIGION: Christianity 97%
EXPORTS: Fish, bananas, animal skins, clothing, fuel

EGYPT

PRONUNCIATION: EE-juhpt
AREA: 386,660 sq. miles
(1,001,450 sq. km)
POPULATION: 70,712,345
CAPITAL: Cairo
CURRENCY: 100 piasters = 1 Egyptian pound (£E)
OFFICIAL LANGUAGE: Arabic
OTHER LANGUAGES: English, French
MAIN RELIGIONS: Islam 94%, Christianity 6%
EXPORTS: Crude oil and petroleum products,
cotton, textiles, metal products, chemicals

MAURITANIA

PRONUNCIATION: maw-ruh-TAY-nee-uh
AREA: 397,955 sq. miles
(1,030,807 sq. km)
POPULATION: 2,828,858
CAPITAL: Nouakchott
CURRENCY: 5 khoums = 1 ouguiya (MRO)
OFFICIAL LANGUAGES: Hasaniya Arabic, Wolof
OTHER LANGUAGES: French, Pular, Soninke
MAIN RELIGION: Islam 100%
EXPORTS: Iron ore, fish and fish products, gold

MALI

PRONUNCIATION: MAH-lee
AREA: 478,652 sq. miles
(1,239,709 sq. km)
POPULATION: 11,340,480
CAPITAL: Bamako
CURRENCY: 100 centimes = 1 CFA
franc (CFAF)
OFFICIAL LANGUAGE: French
OTHER LANGUAGES: Bambara, regional
languages
MAIN RELIGIONS: Islam 90%,
indigenous religions 9%,
Christianity 1%
EXPORTS: Cotton, livestock, gold

BURKINA FASO

PRONUNCIATION: ber-KEE-nuh FAH-soh
AREA: 105,869 sq. miles
(274,201 sq. km)
POPULATION: 12,603,185
CAPITAL: Ouagadougou
CURRENCY: 100 centimes = 1 CFA franc (CFAF)
OFFICIAL LANGUAGE: French
OTHER LANGUAGES: Tribal languages
MAIN RELIGIONS: Islam 50%, indigenous
religions 40%, Christianity 10%
EXPORTS: Cotton, gold, animal products

NIGER

PRONUNCIATION: NEYE-juhr
AREA: 459,073 sq. miles
(1,188,999 sq. km)
POPULATION: 10,639,744
CAPITAL: Niamey
CURRENCY: 100 centimes = 1 CFA franc (CFAF)
OFFICIAL LANGUAGE: French
OTHER LANGUAGES: Hausa, Djerma
MAIN RELIGIONS: Islam 80%, indigenous
religions 14%, Christianity 1%
EXPORTS: Uranium ore, livestock, cowpeas, onions

CHAD

PRONUNCIATION: chad
AREA: 495,752 sq. miles
(1,283,998 sq. km)
POPULATION: 8,997,237
CAPITAL: N'Djamena
CURRENCY: 100 centimes = 1 CFA franc (CFAF)
OFFICIAL LANGUAGES: French, Arabic
OTHER LANGUAGES: Sara, Sango, tribal languages
MAIN RELIGIONS: Islam 50%, Christianity 25%,
indigenous religions and animism 25%
EXPORTS: Cotton, cattle, textiles

SUDAN

PRONUNCIATION: soo-DAN
AREA: 967,500 sq. miles
(2,505,825 sq. km)
POPULATION: 37,090,298
CAPITAL: Khartoum
CURRENCY: 100 girsh = 1 Sudanese dinar (SDD)
OFFICIAL LANGUAGE: Arabic
OTHER LANGUAGES: Nubian, Ta Bedawie, Nilotic,
Nilo-Hamitic, regional languages, English
MAIN RELIGIONS: Islam 70%, indigenous
religions 25%, Christianity 5%
EXPORTS: Oil, livestock, cotton, sesame, peanuts

ERITREA

PRONUNCIATION: ehr-uh-TREE-uh
AREA: 46,842 sq. miles
(121,320 sq. km)
POPULATION: 4,465,651
CAPITAL: Asmara
CURRENCY: 100 cents = 1 nafka
OFFICIAL LANGUAGES: Arabic, Tigrinya, Tigre
OTHER LANGUAGES: Regional languages
MAIN RELIGIONS: Islam 50%, Christianity 50%
EXPORTS: Livestock, sorghum, textiles, food

ETHIOPIA

PRONUNCIATION: ee-thee-OH-pee-uh
AREA: 435,184 sq. miles
(1,127,127 sq. km)
POPULATION: 67,673,031
CAPITAL: Addis Ababa
CURRENCY: 100 cents = 1 birr (Br)
OFFICIAL LANGUAGE: Amharic, Tigrinya,
Oromigna, Guiragigna, Somali
OTHER LANGUAGES: Arabic, English
MAIN RELIGIONS: Islam 45%, Christianity 35%,
animism 12%
EXPORTS: Coffee, leather products, gold, oilseeds, qat

DJIBOUTI

PRONUNCIATION: ji-BOO-tee
AREA: 8,494 sq. miles
(22,000 sq. km)
POPULATION: 472,810
CAPITAL: Djibouti
CURRENCY: 100 centimes = 1 Djiboutian
franc (DF)
OFFICIAL LANGUAGES: French, Arabic
OTHER LANGUAGES: Somali, Afar
MAIN RELIGIONS: Islam 94%, Christianity 6%
EXPORTS: Animal skins, coffee

SOMALIA

PRONUNCIATION: soh-MAH-lee-uh
AREA: 246,154 sq. miles
(637,539 sq. km)
POPULATION: 7,753,310
CAPITAL: Mogadishu
CURRENCY: 100 cents = 1 Somali shilling (SOS)
OFFICIAL LANGUAGE: Somali
OTHER LANGUAGES: Arabic, Italian, English
MAIN RELIGION: Islam 99%
EXPORTS: Bananas, livestock, fish, animal skins

SENEGAL

PRONUNCIATION: sen-i-GAWL
AREA: 75,749 sq. miles
(196,190 sq. km)
POPULATION: 10,589,571
CAPITAL: Dakar
CURRENCY: 100 centimes = 1 CFA franc (CFAF)
OFFICIAL LANGUAGE: French
OTHER LANGUAGES: Wolof, Pulaar, Jola, Mandinka
MAIN RELIGIONS: Islam 92%, indigenous
religions 6%, Christianity 2%
EXPORTS: Fish, peanuts, petroleum products,
phosphates, cotton

GAMBIA

PRONUNCIATION: GAM-bee-uh
AREA: 4,363 sq. miles (11,300 sq. km)
POPULATION: 1,455,842
CAPITAL: Banjul
CURRENCY: 100 bututs = 1 dalasi (D)
OFFICIAL LANGUAGE: English
OTHER LANGUAGES: Mandinka, Wolof, Fula
MAIN RELIGIONS: Islam 90%, Christianity 9%,
indigenous religions 1%
EXPORTS: Peanuts, fish, palm kernels, cotton lint

GUINEA-BISSAU

PRONUNCIATION: gi-nee-bi-SOW
AREA: 13,948 sq. miles
(36,125 sq. km)
POPULATION: 1,345,479
CAPITAL: Bissau
CURRENCY: 100 centimes = 1 CFA franc (CFAF)
OFFICIAL LANGUAGE: Portuguese
OTHER LANGUAGES: Crioulo, African languages
MAIN RELIGIONS: Indigenous religions 50%,
Islam 45%, Christianity 5%
EXPORTS: Cashews, shrimp, palm kernels,
peanuts, timber

GUINEA

PRONUNCIATION: GI-nee
AREA: 94,925 sq. miles
(245,856 sq. km)
POPULATION: 7,775,065
CAPITAL: Conakry
CURRENCY: 100 centimes = 1 Guinean franc (FG)
OFFICIAL LANGUAGE: French
OTHER LANGUAGES: Tribal languages
MAIN RELIGIONS: Islam 85%, Christianity 8%,
indigenous religions 7%
EXPORTS: Bauxite, alumina, diamonds, gold,
coffee, fish, agricultural products

SIERRA LEONE

PRONUNCIATION: see-EHR-uh lee-OHN
AREA: 27,699 sq. miles
(71,740 sq. km)
POPULATION: 5,614,743
CAPITAL: Freetown
CURRENCY: 100 cents = 1 leone (Le)
OFFICIAL LANGUAGE: English
OTHER LANGUAGES: Mende, Temne, Krio
MAIN RELIGIONS: Islam 60%, indigenous
religions 30%, Christianity 10%
EXPORTS: Diamonds and other minerals, coffee,
cocoa, fish

LIBERIA

PRONUNCIATION: leye-BIHR-ee-uh
AREA: 43,000 sq. miles
(111,370 sq. km)
POPULATION: 3,288,198
CAPITAL: Monrovia
CURRENCY: 100 cents = 1 Liberian dollar (L$)
OFFICIAL LANGUAGE: English
OTHER LANGUAGES: Tribal languages
MAIN RELIGIONS: Indigenous religions 40%,
Christianity 40%, Islam 20%
EXPORTS: Iron ore, rubber, timber, coffee, diamonds

CÔTE D'IVOIRE (IVORY COAST)

PRONUNCIATION: koht dee-VWAR
AREA: 124,503 sq. miles
(322,463 sq. km)
POPULATION: 16,804,784
CAPITALS: Abidjan (seat of government),
Yamoussoukro (official)
CURRENCY: 100 centimes = 1 CFA franc (CFAF)
OFFICIAL LANGUAGE: French
OTHER LANGUAGES: Regional languages
MAIN RELIGIONS: Christianity 34%, Islam 27%,
animist 15%
EXPORTS: Cocoa, coffee, timber, petroleum, cotton,
bananas, pineapples, palm oil, fish

GHANA

PRONUNCIATION: GAH-nuh
AREA: 92,100 sq. miles
(238,539 sq. km)
POPULATION: 20,244,154
CAPITAL: Accra
CURRENCY: 100 pesewas = 1 new cedi (₵)
OFFICIAL LANGUAGE: English
OTHER LANGUAGES: Regional languages
MAIN RELIGIONS: Indigenous religions 38%,
Islam 30%, Christianity 24%
EXPORTS: Cocoa, gold, timber, tuna, bauxite,
aluminum, manganese ore, diamonds

TOGO

PRONUNCIATION: TOH-goh
AREA: 21,853 sq. miles
(56,599 sq. km)
POPULATION: 5,285,501
CAPITAL: Lomé
CURRENCY: 100 centimes = 1 CFA franc (CFAF)
OFFICIAL LANGUAGE: French
OTHER LANGUAGES: Regional languages
MAIN RELIGIONS: Indigenous religions 59%,
Christianity 29%, Islam 12%
EXPORTS: Phosphates, cotton, cocoa, coffee

BENIN

PRONUNCIATION: buh-NEEN
AREA: 43,483 sq. miles
(112,621 sq. km)
POPULATION: 6,787,625
CAPITALS: Cotonou (seat of government),
Porto-Novo (official)
CURRENCY: 100 centimes = 1 CFA franc (CFAF)
OFFICIAL LANGUAGE: French
OTHER LANGUAGES: Fon, Yoruba, tribal languages
MAIN RELIGIONS: Indigenous religions 50%,
Islam 20%, Christianity 30%
EXPORTS: Cotton, crude oil, palm products, cocoa

NIGERIA

PRONUNCIATION: neye-JIHR-ee-uh
AREA: 356,669 sq. miles
(923,773 sq. km)
POPULATION: 129,934,911
CAPITAL: Abuja
CURRENCY: 100 kobo = 1 naira (₦)
OFFICIAL LANGUAGE: English
OTHER LANGUAGES: Regional languages
MAIN RELIGIONS: Islam 50%, Christianity 40%,
indigenous religions 10%
EXPORTS: Oil and petroluem products, cocoa, rubber

CAMEROON

PRONUNCIATION: ka-muh-ROON
AREA: 183,591 sq. miles
(475,501 sq. km)
POPULATION: 16,184,748
CAPITAL: Yaoundé
CURRENCY: 100 centimes = 1 CFA franc (CFAF)
OFFICIAL LANGUAGES: English, French
OTHER LANGUAGES: Regional
languages
MAIN RELIGIONS: Indigenous
religions 40%,
Christianity 40%,
Islam 20%
EXPORTS: Crude oil
petroleum products,
timber, cocoa beans,
aluminum, coffee, cotton

EQUATORIAL GUINEA

PRONUNCIATION: e-kwuh-TOR-ee-uhl
GI-nee
AREA: 10,825 sq. miles (28,037 sq. km)
POPULATION: 498,144
CAPITAL: Malabo
CURRENCY: 100 centimes = 1 CFA franc (CFAF)
OFFICIAL LANGUAGES: Spanish, French
OTHER LANGUAGES: Pidgin English, Fang, Bubi,
Ibo, other regional languages
MAIN RELIGION: Christianity 85%
EXPORTS: Timber, cocoa, petroleum

CENTRAL AFRICAN REPUBLIC

PRONUNCIATION: SEN-truhl AF-ri-kuhn
ri-PUH-blik
AREA: 240,534 sq. miles (622,984 sq. km)
POPULATION: 3,642,739
CAPITAL: Bangui
CURRENCY: 100 centimes = 1 CFA franc (CFAF)
OFFICIAL LANGUAGE: French
OTHER LANGUAGES: Sangho, Arabic, Hunsa,
Swahili
MAIN RELIGIONS: Christianity 50%,
indigenous religions 24%, Islam 15%
EXPORTS: Diamonds, timber, cotton,
coffee, tobacco

SÃO TOMÉ AND PRÍNCIPE

PRONUNCIATION: sow tuh-MAY and
PRIN-suh-pee
AREA: 372 sq. miles (963 sq. km)
POPULATION: 170,372
CAPITAL: São Tomé
CURRENCY: 100 centimos = 1 dobra (Db)
OFFICIAL LANGUAGE: Portuguese
MAIN RELIGION: Christianity 80%
EXPORTS: Cocoa, copra, coffee, palm oil

GABON

PRONUNCIATION: ga-BOHN
AREA: 103,346 sq. miles
(267,667 sq. km)
POPULATION: 1,233,353
CAPITAL: Libreville
CURRENCY: 100 centimes = 1 CFA franc (CFAF)
OFFICIAL LANGUAGE: French
OTHER LANGUAGES: Regional languages
MAIN RELIGIONS: Christianity 60%, animism 40%,
Islam 1%
EXPORTS: Crude oil, timber, manganese, uranium

CONGO

PRONUNCIATION: KAHN-goh
AREA: 132,047 sq. miles
(342,002 sq. km)
POPULATION: 2,958,448
CAPITAL: Brazzaville
CURRENCY: 100 centimes = 1 CFA franc (CFAF)
OFFICIAL LANGUAGE: French
OTHER LANGUAGES: Lingala, Monokutuba
MAIN RELIGIONS: Christianity 50%, animism 48%,
Islam 2%
EXPORTS: Petroleum, timber, sugar, cocoa,
coffee, diamonds

DEMOCRATIC REPUBLIC OF THE CONGO (ZAIRE)

PRONUNCIATION: de-muh-KRA-tik
ri-PUH-blik of the KAHN-goh
AREA: 905,356 sq. miles
(2,344,872 sq. km)
POPULATION: 55,225,478
CAPITAL: Kinshasa
CURRENCY: Congolese franc (CF)
OFFICIAL LANGUAGE: French
OTHER LANGUAGES: Lingala, Kingwana,
Kikongo, Tshiluba
MAIN RELIGIONS: Christianity 70%, Islam 10%,
Kimbanguism 10%, indigenous beliefs 10%
EXPORTS: Copper, coffee, diamonds, crude oil

UGANDA

PRONUNCIATION: yoo-GAN-duh
AREA: 91,134 sq. miles
(236,037 sq. km)
POPULATION: 24,699,073
CAPITAL: Kampala
CURRENCY: 100 cents = 1 Ugandan shilling (USh)
OFFICIAL LANGUAGE: English
OTHER LANGUAGES: Ganda or Luganda, Swahili,
other regional languages
MAIN RELIGIONS: Christianity 66%, indigenous
religions 18%, Islam 16%
EXPORTS: Coffee, cotton, tea, fish, iron and steel

KENYA

PRONUNCIATION: KEN-yuh
AREA: 224,960 sq. miles
(582,646 sq. km)
POPULATION: 31,138,735
CAPITAL: Nairobi
CURRENCY: 100 cents = 1 Kenyan
shilling (KSh)
OFFICIAL LANGUAGES: English,
Kiswahili
OTHER LANGUAGES: Regional
indigenous languages
MAIN RELIGIONS: Christianity 66%,
indigenous religions 26%, Islam 7%
EXPORTS: Tea, coffee, petroleum products, fish

RWANDA

PRONUNCIATION: ruh-WAHN-duh
AREA: 10,169 sq. miles (26,338 sq. km)
POPULATION: 7,398,074
CAPITAL: Kigali
CURRENCY: 100 centimes = 1 Rwandan franc (RF)
OFFICIAL LANGUAGES: Kinyarwanda, French, English
OTHER LANGUAGE: Kiswahili
MAIN RELIGIONS: Christianity 87%,
indigenous religions 7%, Islam 2%
EXPORTS: Coffee, tea, animal skins, tin ore

BURUNDI

PRONUNCIATION: boo-RUN-dee
AREA: 10,759 sq. miles (27,866 sq. km)
POPULATION: 6,373,002
CAPITAL: Bujumbura
CURRENCY: 100 centimes = 1 Burundi franc (FBu)
OFFICIAL LANGUAGES: Kirundi, French
OTHER LANGUAGE: Swahili
MAIN RELIGIONS: Christianity 67%, indigenous
religions 23%, Islam 10%
EXPORTS: Coffee, tea, cotton, animal skins, sugar

TANZANIA

PRONUNCIATION: tan-zuh-NEE-uh
AREA: 364,900 sq. miles (945,091 sq. km)
POPULATION: 37,187,939
CAPITALS: Dar es Salaam (seat of government),
Dodoma (official)

CURRENCY: 100 cents = 1 Tanzanian shilling (TSh)
OFFICIAL LANGUAGES: Swahili, English
OTHER LANGUAGES: Arabic, regional languages
MAIN RELIGIONS: Christianity 45%, Islam 35%, indigenous religions 20%
EXPORTS: Coffee, cotton, tobacco, cashews, minerals

ANGOLA

PRONUNCIATION: ang-GOH-luh
AREA: 481,351 sq. miles (1,246,699 sq. km)
POPULATION: 10,593,171
CAPITAL: Luanda
CURRENCY: 100 lwei = 1 kwanza (NKz)
OFFICIAL LANGUAGE: Portuguese
OTHER LANGUAGES: Bantu, other regional languages
MAIN RELIGIONS: Christianity 53%, indigenous religions 47%
EXPORTS: Crude oil, diamonds, refined petroleum products, gas, coffee, sisal (fiber), fish and fish products, timber, cotton

ZAMBIA

PRONUNCIATION: zam-bee-uh
AREA: 290,585 sq. miles (752,615 sq. km)
POPULATION: 9,959.037
CAPITAL: Lusaka
CURRENCY: 100 ngwee = 1 Zambian kwacha (ZK)
OFFICIAL LANGUAGE: English
OTHER LANGUAGES: Regional languages
MAIN RELIGIONS: Christianity 62%, Islam and Hinduism 36%, indigenous religions 1%
EXPORTS: Copper, cobalt, electricity, tobacco

ZIMBABWE

PRONUNCIATION: zim-BAH-bway
AREA: 150,820 sq. miles (390,624 sq. km)
POPULATION: 11,376,676
CAPITAL: Harare
CURRENCY: 100 cents = 1 Zimbabwean dollar (Z$)
OFFICIAL LANGUAGE: English
OTHER LANGUAGES: Shona, regional languages
MAIN RELIGIONS: Syncretic (part Christianity, part indigenous religions) 50%, Christianity 25%, indigenous religions 24%, Islam 1%
EXPORTS: Tobacco, manufactured goods, metals, cotton, gold

MALAWI

PRONUNCIATION: muh-LAH-wee
AREA: 45,747 sq. miles (118,485 sq. km)
POPULATION: 10,701,824
CAPITAL: Lilongwe
CURRENCY: 100 tambala = 1 Malawian kwacha (MK)
OFFICIAL LANGUAGES: English, Chichewa
OTHER LANGUAGES: Regional languages
MAIN RELIGIONS: Christianity 75%, Islam 20%, indigenous religions 5%
EXPORTS: Tobacco, tea, sugar, cotton, coffee, peanuts, timber products

MOZAMBIQUE

PRONUNCIATION: moh-zahm-BEEK
AREA: 309,494 sq. miles (801,590 sq. km)
POPULATION: 19,607,519
CAPITAL: Maputo
CURRENCY: 100 centavos = 1 metical (Mt)
OFFICIAL LANGUAGE: Portuguese
OTHER LANGUAGES: Regional languages
MAIN RELIGIONS: Indigenous religions 50%, Christianity 30%, Islam 20%
EXPORTS: Shrimp, cashews, cotton, sugar, citrus fruit, timber, bulk electricity

NAMIBIA

PRONUNCIATION: nuh-MI-bee-uh
AREA: 318,694 sq. miles (825,418 sq. km)
POPULATION: 1,820,916
CAPITAL: Windhoek
CURRENCY: 100 cents = 1 Namibian dollar (N$)
OFFICIAL LANGUAGE: English
OTHER LANGUAGES: Afrikaans, German, Herero, Oshivambo, Nama
MAIN RELIGION: Christianity 85%, indigenous religions 15%
EXPORTS: Diamonds, metals, cattle, processed fish

BOTSWANA

PRONUNCIATION: bawt-SWAH-nuh
AREA: 231,803 sq. miles (600,370 sq. km)
POPULATION: 1,591,232
CAPITAL: Gaborone
CURRENCY: 100 thebe = 1 pula (P)
OFFICIAL LANGUAGE: English
OTHER LANGUAGE: Setswana
MAIN RELIGIONS: Indigenous religions 50%, Christianity 50%
EXPORTS: Diamonds, copper and nickel, meat

SOUTH AFRICA

PRONUNCIATION: sowth AF-ri-kuh
AREA: 471,008 sq. miles (1,219,912 sq. km)
POPULATION: 43,427,000
CAPITALS: Pretoria (administrative), Bloemfontein (judicial), Cape Town (legislative)
CURRENCY: 100 cents = 1 rand (R)
OFFICIAL LANGUAGES: Afrikaans, English, Xhosa, Zulu, other regional languages
MAIN RELIGIONS: Christianity 68%, Hinduism, Islam
EXPORTS: Gold, diamonds and other minerals and metals, machinery and equipment

SWAZILAND

PRONUNCIATION: SWAH-zee-land
AREA: 6,705 sq. miles (17,366 sq. km)
POPULATION: 1,123,605
CAPITAL: Mbabane, Lobamba (royal and legislative)
CURRENCY: 100 cents = 1 lilangeni (E)
OFFICIAL LANGUAGES: English, Swazi
MAIN RELIGIONS: Christianity 60%, indigenous religions 30%, Islam 10%
EXPORTS: Sugar, wood pulp, cotton, refridgerators

LESOTHO

PRONUNCIATION: luh-SOH-toh
AREA: 11,716 sq. miles (30,344 sq. km)
POPULATION: 2,207,954
CAPITAL: Maseru
CURRENCY: 100 licente = 1 loti (L)
OFFICIAL LANGUAGES: English, Sesotho
OTHER LANGUAGES: Zulu, Xhosa
MAIN RELIGIONS: Christianity 80%, indigenous religions 20%
EXPORTS: Wool, mohair, food and livestock, clothing, footwear, road vehicles

COMOROS

PRONUNCIATION: KAH-muh-rohz
AREA: 719 sq. miles (1,862 sq. km)
POPULATION: 614,382
CAPITAL: Moroni
CURRENCY: 100 centimes = 1 Comoran franc (CF)
OFFICIAL LANGUAGES: Arabic, French
OTHER LANGUAGE: Comoran
MAIN RELIGIONS: Islam 98%, Christianity 2%
EXPORTS: Vanilla, cloves, perfume oil, copra

MADAGASCAR

PRONUNCIATION: ma-duh-GAS-kuhr
AREA: 226,657 sq. miles (587,042 sq. km)
POPULATION: 16,473,477
CAPITAL: Antananarivo
CURRENCY: 100 centimes = 1 Malagasy franc (FMG)
OFFICIAL LANGUAGES: French, Malagasy
MAIN RELIGIONS: Indigenous religions 52%, Christianity 41%, Islam 7%
EXPORTS: Coffee, vanilla, shellfish, chromite, sugar, petroleum products, cotton cloth

SEYCHELLES

PRONUNCIATION: say-SHELZ
AREA: 176 sq. miles (455 sq. km)
POPULATION: 80,098
CAPITAL: Victoria
CURRENCY: 100 cents = 1 Seychelles rupee (SRe)
OFFICIAL LANGUAGES: English, French
OTHER LANGUAGE: Seychelles creole
MAIN RELIGION: Christianity 98%
EXPORTS: Fish, cinnamon bark, copra, petroleum products

MAURITIUS

PRONUNCIATION: maw-ri-shuhs
AREA: 720 sq. miles (1,865 sq. km)
POPULATION: 1,200,206
CAPITAL: Port Louis
CURRENCY: 100 cents = 1 Mauritian rupee (MauR)
OFFICIAL LANGUAGE: English
OTHER LANGUAGES: Mauritian creole, French, Hindi, Urdu, Hakka, Bojpoori
MAIN RELIGIONS: Hinduism 52%, Christianity 28%, Islam 17%
EXPORTS: Textiles and clothing, sugar, cut flowers, molasses

AUSTRALIA AND OCEANIA

AUSTRALIA

PRONUNCIATION: aw-STRAYL-yuh
AREA: 2,967,909 sq. miles (7,686,884 sq. km)
POPULATION: 19,546,792
CAPITAL: Canberra
CURRENCY: 100 cents = 1 Australian dollar ($A)
OFFICIAL LANGUAGE: English
OTHER LANGUAGES: Aboriginal languages
MAIN RELIGION: Christianity 76%
EXPORTS: Coal, gold, meat, wool, wheat, alumina, iron ore, machinery and transportation equipment

PAPUA NEW GUINEA

PRONUNCIATION: PA-pyoo-uh noo GI-nee
AREA: 178,703 sq. miles (462,840 sq. km)
POPULATION: 5,172,033
CAPITAL: Port Moresby
CURRENCY: 100 toea = 1 kina (K)
OFFICIAL LANGUAGES: English, pidgin English, Motu
OTHER LANGUAGES: Regional languages
MAIN RELIGIONS: Christianity 66%, indigenous religions 34%
EXPORTS: Gold, copper ore, oil, lumber, palm oil, coffee, cocoa, lobster, crayfish

NEW ZEALAND

PRONUNCIATION: noo ZEE-luhnd
AREA: 103,736 sq. miles (268,676 sq. km)
POPULATION: 3,908,037
CAPITAL: Wellington
CURRENCY: 100 cents = 1 New Zealand dollar (NZ$)
OFFICIAL LANGUAGES: English, Maori
MAIN RELIGION: Christianity 67%
EXPORTS: Wool, lamb, mutton, beef, fish, cheese, chemicals, forestry products, fruit and vegetables, manufactured goods

SOLOMON ISLANDS

PRONUNCIATION: SAH-luh-muhn islands
AREA: 10,985 sq. miles (28,450 sq. km)
POPULATION: 494,786
CAPITAL: Honiara
CURRENCY: 100 cents = 1 Solomon Islands dollar (SI$)
OFFICIAL LANGUAGE: Melanesian pidgin
OTHER LANGUAGES: English, regional languages
MAIN RELIGIONS: Christianity 96%, indigenous religions 4%
EXPORTS: Fish, timber, palm oil, cocoa, copra

SAMOA

PRONUNCIATION: suh-MOH-uh
AREA: 1,100 sq. miles (2,850 sq. km)
POPULATION: 178,631
CAPITAL: Apia
CURRENCY: 100 sene = 1 tala (WS$)
OFFICIAL LANGUAGES: Samoan (Polynesian), English
MAIN RELIGION: Christianity 99%
EXPORTS: Coconut oil and cream, taro, fish, beer, copra

VANUATU

PRONUNCIATION: van-wah-TOO
AREA: 4,710 sq. miles (12,200 sq. km)
POPULATION: 196,178
CAPITAL: Port-Vila
CURRENCY: 100 centimes = 1 vatu (VT)
OFFICIAL LANGUAGES: English, French
OTHER LANGUAGE: Bislama (pidgin)
MAIN RELIGIONS: Christianity 77%, indigenous religions 8%
EXPORTS: Copra, kava, beef, cocoa, timber, coffee

FIJI

PRONUNCIATION: FEE-jee
AREA: 7,055 sq. miles (18,272 sq. km)
POPULATION: 856,346
CAPITAL: Suva
CURRENCY: 100 cents = 1 Fijian dollar (F$)
OFFICIAL LANGUAGE: English
OTHER LANGUAGES: Fijian, Hindustani
MAIN RELIGIONS: Christianity 52%, Hinduism 38%, Islam 8%
EXPORTS: Sugar, clothing, gold, processed fish, timber

TONGA

PRONUNCIATION: TAHNG-guh
AREA: 270 sq. miles (699 sq. km)
POPULATION: 106,137
CAPITAL: Nuku'alofa
CURRENCY: 100 seniti = 1 pa'anga (T$)
OFFICIAL LANGUAGES: Tongan, English
MAIN RELIGION: Christianity 70%
EXPORTS: Squash, vanilla, fish, root crops, coconut oil

KIRIBATI

PRONUNCIATION: kihr-uh-BAH-tee
AREA: 277 sq. miles (717 sq. km)
POPULATION: 96,335
CAPITAL: Tarawa
CURRENCY: 100 cents = 1 Australian dollar ($A)
OFFICIAL LANGUAGE: English
OTHER LANGUAGE: I-Kiribati
MAIN RELIGION: Christianity 94%
EXPORTS: Copra, coconuts, seaweed, fish

MARSHALL ISLANDS

PRONUNCIATION: MAR-shuhl islands
AREA: 70 sq. miles (181 sq. km)
POPULATION: 73,630
CAPITAL: Majuro
CURRENCY: 100 cents = 1 United States dollar (US$)
OFFICIAL LANGUAGE: English
OTHER LANGUAGES: Marshallese, Japanese
MAIN RELIGION: Christianity 98%
EXPORTS: Coconut oil, fish, trochus shells

FEDERATED STATES OF MICRONESIA

PRONUNCIATION: FE-der-ayt-ed STAYTS of meye-kruh-NEE-zhuh
AREA: 266 sq. miles (689 sq. km)
POPULATION: 135,869
CAPITAL: Palikir
CURRENCY: 100 cents = 1 United States dollar (US$)
OFFICIAL LANGUAGE: English
OTHER LANGUAGES: Regional languages
MAIN RELIGION: Christianity 97%
EXPORTS: Fish, clothing, bananas, black pepper

NAURU

PRONUNCIATION: nah-OO-roo
AREA: 8.5 sq. miles (22 sq. km)
POPULATION: 12,329
CAPITAL: None. Government offices in Yaren district
CURRENCY: 100 cents = 1 Australian dollar ($A)
OFFICIAL LANGUAGE: Nauruan
OTHER LANGUAGE: English
MAIN RELIGION: Christianity 100%
EXPORT: Phosphates

PALAU

PRONUNCIATION: puh-LOW
AREA: 191 sq. miles (495 sq. km)
POPULATION: 19,409
CAPITAL: Koror
CURRENCY: 100 cents = 1 United States dollar (US$)
OFFICIAL LANGUAGE: English
OTHER LANGUAGES: Palauan, Sonsorolese, Angaur, Japanese, Tobi
MAIN RELIGIONS: Christianity 67%, Modekngei religion 33%
EXPORTS: Shellfish, tuna, trochus shells, copra

TUVALU

PRONUNCIATION: too-vah-loo
AREA: 9 sq. miles (23 sq. km)
POPULATION: 11,146
CAPITAL: Funafuti
CURRENCY: 100 cents = 1 Tuvaluan dollar ($T) or 1 Australian dollar ($A)
OFFICIAL LANGUAGES: Tuvaluan, English
MAIN RELIGION: Christianity 98%, Baha'i 1%
EXPORTS: Copra

Territories and Dependencies

THE COUNTRIES LISTED BELOW govern land outside their national borders. These areas of land are known as territories or dependencies. Some territories are governed directly by the country to which they belong. Others receive only protection and financial assistance, and have their own governments and laws.

UNITED STATES OF AMERICA

AMERICAN SAMOA: South Pacific Ocean; 76 sq. miles (197 sq. km); population 68,688
GUAM: Western Pacific Ocean; 209 sq. miles (541 sq. km); population 160,796
MIDWAY: Central Pacific Ocean; 2 sq. miles (5 sq. km); no permanent population
NORTHERN MARIANA ISLANDS: North Pacific Ocean; 184 sq. miles (477 sq. km); population 77,311
PUERTO RICO: Caribbean Sea; 3,515 sq. miles (9,104 sq. km); population 3,888,000
VIRGIN ISLANDS OF THE UNITED STATES: Caribbean Sea; 133 sq. miles (345 sq. km); population 123,498
WAKE ISLAND: North Pacific Ocean; 3 sq. miles (7.7 sq. km); population 124

UNITED KINGDOM

ANGUILLA: Caribbean Sea; 35 sq. miles (91 sq. km); population 12,446
BERMUDA: North Atlantic Ocean; 20 sq. miles (52 sq. km); population 63,960
BRITISH INDIAN OCEAN TERRITORY: Indian Ocean; 23 sq. miles (60 sq. km); no permanent population
BRITISH VIRGIN ISLANDS: Caribbean Sea; 59 sq. miles (153 sq. km); population 21,272
CAYMAN ISLANDS: Caribbean Sea; 118 sq. miles (306 sq. km); population 36,273
FALKLAND ISLANDS AND DEPENDENCIES (SOUTH GEORGIA AND SOUTH SANDWICH ISLANDS): South Atlantic Ocean; 4,700 sq. miles (12,173 sq. km); population 2,967
GIBRALTAR: Southern Spain; 2.25 sq. miles (6 sq. km); population 27,714
GUERNSEY: English Channel; 30 sq. miles (78 sq. km); population 64587
ISLE OF MAN: Irish Sea; 221 sq. miles (572 sq. km); population 73,873
JERSEY: English Channel; 45 sq. miles (116 sq. km); population 89,775
MONTSERRAT: Caribbean Sea; 40 sq. miles (104 sq. km); population 8,437

PITCAIRN ISLANDS: South Pacific Ocean; 18 sq. miles (47 sq. km); population 47
ST. HELENA AND DEPENDENCIES (ASCENSION ISLAND AND TRISTAN DA CUNHA): South Atlantic Ocean; 158 sq. miles (410 sq. km); population 7,317
TURKS AND CAICOS ISLANDS: Caribbean Sea; 166 sq. miles (430 sq. km); population 18,738

FRANCE

FRENCH GUIANA: Northern South America; 35,126 sq. miles (90,976 sq. km); population 182,333
FRENCH POLYNESIA: South Pacific Ocean; 1,609 sq. miles (4,167 sq. km); population 257,847
GUADELOUPE: Caribbean Sea; 852 sq. miles (1,507 sq. km); population 435,739
MARTINIQUE: Caribbean Sea; 425 sq. miles (1,101 sq. km); population 422,277
MAYOTTE: Mozambique Channel, Africa; 144 sq. miles (373 sq. km); population 170,879
NEW CALEDONIA: South Pacific Ocean; 7,367 sq. miles (19,081 sq. km); population 207,858
RÉUNION: Indian Ocean; 969 sq. miles (2,510 sq. km); population 743,981
ST-PIERRE AND MIQUELON: North Atlantic Ocean; 93 sq. miles (241 sq. km); population 6,954
WALLIS AND FUTUNA ISLANDS: South Pacific Ocean; 106 sq. miles (275 sq. km); population 15,585

THE NETHERLANDS

ARUBA: Caribbean Sea; 69 sq. miles (179 sq. km); population 70,441
NETHERLANDS ANTILLES: Caribbean Sea; 371 sq. miles (961 sq. km); population 214,258

NORWAY

BOUVET ISLAND: South Atlantic Ocean; 22.6 sq. miles (58.5 sq. km); no permanent population
JAN MAYEN ISLAND: North Atlantic Ocean; 144 sq. miles (373 sq. km); no permanent population
SVALBARD: Arctic Ocean; 23,958 sq. miles (62,052 sq. km); population 2,868

DENMARK

FAROE ISLANDS: North Atlantic Ocean; 540 sq. miles (1,399 sq. km); population 46,011
GREENLAND: North Atlantic Ocean; 836,326 sq. miles (2,166,086 sq. km); population 59,900

AUSTRALIA

CHRISTMAS ISLAND: Indian Ocean; 52 sq. miles (135 sq. km); population 474
COCOS (KEELING) ISLANDS: Indian Ocean; 9 sq. miles (23 sq. km); population 632
HEARD AND MCDONALD ISLANDS: Indian Ocean; 159 sq. miles (412 sq. km); no permanent population
NORFOLK ISLAND: South Pacific Ocean; 13 sq. miles (34 sq. km); population 1,866

NEW ZEALAND

COOK ISLANDS: South Pacific Ocean; 92 sq. miles (238 sq. km); population 20,811
NIUE: South Pacific Ocean; 100 sq. miles (259 sq. km); population 2,134
TOKELAU: South Pacific Ocean; 4 sq. miles (10 sq. km); population 1,431

DISPUTED TERRITORIES

GAZA STRIP (PALESTINE): Middle East; disputed by Israel and Palestine, Palestinian interim self-government; 139 sq. miles (360 sq. km); population 1,225,911
KASHMIR: Southern Asia; disputed by India and Pakistan; 85,085 sq. miles (222,236 sq. km); population 7,718,700
TURKISH FEDERATED STATE OF CYPRUS: Mediterranean Sea; disputed by Turkey and Cyprus; 1,295 sq. miles (3,355 sq. km); population 177,120
WEST BANK (PALESTINE): Middle East; disputed by Israel and Palestine, Palestinian interim self-government; 2,263 sq. miles (5,860 sq. km); population 1,612,000
WESTERN SAHARA: Northwestern Africa; disputed by Morocco and separatist movement; 102,703 sq. miles (266,001 sq. km); population 256,177

Glossary

acid rain ~ Rain that has combined with pollution in the atmosphere to form an acid. Acid rain can kill plants and damage buildings.

adaptation ~ A change that occurs in a plant's structure or in an animal's body or behavior to allow it to cope better with its environment.

agriculture ~ The use of the land to grow crops and raise animals. Agriculture is another word for farming.

altitude ~ The height of a place or object above sea level.

ancestor ~ A member of a person's family who lived a long time ago.

Antarctic Circle ~ A line of latitude at 66.5° south which marks the boundary of Earth's southern polar region. South of this line there is continuous daylight in midsummer and continuous darkness in midwinter.

archipelago ~ A large group of islands.

Arctic Circle ~ A line of latitude at 66.5° north that marks the boundary of Earth's northern polar region. North of this line there is continuous daylight in midsummer and continuous darkness in midwinter.

arid ~ Having low rainfall and, as a result, little vegetation. Very arid areas are called deserts.

atoll ~ A low, ring-shaped, sandy island enclosing a lagoon. An atoll is usually formed by the growth of a coral reef on top of an undersea mountain.

axis ~ An imaginary line through the center of Earth around which the planet is constantly rotating.

---

basin ~ 1. A wide, bowl-shaped depression in the landscape. 2. An area of land that is drained by a river and its tributaries.

bay ~ A body of water partly enclosed by land.

bight ~ A recess in a stretch of coastline which forms a large bay.

border ~ A line that separates one country from another.

---

canal ~ An artificial waterway, normally created by digging a large ditch to carry water to an irrigation area or to create a transportation route for shipping.

canyon ~ A deep, steep-sided valley formed by a river.

cape ~ A piece of land that juts out into a lake or sea.

capital ~ The city where a state or country's government is located. Sometimes a country has more than one capital because parts of its government are located in different cities.

cartographer ~ A person who makes maps. The science of making maps is known as cartography.

channel ~ A narrow stretch of water between two landmasses.

climate ~ The pattern of weather that occurs in a place over an extended period of time. Earth can be divided into a number of climate zones.

compass ~ 1. A device that contains a magnetic needle which indicates the direction of north. 2. An arrow or similar icon that indicates the direction of north on a map.

coniferous ~ Coniferous trees are evergreen trees that produce seeds inside cones and usually have thin, needle-shaped or scaly leaves.

continent ~ One of Earth's seven major landmasses: Europe, Asia, Africa, North America, South America, Australia and Antarctica.

coral ~ A hard, rocky material formed by the skeletons of tiny creatures called coral polyps.

crop ~ A plant that is grown in large quantities by farmers. Crops include foods such as cereals and vegetables as well as other plants such as cotton and tobacco.

crust ~ The hard, thin rocky layer that covers the surface of Earth. The crust is broken into segments called plates.

culture ~ The shared traditions and way of life of a people.

currency ~ The kind of money used in a country.

---

dam ~ A wall-like barrier built to hold back the water of a river and create an artificial lake called a reservoir.

deciduous ~ Deciduous trees shed their leaves every year, usually in fall. The tree remains bare during winter but grows new leaves in spring.

deforestation ~ The cutting down of forest trees for timber, or to clear land for farming or building.

delta ~ A fan-shaped area of land formed by silt deposited by rivers where they empty into the sea.

dependency ~ A region or landmass governed by another country.

descendants ~ The offspring of a person, including his or her children, children's children, and so on.

desert ~ A dry area with low rainfall and sparse vegetation that is adapted to withstand drought.

---

earthquake ~ A shaking of the ground caused by the sudden movement of part of Earth's crust.

ecosystem ~ A community of plants and animals and the environment to which they are adapted.

endangered ~ An animal or plant species that is in danger of becoming extinct.

environment ~ The natural surroundings of a community of plants and animals, particularly the shape of the land, the climate and the soil.

equator ~ An imaginary line that circles the globe midway between the North and South poles. The equator divides the world into the Northern and Southern hemispheres.

ethnic group ~ A group of people sharing the same origin, language, nationality and lifestyle.

evergreen ~ An evergreen tree is a tree that does not shed its leaves in winter.

evolution ~ A process of gradual change, especially in living things.

exports ~ Goods that are sold to other countries.

extinct ~ An extinct species of animal or plant is one that no longer exists because all the individual animals or plants died.

---

federation ~ A union, by mutual agreement, of states or territories to form one country.

fertile ~ Fertile land is land with good soil. Plants grow well in fertile land if there is good rainfall or irrigation.

fjord ~ A deep, steep-sided valley gouged out by a glacier and later flooded by the sea to form a narrow inlet.

forestry ~ The science of making use of and managing forest resources.

fossil ~ The remains or traces of a prehistoric plant or animal, normally found between layers of rock.

fossil fuel ~ Fuel found deep underground which formed from the decayed remains of prehistoric plants and animals. The most common fossil fuels are coal, oil and natural gas.

---

gazetteer ~ An index of place names.

geyser ~ A spring that boils and emits hot water and steam.

glacier ~ A large mass of ice that moves slowly down the side of a mountain or along a valley, and is constantly replenished by snowfall at the top of the mountain.

gorge ~ A deep, steep-sided, rocky valley.

grassland ~ A large area of land covered with grass plants.

Greenwich meridian ~ An imaginary line that extends from the North Pole to the South Pole through Greenwich, England, and that marks 0° longitude.

gulf ~ A large bay.

---

hemisphere ~ One half of the world. Earth is divided into Northern and Southern hemispheres by the equator, and into Eastern and Western hemispheres by the Greenwich meridian (0°) and 180° line.

high-tech industries ~ Industries that produce electronic goods such as computers.

hydroelectricity ~ Electricity produced using the power of running water.

---

iceberg ~ A large block of ice floating in the sea. Icebergs break off the ends of glaciers and ice sheets. The part of an iceberg under the surface of the sea is usually eight times as large as the part above the surface.

ice cap ~ A sheet of ice and snow that covers an area permanently. Ice caps are found in polar regions and on some high mountaintops.

immigrant ~ A person who has come from one country to live in another.

independent ~ Not governed by another country.

inlet ~ A narrow bay.

irrigation ~ The process of providing water to farmland by artificial means, such as pumping water from rivers, lakes and dams, or diverting water through channels and pipes.

island ~ An area of land surrounded by water.

kingdom ~ A country whose ruler or head of state is a king or queen.

lagoon ~ 1. A shallow area of salt water separated from the sea by a strip of land. 2. Inland bodies of water that were previously part of a river.

landmass ~ A large area of land not covered by water.

latitude ~ Distance north or south of the equator measured in degrees.

livestock ~ Animals, such as cattle or sheep, raised by farmers.

longitude ~ Distance east or west of the Greenwich meridian measured in degrees.

marsh ~ An area of wet land containing plants adapted to growth in water. Also called a swamp or wetland.

manufacturing ~ The making of useful products from raw materials.

migration ~ Movement of people or animals to another country or region. Many animals migrate to find food or avoid severe weather.

mineral ~ A substance occurring naturally in Earth's crust that is neither plant nor animal. Well-known minerals include chalk, clay and many metals.

native people ~ The original human inhabitants of a region or country.

nomad ~ A person who does not live in one place but continually moves around. Nomads often move in search of food and water for themselves and their animals.

North Pole ~ see pole

oasis ~ A patch of land in a desert where there is water and more vegetation than elsewhere.

peninsula ~ A long strip of land that extends outward from a larger landmass and is almost surrounded by water.

plain ~ An area of flat or rolling land with shallow river valleys.

plantation ~ A piece of land where a particular tree crop is grown. Such crops include forest trees, rubber and coconut palms.

plate ~ One of the segments of Earth's crust.

plateau ~ An area of flat or rolling land with deep river valleys, gorges and canyons.

pole ~ The points on Earth's surface representing the ends of the planet's axis, around which it is constantly rotating. The North Pole is Earth's most northern point. The South Pole is the most southern point. The regions around the poles are known as the polar regions.

population ~ 1. The people who live in a place. 2. The total number of people living in a place.

populous ~ A populous country is a country with a large population.

principality ~ A country whose ruler or head of state is a prince or princess.

radioactive ~ Radioactive materials emit high-energy particles in the form of invisible rays. Some natural substances, such as uranium, are radioactive.

rain forest ~ A type of dense forest that grows in regions of high rainfall.

range ~ 1. A chain of mountains. 2. An area of open grassland where animals graze.

raw materials ~ Natural substances which can be turned into useful products. Examples include timber, coal and coffee beans. Raw materials are also known as resources.

reef ~ A ridge of rock, sand or coral lying just below the surface of the sea.

republic ~ A country led by an elected representative called a president.

reservoir ~ An artificial lake, usually created by building a dam across a river.

resources ~ Substances or materials that occur naturally in a place and are of value to the area's inhabitants. Resources that can never be used up, such as water and waves, are called renewable resources. Resources that will eventually be used up, such as coal and other minerals, are known as nonrenewable resources.

river basin ~ An area of land drained by a river and its tributaries.

rural ~ Relating to the countryside. Rural industry means industry located in country areas.

savanna ~ A type of grassland with scattered trees. Most savannas occur in tropical areas that have a distinct summer wet season.

scale ~ An indication on a map of how distances on the map relate to actual distances.

scrub ~ An area of land covered with shrubs and low trees.

sea level ~ The average height of the surface of the sea, which is used as a base point for measuring altitude.

South Pole ~ see pole

species ~ Animals or plants of the same type.

steppe ~ A type of dry grassland that covers parts of eastern Europe and central Asia.

strait ~ A narrow strip of water that connects two larger bodies of water.

swamp ~ An area of wet land containing plants adapted to growth in water. Also called a marsh or wetland.

technology ~ The use of scientific knowledge to carry out certain tasks or solve certain problems. Using machines in industry is an example of technology.

temperate ~ Neither hot nor cold. Most of Earth's temperate regions are located between the tropics and the polar regions.

territory ~ 1. A large area of land. 2. All the land and sea governed by a country or state. 3. A region or landmass governed by a country that is located in another part of the world.

textiles ~ Woven or knitted fabrics.

time zone ~ A region in which everyone uses the same time. The world is divided into 24 time zones. The time in each zone is usually one hour earlier than the zone to its east.

trade ~ The buying and selling of goods.

tributary ~ A stream or river that flows into a larger stream or river.

Tropic of Cancer/Capricorn ~ see tropics

tropics ~ 1. The hot, wet regions of Earth that lie near the equator. 2. Either of two lines of latitude: the Tropic of Cancer at 23.5° north and the Tropic of Capricorn at 23.5° south. Because Earth is tilted at an angle of 23.5°, these lines mark the point at which the Sun is directly overhead in summer.

tundra ~ A cold, barren area where much of the soil is frozen and the vegetation consists of only mosses, lichens and other small plants adapted to withstanding intense cold. Tundra is found near the Arctic Circle and on mountaintops.

urban ~ Relating to cities. A country's urban population is the number of people that live in its cities.

valley ~ A long, narrow depression in the land along which a river usually flows.

vegetation ~ The community of plants that is characteristic of a particular region.

volcano ~ A mountain that has been built up from molten rock erupting through a hole in Earth's crust.

wetland ~ An area of wet land containing plants adapted to growth in water. Also called a swamp or marsh.

woodland ~ An area of land covered with widely spaced trees and shrubs.

Index and Gazetteer

Acknowledgments

Weldon Owen would like to thank the following people for their assistance in the production of this book:
Helen Bateman, Anthony Burton, Alastair Campbell, Jo Collard, Melanie Corfield, Simon Corfield, Sharon Dalgleish, Libby Frederico, Kathy Gammon, Kathy Gerrard, Janine Googan, Greg Hassall, Lynn Humphries, Chris Jackson, Megan Johnston, Ralph Kelly, Jennifer Le Gras, Rosemary McDonald, Kylie Mulquin, Nicholas Rowland, Rachel Smith, Julie Stanton, Dawn Titmus, Greg Tobin, Wendy van Buuren, Michael Wyatt

Cartographic sources: U.S. Central Intelligence Agency; International Boundaries Research Unit, Durham University, United Kingdom; U.S. Geographer General

Photographic credits: 14 bottom left, **David Weintraub**/The Photo Library—Sydney; 14 bottom center, **Stephen Wilkes**/The Image Bank; 14 bottom right, **Mats Wibe Lund**/Icelandic Photo; 15 center far right, **David Hardy**/SPL/The Photo Library—Sydney; 15 bottom left, **Francois Gohier**/Ardea London; 15 bottom center, **B. McDairmant**/Ardea London; 15 bottom right, **International Photo Library**; 16 top far right, **Robert Harding** Picture Library; 16 bottom, **David W. Hamilton**/The Image Bank; 17 top left, **Jeffrey C. Drewitz**/The Photo Library—Sydney; 17 top center left, **Sobel/Klonsky**/The Image Bank; 17 top center, **Horizon International**; 17 top center right, **Staffan Widstrand**/Bruce Coleman Limited; 17 top right, **Christer Fredriksson**/Bruce Coleman Limited; 19 top center, **Alain Compost**/Bruce Coleman Limited; 27 top, **Horizon International**; 27 center, **Shone/Gamma/Picturemedia**; 27 bottom, **Witt/Sipa Press**/The Photo Library—Sydney

The Polar Regions
102

Northern
Europe
72

Northe
Euro
72

The United
Kingdom and the
Republic of Ireland
56

The Low
Countries
62

Western Central Europe 6

France 60

Spain and Portugal
58

Italy

Northern
Africa
92

Western Canada
and Alaska
34

Eastern Canada
36

Central
United
States
42

Western
United
States
44

38 Northeastern
United States

Southern
United States
40

Mexico,
Central America
and the Caribbean
46

Northern
South America
50

Southern
South America
52